The Voice of Rolling Thunder

A MEDICINE MAN'S WISDOM FOR WALKING THE RED ROAD

SIDIAN MORNING STAR JONES AND
STANLEY KRIPPNER, PH.D.

Bear & Company
Rochester, Vermont • Toronto, Canada

Bear & Company
One Park Street
Rochester, Vermont 05767
www.BearandCompanyBooks.com

Text stock is SFI certified

Bear & Company is a division of Inner Traditions International

Library of Congress Cataloging-in-Publication Data
Jones, Sidian Morning Star.
  The voice of Rolling Thunder : a medicine man's wisdom for walking the red
road / Sidian Morning Star Jones and Stanley Krippner.
       p. cm.
  Summary: "Rolling Thunder's life and wisdom in his own words and from
interviews with those who knew him well" — Provided by publisher.
  Includes bibliographical references (p.) and index.
  ISBN 978-1-59143-133-6 (pbk.) — ISBN 978-1-59143-808-3 (e-book)
  1. Rolling Thunder. 2. Indians of North America—Biography. 3. Cherokee
Indians—Biography. 4. Indians of North America—Medicine. 5. Indians of
North America—Religion. I. Krippner, Stanley, 1932– II. Title.
  E90.R74J66 2012
  299'.7—dc23
                                                                    2012011943

Printed and bound in the United States by Lake Book Manufacturing, Inc
The text stock is SFI certified. The Sustainable Forestry Initiative® program
promotes sustainable forest management.

10 9 8 7 6 5 4 3 2 1

Text design by Jack Nichols and layout by Brian Boynton
This book was typeset in Garamond Premier Pro with Willow and Swiss used as
display typefaces
All images courtesy Stanley Krippner unless otherwise noted.

To send correspondence to the authors of this book, mail a first-class letter to the
authors c/o Inner Traditions • Bear & Company, One Park Street, Rochester, VT
05767, and we will forward the communication.

You can also contact the authors directly at **sidianmorningstar@gmail.com** or
through Sidian Morning Star's website **OpenSourceReligion.net** or through
Stanley Krippner's website **www.stanleykrippner.weebly.com**.

The Voice of Rolling Thunder

"Rolling Thunder, an intertribal medicine man, never claimed to be a shaman himself but played an important role in reconnecting contemporary healing with shamanic traditions. This wonderful book honors his memory and reveals both his extraordinary talents and his very human strengths and frailties."

JURGEN KREMER, PH.D., PRESIDENT OF THE SOCIETY FOR THE STUDY OF SHAMANISM, HEALING, AND TRANSFORMATION

"This book is an accessible, authoritative, and interesting treatise on Native American healing. I found it thoroughly enjoyable, valuable, and provocative."

RICHARD CLEMMER-SMITH, PROFESSOR AND CURATOR OF ETHNOLOGY AT THE UNIVERSITY OF DENVER MUSEUM OF ANTHROPOLOGY

"Rolling Thunder was a catalyst for serious pioneering scholarship in the shamanic healing arts."

OSCAR MIRO-QUESADA, FOUNDER OF HEART OF THE HEALER

"In many ways, Rolling Thunder was the most traditional of all the medicine people I have known."

KENNETH COHEN, AUTHOR OF *HONORING THE MEDICINE*

Sidian Morning Star Jones dedicates this book to Stanley Krippner, "who believed in me from the very beginning and accepted me for exactly who I am."

Stanley Krippner dedicates this book to Edwin Stronglegs Richardson, the first Native American to receive a Ph.D. in clinical psychology, "for his dedication to the preservation of Native American traditions and his service to humanity and the planet Earth."

Contents

Acknowledgments

The authors would like to express their gratitude to the Saybrook University Chair for the Study of Consciousness of San Francisco, California, and the Floraglades Foundation of Labelle, Florida, for their support in the preparation of this book, and to the Woodfish Foundation of San Francisco, California, for the award that honored its concept and execution.

Foreword

CAROLYN FIRESIDE

Some called him a shaman; others called him a fraud. He was said to be a healer—or a snake-oil salesman. He was either a Native American spiritual force of unparalleled power—or a supremely gifted flimflam artist. Whatever one thought of Rolling Thunder, one thing is certain: anyone who interacted with him would never forget the experience and would never be quite the same again.

Early in life, Rolling Thunder was given the name John Pope in Stamps, Arkansas, where he was born on September 19, 1916. His mother was Caucasian, and his father was Cherokee and Cajun. According to the sources I consulted, his father's Native name was Yankkiller, and RT's grandfather used the same name. RT often stated, "My grandfather, a traditional Indian chief, was murdered by soldiers and agency police." This family tragedy set RT on his course of social activism as the years proceeded.

Another precursor to RT's activism was the fact that RT's father belonged to a Cherokee resistance group called Snake and was killed during one of their protests. RT was raised on a reservation in Oklahoma, where he began to learn the ways of the medicine people.

He led a hard laborer's life, working as a brakeman for the Southern

Pacific Railroad for thirty-six years. He had an early marriage to a Native woman of the Miwok tribe, Marlene Pope, and they had three children. They lived in Carlin, Nevada, in a trailer home. One tragic day, their home caught on fire, probably due to defective wiring; Marlene ran back into the trailer to save their baby, but they both perished. RT tried in vain to save them, burning his hands in the process. The local physicians said that they would have to amputate both his hands to save his life, but RT refused. Instead, he had a vision of a plant that could be found in the Nevada mountains and that it would make itself known to him. RT walked into the mountains, found a plant that was literally glowing, and applied it in poultices. His skin was virtually absent but began to grown back, and his hands were saved. But the effects of the fire were apparent on his hands for the rest of his life.

RT learned Indian medicine from two renowned teachers, Silver Wolf and Phillip Grey Horse, both of whom lived in Nevada. Later he found other teachers, including Frank Fools Crow, Mad Bear Anderson, Aminitus Sepuoia, and David Monongye—who lived to be more than one hundred years old.

His other two children, Jesse and Iris Pope, survived the fire. Rolling Thunder continued to live in Carlin with Spotted Fawn, his second wife, a Western Shoshone. (Please see plate 11 of the color insert, wherein Spotted Fawn is depicted.) When they married, he became an adopted member of a branch of the Shoshone Nation. They had six children, four of whom survived: Mala Spotted Eagle, Buffalo Horse, Bundy Morning Star Whittaker, and Patricia Mocking Bird Acre. In the meantime, RT spent considerable time learning about Native American healing traditions, and his reputation as an effective healer gradually spread.

In 1971 Rolling Thunder was invited by Stanley Krippner to speak at a conference sponsored by the Menninger Foundation of Topeka, Kansas. He met Doug Boyd at the conference, and Boyd's 1974 biography, *Rolling Thunder*, brought the medicine man to international attention. Shortly after the book's publication, Rolling Thunder retired from his job on the railroad and devoted the rest of his life to "walking the Good Red Road" as an intertribal medicine man, serving people in need and preserving the culture of Native Americans.

The road that he traveled took several forms. He attended several concerts featuring Joan Baez, Joni Mitchell, and Bob Dylan as part of their Rolling Thunder Revue in 1975 and 1976. Family legend attributes the name to Dylan's appreciation of a sunrise ceremony conducted by RT, but this cannot be verified. However, RT was a comrade of the Grateful Dead rock band and had a backstage pass to many of their concerts.

RT spoke to audiences at many conferences in the United States as well as in Sweden, Austria, Denmark, Canada, and Germany. In Europe he often gave public talks, speaking to standing-room-only crowds of several thousand people. His fame resulted from the convergence of several historical developments. Shamanism had been brought to popular attention by Carlos Castaneda's books, even though Castaneda's semi-fictional protagonist, don Juan Matus, was more of a village sorcerer than a shaman. Because the Castaneda books were of dubious authenticity, there was a need on the part of many spiritual seekers to encounter an actual native shaman in face-to-face settings. Rolling Thunder met this need, especially in Europe, where Native Americans were considered to be more "exotic" than they were in the United States.

Rolling Thunder's connection with rock musicians and the fact that he was the central figure in a popular book provided extra dimensions to his luster. He was highly respected by other well-known Native American shamans such as Mad Bear Anderson (with whom, as previously mentioned, he studied), Running Deer, Wallace Black Elk, and Leslie Gray. RT was a medicine man not a chief, and he resented it when people called him Chief Rolling Thunder. He also considered himself to be a teacher, and at one time he was an official spokesperson for Chief Temoke, a traditional Shoshone elder. When asked whether Indians were American citizens, he responded, "In 1924 Indians were made U.S. citizens by an act of Congress, without being asked, just so they could tax us and draft us."

From 1975 to 1985 he was the spiritual leader of Meta Tantay, a 262-acre community he developed in northeastern Nevada, which was devoted to maintaining Native American traditions (see plate 3 of the color insert). In the 1970s he appeared in *Billy Jack, The Trial of Billy Jack,* and *Billy Jack Goes to Washington,* three independent films that increased their viewers' appreciation of contemporary Native American lifestyles. A video, *Rolling Thunder: Healer of Meta Tantay,* was released in 2005 and contains interviews with RT and with a family appearing to be living happily in the community.

The sweat lodge, a central focus of the Meta Tantay community, began to be used more frequently for sacred ceremonies and healing rituals (please see plate 5 of the color insert for an example of a sweat lodge). As a medicine man, Rolling Thunder also utilized the herbs, teas, and natural substances he had collected in his travels or that were given to him by other medicine people or, from time to time, by Western physicians. He described a "Rolling Thunder's Diet" for "Thunder People," which consisted of "organic" foods that had not been contaminated by preservatives, radiation, or microwaves.

His refusal to have anything to do with the U.S. Department of Indian Affairs was always a center of contoversy. He claimed that his father's band, the Chickamauga Cherokee, had refused to register with the department also, as a means of protest against white domination. Because of this, RT's authenticity as a Native American was challenged by Ake Hultkrantz and Hans Peter Duerr, two prominent German anthropologists, and various anthropologists in the United States, two of whom threatened to file a lawsuit against RT for fraud. These charges were answered by data collected by Stanley Krippner and others, whose descriptions of Rolling Thunder emphasized his political activism and his opposition to the federal U.S. bureaucracy. The lawsuit did not materialize, but RT's legitimacy as a traditional medicine man was never accepted in some anthropological circles on both sides of the Atlantic Ocean. RT always answered in the same way: "I could have been enrolled, but I chose not to be. I've spent my entire life without a roll number. I know who my relations are and can prove my lineage."

Rolling Thunder opposed the forced sterilization of Native American women, the "kidnapping" (as he called it) of Native American children and their relocation to Euro-American homes and schools, and the devastation of the natural environment by corporations and industrial firms. He garnered both sympathy and attention for his efforts to stop the destruction of pinyon nut trees and to prevent the use of Indian lands as atomic waste dumps and storage sites.

After Rolling Thunder's death, his third wife, Carmen Sun Rising Pope, collected several of his talks and published them in a book titled *Rolling Thunder Speaks: A Message for Turtle Island.* Turtle Island is a name used by many Native American tribes for the North American continent.

In retrospect, the importance of Rolling Thunder is more apparent now than it was during his lifetime. As a medicine man, political activist, spiritual leader, popular lecturer, media celebrity, preserver of Native American traditions, advocate of the natural environment, and spokesperson around the globe for indigenous ways of life, he was instrumental in drawing serious attention to shamanic traditions. He helped to lay the groundwork for Michael Harner's Foundation for Shamanic Studies, for the popular magazine *Shaman's Drum,* and for international conferences on shamanism, following the success of the first such conclave held in Alpbach, Austria, in 1982, where he was one of the central figures.

Rolling Thunder did not deliberately carve out this historic role for himself and he never referred to himself as a shaman. However, his personal qualities of shrewd insight, understated showmanship, extensive herbal knowledge, and a combination of humor and militancy allowed him to put his own stamp on a growing interest in indigenous ways of knowing and being. In describing his background in 1981, he told an interviewer for *Plowboy Magazine:*

Rolling Thunder: I was raised in eastern Oklahoma, in a range of the Ozarks called the Kiamichi Mountains. I've been told that before I was born—during my father's youth—those hills had all been Indian territory, but the land was gradually taken away from our tribe, and we retreated to the wooded areas to live. The Great Depression was on when I was a youngster, so we had to make a living practically with our bare hands, just as our ancestors had done. At about the age of fifteen, I built my first house, a log cabin with a separate smokehouse and a corral for goats and hogs. I lived alone there for quite a while and worked about an acre of land with a hoe and a shovel.

Those were mighty rough times, but they taught me a lot about nature and about ways of living in harmony with Mother Earth. I learned how to forage for nuts, berries, and roots in the forest and how to catch fish by setting traps in the water. I also taught myself to recognize all the local woodland plants, although I never got to know many by their English or Latin names. Instead, I made up my own labels for each one, and I learned how to use them for food and medicine. So you see, a lot of my early training took place during that period, and that education helped me once I learned that I was meant to become a medicine man.

Plowboy Magazine: When did you first become aware of—or "feel"— your ability to heal, and where do you believe the power comes from?

Rolling Thunder: All I can say is that I woke up one morning, and this force was with me for the first time. I'd been doctored—in my sleep—the night before by a Sun God and his helpers, and when I awoke I knew something was different. I felt this great power within me! But I had to learn to live with the tremendous force, to watch every thought or emotion I had, twenty-four hours a day. Since the force is so strong, you see, it has a great potential for misuse, and it could really hurt someone if it were employed in a negative or destructive way. It's difficult for a healer to adjust to that newfound power. . . . We all have to learn to guard every thought, every word, and every feeling, since the power could use any such "channel" to affect someone in one way or another.

I believe the healing force contains the strength of the Creator—

or Great Spirit—as well as the energy of the thunder and the lightning and that of all living beings. I sometimes also ask the stars or the sun to help me, or I may call on the great medicine men and tribal chiefs of the past. As a medicine man, I attempt to bring such forces together so they'll convey their healing power to the sick person.

Those words from the magazine interview serve as a tantalizing introduction to the tales recounted in this book. *The Voice of Rolling Thunder* is quite different from other books and articles written about RT. His life was marked by an abundance of remarkable interactions with a wide variety of people. Many incredible stories have come down to his grandson Sidian Morning Star Jones, an open-minded and self-educated skeptic regarding anecdotes about extraordinary happenings. In this book Sidian invites the reader to join him on a journey in which he shares these precious, often outrageous stories of a Native American medicine man. Readers are also asked to consider Sidian's reflections on the implications of these accounts as well as their credibility as he explains their role in clarifying his own quest for understanding the world and his place in it.

Stanley Krippner facilitates Sidian's quest, contributing his own memorable reminiscences about Rolling Thunder, as well as introducing Sidian to dozens of people whose lives were touched by his grandfather. Stanley Krippner places these stories in the context of North American shamanism, pointing out how Rolling Thunder carried out a centuries-old tradition of healing, service, and activism.

Plowboy Magazine, in the above-mentioned interview with Rolling Thunder, observed that one meaning of his traditional name is "speaking the truth." The *Plowboy* author added, "When someone speaks the truth, others should listen." Sidian once remarked, "I am on a warpath for truth. That is what motivated me to create this book. I want people to listen to the Rolling Thunder." Stanley Krippner, a psychologist and scientist, has been on this "warpath" all of his professional life, beginning his studies of shamanism when its practitioners were seen as frauds, at best, and schizophrenics, at worst.

Stanley Krippner and Sidian Morning Star Jones join forces in this book—Sidian with his personal agenda and Stanley with his scholarly agenda. Their readers can choose one agenda or both, or can invent agendas of their own as they listen to the Rolling Thunder.

CAROLYN FIRESIDE has been a staff copywriter and editor at firms such as G. P. Putnam, HarperCollins, and Random House as well as a publishing executive, collaborating on and editing many successful works of nonfiction and fiction. She is also the author of award-winning novels. She has edited fiction ranging from medical horror to women's romance. Authors she has worked with include Jerzy Kosinski, Jay Presson Allen, Nobel Prize–winning scientist Dr. Louis J. Ignarro, Picasso scholar John Richardson, James Michener, Dave Barry, Dean Koontz, Dick Francis, and LaVeryle Spencer.

PREFACE

The Genesis of This Book

STANLEY KRIPPNER, PH.D.

In 1967 I met Mickey Hart, one of two drummers who played incredible music with the Grateful Dead. Over the years he and I have become good friends, and one thing that we share is our love of music. In addition, Mickey is always eager to engage in intellectual conversation. When I told him about the brain research studies that revealed how steady drum rhythms can alter consciousness, he became so intrigued by this idea that he organized a small seminar during which the leading researchers in this field came together to share and discuss their data.

Another of our topics of conversation was Native American shamanism, an area that I had researched for several years. I had been interested in Native Americans since my successful hunts for Indian arrowheads as a boy growing up on a farm in Wisconsin. Mickey would tell me about his friend, the intertribal medicine man Rolling Thunder, who lived in Carlin, Nevada, but who frequently visited the San Francisco area. Mickey remarked, "I would like you two to meet, and one of these days I am going to bring him to the ranch when you are here."

That day turned out to be April 18, 1970. I was on my way to Sacramento for a seminar and accepted Mickey's invitation to stay at his ranch for a few days before the seminar began. The day after I arrived, Mickey and several members of the band were scheduled to play at a San Francisco venue, the Family Dog, under the name of Mickey Hart and the Heartbeats, a sobriquet often used when members of the Grateful Dead were trying out new material. Mickey told me that Rolling Thunder would be a guest of his at this gig, and we would finally be able to meet. To that end, Mickey dispatched a private plane to the Elko, Nevada, airport to pick up Rolling Thunder and bring him to San Francisco.

Later, at the Family Dog, Mickey Hart and the Heartbeats played a memorable first set. During intermission I observed a colorful trio walking down the side aisle of the hall. It consisted of a handsome middle-aged man bedecked with beads and feathers with a lovely young woman on each arm. The other people at the Family Dog probably thought that this striking gentleman was an aging hippie showing off his harem. But I immediately knew that he must be Rolling Thunder, the intertribal medicine man.

I walked over and introduced myself, and RT's first response was, "Mickey has told me a lot about you." I answered, "Same here." The trio walked on, greeting several young people who had driven to the concert from Nevada, and then the second set began. Of course, almost everyone in the audience was a Deadhead and knew the true identity of the Heartbeats, hence the full house. The new material was well received, and much of it found its way into future Grateful Dead concerts.

After the show we all went back to Mickey's ranch. The Nevada retinue gathered around a campfire, gently tripping on some LSD they had obtained at the show. RT was pleasantly engaged in a private room with one of the young women I had met earlier. Mickey was holding court with his own friends, getting feedback on the new material that had been heard publicly that night for the first time. I was happy to retire early—and alone.

RT was otherwise occupied on April 19, and I spent much of the day preparing for my upcoming seminar. Mickey and I also engaged in one of our intense discussions, this one about how he could help enhance the creativity of his students through hypnosis. RT awakened early the following morning, because he had promised Mickey that he would lead one of his traditional sunrise services for the group. These ceremonies were held early in the morning, just as night was turning into day. We assembled on top of a hill on Mickey's property, and RT prayed to the four winds, thanking each of the winds for its special gifts. He also allowed Mickey to record this prayer, which was used to open Mickey's first solo album, released in 1972, and which he appropriately named *Rolling Thunder*.

This early-morning invocation was followed by the burning of sage. It was a splendid way to open the day, and when it was over, the group saw me off as I left for Sacramento and my seminar. In retrospect, it was the beginning of a beautiful friendship between Rolling Thunder and me.

Many observers called RT a shaman, a term that was originally a Siberian word. Gradually the term *shaman* was applied to spiritual practitioners who engaged in similar activities around the world. RT, however, refrained from calling himself a shaman. Most Native American practitioners I have met prefer the terms *medicine man* or *medicine woman,* or use the tribal word for a medicine man or medicine woman. The term *shaman* is seen as a description imported from another time and place and a threat to the tradition and integrity of Indian medicine. We will, however, use the term *shaman* in this book when citing anthropological literature on the topic and will try to avoid overusing the label.

From an anthropological perspective a shaman is designated by a community, and the only time that RT had a clearly designated community was when he was ensconced at Meta Tantay, the vibrant group of people who erected structures and lived communally on land that the Grateful Dead and other supporters had bought for RT near his hometown. (Please see plate 7 of the color insert.) One might say that he served as Meta Tantay's shaman, because he gave the camp its spiritual direction and also practiced the Native American medicine he had cobbled together over the years.

RT never called himself a "Cherokee medicine man" or a "Shoshone medicine man," although he had ties to both of these tribal groups. The

officials of the Cherokee Nation and the Shoshone Nation make a justi-
fied protest when these terms are incorrectly used. RT studied Native
American medicine with a variety of medicine people but did not enter
into the type of apprenticeship that would enable him to use a tribal
name to describe what he did. RT often used the phrase "I doctor people," and that colloquial statement is as good a descriptor as any.

It is important that we share some information on North American
shamanism with our readers in order to provide the proper context for
an in-depth understanding of Rolling Thunder, his activities, and how
his activities attained legendary status during his lifetime. We should
add that we have used the terms *Native American* and *American Indian*
interchangeably for variety; RT used the word *Indian* far more often
than such words as *Native* or *Native American*.

We have also used the word *indigenous* to refer to people who have
long inhabited a particular region; the term *First Nations* as applied to
American Indians has a similar connotation, as does the term *Native*.
We have not used First Nations because the term is highly politicized,
especially in Canada, as is the term *aboriginal,* meaning the first people
to occupy a particular land. The issue of labels can be cumbersome.
What was an African American called by Native Americans when they
arrived as slaves? One description, quite accurate in its own way, was
"black white man."

The same weekend in 1970 that I met Rolling Thunder I also met
his daughter Morning Star, or "Bundy," and her fiancé, Russell Jones.
Their marriage would prove to be a tumultuous one, and although it
did not last very long, it produced their remarkable son, Sidian. Because
I enjoyed a strong rapport with Rolling Thunder, I would become fast
friends with him and Bundy over the years. Every Christmas, Bundy
and I exchanged Christmas cards, and I would frequently see her when
I visited RT or when she and her mother, Spotted Fawn, came to San
Francisco.

In 1989 it was Bundy who alerted Mickey Hart that her father
was seriously ill, and her phone call prompted Mickey and me to fly to
Nevada in a private plane to take RT for an emergency operation that

prolonged his life. On that occasion and on others as well, Bundy urged me to come to Boise to meet her family, which I finally did. It was at this family gathering that I had the pleasure of meeting Sidian, not yet twenty years of age, for the first time.

He and I stayed in touch by e-mail, and as our friendship grew, I invited him to San Francisco. Sidian was, at this point, already an accomplished artist, and it was clear to me that he had abundant creative gifts.

RT died in 1997, and after his passing I heard that there were plans being made by an old friend known as Everlight to write a book about him. However, shortly thereafter, Everlight contacted me to tell me that she had taken on a new job and thus would not be able to devote sufficient time to what she had hoped would be an anthology of reminiscences written by RT's friends. With Everlight's approval, the next time I was in touch with Bundy, I suggested that Sidian and I write our own book. Bundy was pleased that I thought her son was accomplished enough for the job.

On subsequent visits to San Francisco, Sidian and I began to interview family, friends, and associates of RT and to have transcripts made of these interviews. It is what RT would have referred to as "tales" that, along with transcripts of several of RT's lectures, formed the raw material for this book. When Sidian sent me his comments on the interviews, I could see that he was thoughtful and articulate.

Once we started to work with the interviews, Mickey Hart loaned us several audiotapes of some of Rolling Thunder's lectures. This gave us access to some material that was not available in the earlier RT books by Doug Boyd and Carmen Sun Rising Pope. We have not used the anecdotes described in their books; indeed, many of the stories in this book have never been published.

Sidian conducted most of the interviews, and in so doing became familiar with the "Good Red Road" of traditional Indian spirituality that his grandfather had walked on. RT truly deserves the accolade given him by the Cherokee medicine man Running Wolf, who directed the Native American Spiritual Center in New Mexico. In a 2007 online interview in *The Light Connection,* Running Wolf remarked, "Rolling Thunder, in my opinion, was the most powerful medicine man in the last century. It was an honor for me to have him as a teacher and to be recognized by him."

It is likewise an honor for me to be coauthor of this book, together with Sidian Morning Star Jones, about this most remarkable man.

INTRODUCTION

Listen to the Rolling Thunder

SIDIAN MORNING STAR JONES

At length, it may be said, all will come to know their greatest creator. But in this way, are we not seeing the forest for the trees? For all the while we strive to be closer to the Great Spirit, we seem to be passing up the very essence of it. This essence is the very continuation of every hour we live.

Vision, the myriad sacred pacts with Nature and the ineffable relationship with dream cognizance, is contained within the enduring insights of Native Americans in the eyes of millions. Those who open their heart to such a lifestyle can only begin to ask, "What have we lost in our isolation from Nature? Do those who honor the dream lead more awakened lives? What is it to be *more* awake?"

There are those who have tried to answer these questions. My grandfather, Rolling Thunder, was one of them. Vision has always been the compass and the map to our curious quest for peace and wisdom. In the very middle of this era, during the greatest spiritual excitement of the time, Rolling Thunder was practicing what he had known for years: the ways of the medicine man.

This book attempts to contribute to the field of the Indian spirit as it brings its readers a number of eyewitness stories, anecdotes, and

1

factual accounts of RT, most of which have never before been published. Natives told me some of these stories, but not the majority. All of these people had contact with RT, encounters during which they listened to the Rolling Thunder.

1

The Long Journey

Dr. Alberto Villoldo, a medical anthropologist and former student at Saybrook University of Stanley Krippner, this book's coauthor, had several interactions with Rolling Thunder, usually during RT's visits to California. RT was one of the elders who inspired Alberto to start the Four Winds Foundation. One of the foundation's activities is to take people to such sacred places as Machu Picchu, Peru, where traditional practitioners share their legacy with visitors. Alberto has coauthored two books with Stanley, as well as half a dozen books that apply traditional teachings to their readers' lives. Alberto participated in several of the rituals, ceremonies, and healing sessions that Rolling Thunder conducted over the years.

We asked Alberto to tell us about one of his more memorable encounters with Rolling Thunder. Alberto recalled a crowded ride in a Volkswagen car from San Francisco to Carlin, Nevada, in 1974.

The journey was a long one. Five of us were squeezed into a Volkswagen with our sleeping bags and packs filling the trunk and what room was left on the floor. I was thinking about my previous encounters with RT and the many times I had heard him criticize the Bureau of Indian Affairs and the manner in which the European settlers and their descendants had destroyed the natural environment. RT had stated that the Earth does not belong to anyone.

When the Europeans came to the Western Hemisphere, the Indians were willing to share their knowledge of natural medicine as well as the skills they had developed in cultivating the land and in hunting. But the Europeans were not interested in sharing the land, only in owning it. They were not interested in cooperating with nature, but sought to master and exploit it. "Now the white man is realizing that he has made the land barren and polluted the environment," RT would say, "and he has also contaminated his heart and left his spirit barren."

That evening we arrived at RT's home in Carlin. He was out on a run with the railroad, where he worked as a brakeman. We pitched camp in the huge backyard that extends into the distant foothills, rolled out our sleeping bags, enjoyed the Nevada sunset, and greeted RT when he returned later that evening. We also enjoyed a delicious pasta dinner.

The next day was spent discussing RT's current activities as both a medicine man and a political leader. That evening he declared that there were so many lovely ladies with us that we could not pass up the opportunity for a dance. During that time of year there was little rain in Nevada, it being the dry season, yet Native American tradition holds that before one initiates a dance there should be a brief shower to settle the dust on the dance ground; moreover, after the dance there should be a stronger rain to wash away the tracks of the dancers.

At sunset we climbed into three cars and headed for an abandoned ranch in a valley a few miles away. On our way to the valley I gazed at the stars, which were shining brightly in the clear sky. Not a cloud was in sight. Suddenly the driver slammed on the brakes and drew our attention to the road ahead of us. Three deer were standing by the side of the road, recovering from their surprise upon seeing our headlights. They took off in a trot, leaping gracefully into the hills.

Just a few seconds had elapsed, but when we looked into the sky again, we observed small, puffy clouds gathering in front of us. A few minutes later we turned on the windshield wipers. The shower stopped as we arrived at the dancing ground. There were no puddles, yet the water had settled the dust. We learned later that a rain dance is not seen as "causing" rain, because that concept reflects Western cause-and-effect thinking. The rain dance attempts to restore balance to the system, and any rain that falls is a result of the restoration of that balance. In fact, as the rain approached, RT exclaimed, "Listen to the Rolling Thunder. That thunder is really rolling in the sky."

We danced for hours as RT's retinue played drums and sang. RT taught us *what he called the snake dance. The sky was still clear as we finished our dance, but on the way to our cars, dark clouds gathered over the clearing. Thunder began to crackle, lightning closely followed, and a heavy rain poured down as we ran the last few yards to our cars. RT observed, "It's not good to leave our prints behind. We don't want the white folks to think that a bunch of savages and hippies were doing some kind of pagan ceremony."*

From an observer's viewpoint it may seem as though RT could have caused the rain to come before and after the dance. To RT, however, it was not a matter of magic or manipulation but a matter of aligning himself with natural laws and subtle energies. A kind of harmony emerges, like a leaf that rides a river and not a fish that swims against it.

Stanley's Comments

I was not present during this incident, arriving in Carlin some time later, but I know that Alberto Villoldo is an acute observer. RT's behavior was typical of North American shamanic practitioners in several ways. The appearance of several "lovely ladies" stimulated RT's suggestion for an outdoor dance. There is a tradition of Elk Power in many Native American shamanic traditions, where sexual attraction is sublimated into spiritual pathways through dance, music, and ritual. RT sometimes fell short in the sublimation process, but on this occasion he manifested his most appropriate social behavior.

The appearance of Deer could be interpreted as the arrival of traditional "power animals," another shamanic tradition, especially in the Americas. Each animal has something to teach its human relatives; for example, Deer is often associated with quick action and clever escapes. When RT commented that the rain would cover the tracks of the dancers, he was reflecting an attribute of Deer. (When referring to a power animal or animal ally, the singular form of the word is often used to emphasize the animal's symbolic essence.)

Many of the people we interviewed for this book had attended one or more of RT's ceremonies. Gary Sandman, an acquaintance of Rolling Thunder, helped him to schedule the lectures and workshops that took him all around the United States and to many parts of the world. Here Gary Sandman gives his account of an early-morning sunrise ceremony with Rolling Thunder and then goes on to discuss Rolling Thunder's early training, what a vision quest is, various people's places in Native society, and as other aspects of the Native American culture.

We gathered one early morning in Santa Barbara, California, to do a sunrise ceremony. It was about fifteen minutes before sunrise, so we started a fire in the fire pit and formed a circle around it, warming ourselves in the chilly weather. RT pulled out a pouch of Five Brothers Tobacco, pure tobacco with no artificial ingredients. He passed the pouch around, each of us taking a little bit of tobacco in our hands. RT then led us in a prayer, starting out with Father Sun, Mother Earth, Grandmother Moon, and All My Relations. He would include "the East where the Sun rises, to the South where the heat comes from, to the North where the cold comes from, and to the West where the Sun sets." RT would vary the order and the wording from time to time, just to maintain our attention, often repeating the prayers to the Sun, Earth, and Moon.

Medicine men and women live in both worlds, thus painting a very different picture of the cosmos. RT was a medicine man. He could see the unseen and interact with the unseen. Part of his training was to take on different illnesses, different challenges—the biggest challenge being life over death. RT's teacher trained him to communicate with Nature, to heal. When RT was ready, his teacher told him, "You're going to go out into the wilderness, and you're going to see two trees ripe with berries. These berries will be identical. One tree will bear poisonous berries, and one will bear berries that you can eat that will nurture you. You are going to learn which one is a poison and which one is edible." And so RT went out into the woods to find these trees, and when he did he sat with them until he knew which one to eat, and then he ate, choosing the berry that would nurture him.

For another training his teacher told him, "You are going to go out into the plains. A donkey will be there. I want you to take that donkey and go up into the *hills. You will find a cave, and it will be full of rattlesnakes. Find the king snake and bow to it. He will offer you his venom; I want you to take it." And so he got on the donkey and went up into the hills and into the snake den. Snakes covered the cave, and for a moment RT just stood there admiring them. Just then a huge rattlesnake, the biggest RT had ever seen, emerged, coming straight to him. He said a prayer, and then the snake bit him. RT recalls passing out and being transported to the "other side," where he literally fought to come back to "this side." From his training and what he was taught, he was able to win that battle and return. The snake's venom is now his medicine, which also allows him to take snakebites and be unaffected by them.*

At one time RT was asked to be part of a movie that was being made about his life story. It was called Billy Jack. *They reenacted a snake ritual and used RT's actual leg for the shot. RT was able to take that venom because of his medicine.*

When RT talked about Indian society, it seemed idyllic. Everybody had a place. Part of growing up involved taking the time to determine who someone's spirit guides were. To determine your spirit guide, you went out into the woods by yourself on a three-day fast. This was a part of your vision quest. It allowed you to understand what your passion was, your identity, to find your place within your tribe. This way you gave your best, because it was your passion, your joy.

Once your Medicine Wheel was drawn, it was put on a shield. Your Medicine Wheel wasn't put there to protect you but to identify you. Your Medicine Wheel was displayed, so when a member of the community came to visit they saw you, your true identity. It was your welcome and said "This is who I am, come celebrate who I am with me." Instead of hiding who you were, you celebrated it and were open to it.

The term Medicine Wheel *has many manifestations. It can refer to a personal icon, which most often is constructed by a medicine person, a person who has charted that person's path. It can also refer to a circular design that a medicine person created as part of a healing ceremony. It can also take a more permanent form, appearing in the form of a circular pattern of rocks representing the relationship between Mother Earth and the rest of the cosmos.*

Everyone had their place in Indian society, even those that seemed to be of no use. When somebody was said to be insane in a community, they didn't put him away in a mental hospital and medicate him. They would allow him to be part of the community. When he talked crazy the medicine man would listen, because he alone was able to translate what was too much for the other community members to understand. The medicine man believed the insane person saw the other side but lacked the training to understand it, so it overwhelmed him. The medicine man would translate these rants and use that information to help the tribe.

The sick had their place as well. When someone was sick, everyone would take care of him or her, as well as the medicine man. It was also a part of the medicine man's role to help if there were arguments or misunderstandings. The medicine man was trusted to have an overview of what was best for the tribe and was careful of energies that could weaken the tribe. When the tribe had to move, the medicine man read the land and decided where they were going to go. He would instruct the tribe to where the proper places were to put the sweat lodge, store the food, and where you could sleep so you were not on a negative energy spot. The medicine man had the eyes to see the unseen and could help settle the village before it had even reached its new destination.

RT saw all forms of behavior as a blessing from the Great Spirit. If there was an early snowstorm, it was a blessing. Everything was a blessing. From the morning prayer to eating, to raking leaves, to hunting a deer, to cracking ice on the water so that the animals can drink, to making love. He said every aspect of what we do can be a prayer to the Great Spirit.

For example, he explained that Native Americans pray for game before a hunt, negotiating with the Creator of the animals to request that a particular animal should sacrifice itself so that the people can eat. In return, the Creator will demand certain obligations, such as using the energy generated by the animal's flesh for constructive purposes. Rolling Thunder said, "We are dancing with the Spirit in everything that we do. It's a part of every aspect of our lives. So why do American white people go into a building to celebrate God?" He thought that a church was kind of strange, because God was in Nature and the Spirit expressed itself everywhere. So why would we go inside instead of staying outside? He thought white people had peculiar habits and patterns.

Rolling Thunder believed that ritual was important in that the ritual itself was an important element in building community. If visitors had never been to RT's home and if they participated in a dance with members of his family and his companions or "spiritual warriors," they were seamlessly inaugurated into the events that would unfold during the rest of their visit. The assiduous scholar of shamanism Christina Pratt writes that the term *spiritual warrior* is a metaphor. It refers to people who fight their own internal enemies as well as those external forces that endanger them and their community. RT taught his entourage how to develop themselves spiritually while, at the same time, being on the lookout for threats from the outside world, whether they were metaphysical, political, or psychological.

A ceremony is what chaos theorists would liken to a "strange attractor," an influence that the rest of the system weaves and dances around, never escaping from its influence. Therefore, the system itself generates its own complicated behavior. When the ceremony begins, time is created for the ceremony. From that moment on, time is sent backward into the past and forward into the future. The strange attractor of time can be generated out of the rhythms and relationships within the world of Nature and Spirit.

A shamanic ceremony is an important community event. Ceremonies consist of a number of rituals, a term applied to those activities considered sacred that carry deep meaning to those who practice them. Quite often these ceremonies are nocturnal activities that unite a community through the use of dancing, singing, chanting, drumming, clapping, and other shared behaviors. Power animals are often evoked and sometimes appear spontaneously, as described by Alberto in his narrative. In fact, many animals appear to "drum," using their bodies to produce vibrations that communicate information to other members of their species.

By drumming, animals often warn members of their group that an enemy predator is nearby. But drumming can also be used in mate selection, especially by male animals who announce their availability and show off their prowess through this type of body signaling. The presence of lovely ladies often stimulated Rolling Thunder's ritual activities, just as the presence of an attractive female often evokes drumming, preening, and courting behavior on the part of male animals.

Shamanic ceremonies and rituals stimulate the release of body opioids and other internal chemicals through repetitive physical activities such as dancing and clapping, extreme body reactions such as sweating (as in the sweat lodge), self-inflicted wounds (as in some versions of the sun dance), emotional reactions (as in wearing or viewing terrifying masks), and suggestion (as in storytelling that creates positive expectations). The body's opioids reduce pain and discomfort, and their production is highest at night.

Sometimes a nighttime activity would continue until the shaman collapsed. Upon recovery the shaman often would report an out-of-body experience that carried him or her into another world. The shaman would bring back information deemed useful to the community. These cognitive processes were animal-like in that they involved hunting and food procurement, as well as protection from the tribe's enemies. The animals that were venerated during these ceremonies could be admired for their power or for their sacred qualities.

These animals were helping spirits who augmented the shaman's power and skills. But these animals were also sacred; they were prayed to, hoping they would intercede in human affairs. Sometimes Deer, Bear, or Eagle were admired for their power and sometimes for their sacred qualities, as when a hunter uttered a prayer of thanks over a recently killed prey, vowing to use its flesh to feed the hunter's family and community. In Rolling Thunder's words, "We give thanks for everything. We offer thanks to the game we have killed, and we express our gratitude to the vegetables we grow in our garden." It is as if Indians knew that hunter and prey were engaged in a mutual dance, one that involved obligations and thanks.

More often than not, the shaman would spend some time during the ceremony recounting mythic stories. During certain rituals the shaman would converse with animal spirits, using a language that other community members did not understand, a language punctuated by animal or bird sounds. Some shamanic rituals would implore malevolent spirits to cease their afflictions or would ask benevolent spirits to locate game, heal the sick, or protect the entire group. Rolling Thunder believed that evil spirits could be kept away through burning incense and playing traditional Indian music; he felt that these spirits were ignorant and could not relate to the smell of incense, sage, and sacred fragrances.

Anthropologists have noticed a similarity between shamanic rituals and certain animal behaviors. There are animal practices that serve as social signals, whether they are for mating, for locating food, or for warning about the presence of predators. These are instinctual behaviors, genetically programmed, that are essential for survival. They served adaptive purposes over the course of evolution. For example, chimpanzees protect their territory against other groups through group shouting, hooting, and jumping up and down on tree stumps. These signals can be heard at a distance and allow dispersed group members to stay in touch with each other during travel. Synchronous group vocalization is found in chimpanzees and other groups, promoting social well-being.

The human expressive capacity of music has deep evolutionary roots and provides a means of communicating information to other members of the group. Musical capacities play an important role in enhancing human functioning at a number of levels, particularly in promoting social solidarity and providing healing mechanisms. Music, through the positive effects of tone and sound on emotions, has positive effects on mental and physical health. Music also influences synchronization. It does this in several ways, ranging from the coordination of emotions through promoting a common sense of intention among group members. The anthropologist Michael Winkelman adds that music synchronizes brain waves, has positive vibratory effects on the body, and impacts the brain's positive emotional processing centers. Therefore, music heals through the elicitation of positive emotions as well as by providing a means for catharsis and the relief of troubling emotions and repressed feelings.

The precursors of the use of music and dancing by shamans can be seen in the rhythmic activities of chimpanzees and other apes. Observers have noted how chimpanzees will engage in foot stomping, marching around a post, and revolving in a circular form while spinning like tops. Males run up and down hills, breaking branches as they go, hooting and throwing rocks. They may even drum on trees or tree stumps, beat on the ground, and wave branches.

Primates exploited this group orientation through mimesis, the deliberate use of communication through imitation. Basic to shamanic rituals are mime, dancing, chanting, singing, percussion, and enacting struggles with one's enemies. Mimesis provides the shaman and the tribe an opportunity to entrain the body, using body movements, facial expressions, and gestures as a form of symbolic communication. Vocal imitation of animals was one of the first examples of human mimesis. Fundamental emotions are expressed in rituals and serve to coordinate the group.

The links among community relations and intercommunity alliances helped shamanism contribute to human survival. When there were droughts only those humans who were able to forge emotional bonds with other people and other communities survived. The tendency to distrust strangers and maintain in-group boundaries was transcended in order to create a common identity. Those early humans who manifested this ability survived in inhospitable environments. At the same time, disruptive members of a community could not be tolerated because they threatened group cohesion. To be banished from a community was seen as a more severe punishment than incarceration or execution, but it had to be done for the protection and survival of the social group.

Shamans facilitated relationships among members of their tribe or clan in several ways. They told creation stories that provided a mythological account of how the group came into being. They told survival stories—mythic talks of how the tribe overcame natural catastrophes, plagues, and warfare. But when it was expedient for the tribe to have peaceful relations with neighboring tribes, shamans would arrange ceremonial bondings, such as passing around a peace pipe filled with sacred herbs, or helping tribal warriors procure enough game and other food for magnificent feasts.

A central aspect of shamanism is community service. Ritual reinforces the biological need for human communication that evolved to provide attachment bonds between infants and those who nurture and protect them. Humanity's evolutionary ancestry produced a neuropsychology for a social world, a need for a shared emotional life that is wired into the human nervous system. Shamanic ritual provided a group identity and a social support system, both of which could be called on when healing was required. In these chapters we will often return to the discussion of evolution, because the human brain and body developed skills that were useful to survival and thus were carried down to future generations. Charles Darwin observed how cooperative activities were much more frequent than aggressive activities; in his book about the ascent of human beings he uses the term *love* or its equivalent dozens of times.

Native Americans experienced being a part of the universe, an integral part of the cosmos in which the lines between past, present, and future were dissolved. The contemporary Western individual's urge to restore this lost unity is an essential factor in such contemporary human activities as meditation, prayer, nature walks, and—for some people—sexual union. Rolling Thunder was a staunch advocate of the powers inherent in sexual activity, believing it facilitated his abilities to "doctor," as he referred to his healing sessions.

When RT talked about sex, he observed, "In the Indian way, sex is a part of Nature and is considered a natural function for people and must be treated with respect. It was not pornography or evil. People were healthy and had healthy minds. That's why we didn't have a lot of so-called sexual problems that a lot of modern people are having." As for women's liberation, RT observed, "Women's liberation was already a fact among Native Americans before Columbus or any other illegal immigrant had become a fact of life and the law of the land." As for love, "True love extends to Mother Earth, Father Sun, Grandmother Moon, stars in the sky that guide our way and give us messages, all animal life, all plant life, and people of different tribes, nationalities, and races."

Sidian's Comments

Weather prediction isn't exactly an enigma with modern technology, given the tons of scientific data at our disposal. However, RT's foresight in Alberto Villoldo's story, like so many other stories I've heard, is uncanny. The timing and the symbolic meaning were integrated very tightly and coincide not only with RT's own words but also with Native American lore in general. Even the degree of intensity of each rain shower proved appropriate to the circumstance.

If one simply accepts the story at face value it only seems to raise more questions, and this can be frustrating. How does one align with such subtle energies, thereby gaining what might be called a clairvoyance of Nature? Have we, as humans, torn ourselves from these connections by constructing and inhabiting antiseptic suburbs and cemented cities? Or are all these events the clever deceptions of a trickster?

For example, before a healing session, a Yuippie medicine man will ask tribal members to bind him very tightly and cover him with a blanket. If he emerges from the blanket, it is a sign that the healing will be successful. If people were to see this feat performed in Las Vegas, they might applaud the expertise of an escape artist. But if many of the same people were to see it performed at a Native American ceremony, they could conclude it was an example of shamanic power. But of course, in this example, the medicine man has control over many variables, such as setting, helpers, items, and so on. In Alberto's story, Rolling Thunder seems to have had little control over any of these things.

These dilemmas seem to permeate every tale I've been told by the countless people who have talked to me about my grandfather. Their validity cannot be known empirically, but the stories can be deeply considered as something worthy of investigation and personal reflection. This is one thing I learned while interviewing people for this book. Even when those men and women I interviewed were present at the same time and place, there were differences in their accounts. Usually the variations provided a fuller account of the event than was present in a single description.

❖

Now let's take a look at a different account of the 1974 "long trip" to Carlin, Nevada, this time through the eyes of Michael Bova, an art therapist and "psychic healer" who accompanied Alberto Villoldo and his group. Michael's account complements what Alberto already described as "a long journey."

In 1974, I was one of five men and women who traveled in a cramped Volkswagen through the Nevada desert to visit Rolling Thunder. When we arrived I remember seeing a sign with the approximate wording, "No Drugs, No Alcohol Allowed on Land" (please see plate 6 of the color insert). Rolling Thunder had not returned from work, but we met RT's wife Spotted Fawn and were invited to wait in the backyard area, where we joined several others who were cutting and drying apples. We joined them in slicing apples, and these slices were placed to dry on the house's hot tin roof. The two young men whom we helped were brothers who introduced themselves as Wild Cat and David Leaping Horse.

Wild Cat, a large man with long hair, said he was a "spiritual warrior" who was apprenticing under Rolling Thunder. He told us that he was learning how to harness lightning and talked a bit about how this ability could be put to practical use. I recall many of his thoughts were about using lightning in terms of civil protests against the Bureau of Indian Affairs. When I introduced myself Wild Cat showed great respect and deference to my work in psychic healing. I clearly remember the part of the ride where there was lightning and heavy rain. I remember the wipers pushing the rain off the windshield as well as the wide horizon with lightning coming down in the distance all around us. The weather is a vivid memory as well as my wondering if Wild Cat's harnessing lightning was at play. This vivid memory bolstered my feeling of discomfort, along with awe, that this "cultural belief" was a reality and I had found myself to be a part of it.

David seemed to be the quieter brother. I recall that he and Wild Cat were always seen together. Both were deeply involved in the ceremonies and activities that took place during the several days of our stay. These included Rolling Thunder's "fireside chat" in his living room, his sunrise ceremonies, his preparation for the sweat lodge and healing ceremonies, and the evening dance.

When Rolling Thunder was ready, all of us visitors were invited into his living room along with Rolling Thunder's family, friends, and spiritual warriors, including Wild Cat and David. RT spent quite awhile talking about many topics relating to the experience of Native Americans, Native American medicine, and his own experiences as a medicine man. In that day's mail a letter had arrived from a young man who had been psychiatrically hospitalized but was now on the mend. He thanked RT for his healing intervention at the hospital. RT told us that the doctors at the hospital told him that this teenager was hopelessly unresponsive to treatment, and it was only after RT physically wrestled the evil spirit out of him as part of his "doctoring" that he began to do better. Spotted Fawn added that RT's intervention in local hospitals was acceptable for many doctors in that part of Nevada.

When RT was talking, at times he seemed to meander among different topics that seemed only loosely connected. But during this time of meandering, when he looked at me RT seemed to look right through me, and his words seemed to directly respond to my unasked questions. I remember telling this to Gary Sandman, another visitor, and he agreed. Sandman told me that he also experienced RT and his conversations in this way. Even though the topic might seem unrelated to what had gone before, it made sense to the person on whom RT fixated his gaze during that part of the conversation.

That night Spotted Fawn; Carie Harris, Stanley Krippner's stepdaughter; and Christine Armstrong, another member of our entourage, prepared a sumptuous meal of lasagna, a very appropriate dish for an Italian American visitor to a Native American home. At the end of the meal I was excited to hear Rolling Thunder's plan for the following night. He had planned to take us dancing, which I assumed would be outdoors. Soon after this announcement on the back steps of his home there was a slight drizzle, and I told RT that I assumed the dance would have to be canceled if there was rain. He said that rain was typical before an Indian dance to settle the dust. But he also remarked that there would be no rain for our dance. Instead, it would rain harder when we were finished to wash away our tracks so the locals will not think there had been a bunch of Indians and hippies dancing in the desert. I thought that was a quaint notion, but all the same I decided to bring my hat along. I had been given a bunk in a trailer in RT's backyard and fell asleep immediately.

We arose early for the sunrise ceremony that Rolling Thunder held each morning with the accompaniment of Wild Cat and David. Rolling Thunder and his words met the morning's stillness and the desert's beauty with Five Brothers Tobacco in his cupped hands as he acknowledged the Great Spirit and the Four

Directions—North, South, East, West—as well as Father Sun, Mother Earth, Grandmother Moon, and All Our Relations, in other words, all other forms of life. It was one of the most moving ceremonies I had ever been a part of, and it set the tone for the entire day.

After breakfast Rolling Thunder shared many of his thoughts and opinions about Euro-Americans' treatment of the Earth. Regarding pollution, RT remarked that one of the worst hazards not realized by many is electronic pollution. The waves given out by radios, television sets, microwave ovens, and other electrical appliances were polluting the air. RT said that the atmosphere is being swamped by these electronic emissions, but few people are paying attention to the effect they are having on us. This pollution interferes with the workings of the mind as well as the body. There are some "power places" in the Sierra Nevada that are far away from radio waves, and those are very special places. Medicine people often go there to rest and restore their energy because there are no distractions, especially electronic ones. They also take people they are "doctoring" there because they can heal faster in this environment.

Spotted Fawn served refreshments, and we took them outside, where we sat down in the shade to discuss the many pressures, tensions, and craziness of life in America's big cities. RT attributed part of these problems to electronic pollution, with city noise coming in a close second.

Suddenly I noticed a spider sitting next to me. I was about to whack it when Spotted Fawn stopped me and gently scooped it up and put it outside, saying that it could be the spirit of an ancestor. I could not tell if she was joking, or if I was meant to take her seriously. After I got to know her better, I suspected that she had been joking.

Rolling Thunder spent most of the day with fellow activists from nearby tribes, and the rest of us enjoyed talking with each other and swapping stories with the spiritual warriors who were on hand to help with chores and yard work. As the sun set I felt a few raindrops and remembered that I had planned to bring my hat along to the dance.

When we arrived at the location chosen for the dance a huge fire had already been built by David and Wild Cat, who were there to greet us. I later learned that lighting a fire is used to begin a cycle; when the cycle is ended and the people are about to disperse, the fire is put out.

The rain had suddenly stopped, and the next few hours were spent dancing Native dance-steps to David and Wild Cat's drumming, which we accomplished with some quick dance-step lessons. We laughed, danced, and had a great time for several hours, and when we finished the last dance we all whooped and fell to the ground in delightful exhaustion. As soon as our butts hit the ground the rain came down. It was immediate, and we quickly readied ourselves up to get back to the cars. I was amazed that the weather changed just as Rolling Thunder had forecast, and I found this both beautiful and disconcerting. A part of me could not make peace with this new reality that I had entered the previous day.

I was also dealing with a very different problem. I did not want to offend Rolling Thunder, but during one of his talks RT stated that it was disrespectful for one healer to conduct healings on another healer or medicine person's land without permission. During the dance I felt deeply in harmony with the experience and found myself moving into the meditative healing state I had learned from Lawrence LeShan, a New York psychologist and parapsychologist, in my seminars with him. I tried very hard to repress this state but was not able to do so completely. As we readied to leave the dance area and go back to our cars I asked Rolling Thunder for some guidance about what I was going through. Rolling Thunder asked me what spirits I call on during healing, and I told him that I did not call on spirits but went into a state of union with another person that was based on love. Rolling Thunder said, "Well, there's nothing wrong with loving someone." So, that was that. It was okay.

This encounter should have helped me to feel better, but once again I felt confused. This special, loving, meditative state that I had dutifully practiced for years was a special state that mystics and saints drew from. I sensed that it was just a warm and fuzzy feeling to Rolling Thunder. At least that's how I saw it at the time. Yet this remarkable man seemed to move in synchrony with atmospheric conditions as we danced. This was something that I never even imagined that I would experience.

That night I went to my sleeping quarters in a trailer that seemed to be kept for guests and for storage. As I walked in, right by the door was a huge plant of some kind that had been pulled from the ground and had been placed there, possibly to dry or for future use. I remembered the books I had read that emphasized Native Americans' awareness of a plant's spirit and its power. That awareness gave respect to these plants, and I felt this plant had been taken from the Earth, possibly by Rolling Thunder or his family members. So my respect for the plant would be enacted by greeting it and not stepping on it as I went toward the bed. I did this little ritual and, again, went immediately to sleep.

A knock on the door awakened me. Another visitor who had no place to sleep asked to share my bed. I told her that it was fine, but before I could warn her about the plants she walked right into the trailer, stomping all over them. My warnings were too late, and before long she was in bed. We lay there for a while talking about the amazing day that we experienced. It was a warm night with only a small open window to mitigate the heat. Suddenly, a small, compact breeze began blowing through the trailer, seeming to ricochet within it. The wind traveled through the trailer faster and faster, which startled us both. I remembered reading a book by Carlos Castaneda in which he became vulnerable to wind currents by cutting down too many plants. I remembered that Castaneda had used balled-up clothing to cover his abdomen, and we mimicked this protection with pillows protecting our bellies until this breeze seemed to leave.

Stan Krippner and Corinne Calvet arrived the following day. Corinne was a friend of Stan's who had hoped that her young son Robin would receive a healing from RT. When Robin refused, Corinne used the airplane ticket herself, planning to ask RT if he could bring relief to an abdominal pain that had resisted the ministrations and medications of a half-dozen Hollywood physicians. Corinne, born in Paris, was an accomplished actress who had appeared on the French stage before being brought to Hollywood to costar in a 1949 film, Rope of Sand, *with Burt Lancaster. Her later costars included Danny Kaye, Joseph Cotten, James Cagney, Alan Ladd, and James Stewart. Later I discovered that Spotted Fawn had seen one of Corinne's films on television the night before her surprise arrival and interpreted this coincidence as a "sign" that RT should agree to her request for a healing. Stan had met Corinne in New York City, where she played an active role in the Arica Foundation, which promulgated the teachings of Oscar Ichazo, a South American spiritual teacher.*

Stan and I spent some time catching up on our activities since our last meeting, and I enjoyed meeting the charming Corrine Calvet. When I was introduced to Rolling Thunder, I was struck by his charisma as well as his great personal power. I brought tobacco to him, as was the custom, and a necklace made of coconut and sea urchins. He liked the necklace and wore it in a frequently reproduced photograph taken that weekend, flanked by two beautiful women, Corrine Calvet and Carie Harris. I had bought the necklace in Manhattan's Union Square; a friend thought that RT would like it because the urchins were from the sea and there was no sea in Nevada.

Rolling Thunder had told us that he usually waits three days before making a decision whether to "doctor" someone who requests help. But Spotted Fawn encouraged him to make an exception in the case of Corrine, based, in part, on the film she had watched while the rest of us were dancing. As a result, RT announced that he would "doctor" Corrine after dinner. RT did not spell out this plan for the evening, but it unfolded later. The men would participate in a sweat lodge purification ceremony, followed by the women. All of us would then do a snake dance around Rolling Thunder and Corrine as he performed the healing ceremony. The plan changed, however; at the end of another delicious dinner it was apparent that there would not be enough time for the women to enter the sweat lodge. But RT pointed out that this was not absolutely necessary because almost all of the women there had purified themselves once a month during menstruation.

There were two small domes, or wickiups, in the backyard area. One was the home of one of RT's children, Buffalo Horse, and the other was the sweat lodge. All the men were instructed to remove their clothing, after which we stood around the fire receiving instructions from Wild Cat. We were to enter the wickiup in a line and sit inside facing the center in a circle. Wild Cat told us that if the steam-filled wickiup gets too hot there are several methods to bear the heat. First, you could cup your hands over your nose, mouth, and chest, keeping your head down to breathe air that is close to your body. Second, you could bend forward and breathe the air closer to the ground. It was important to remain in the ceremony, but if the heat was completely unbearable for someone, this should be announced, and the whole group would leave in formation and the heat-struck person would drop out of the line. Then the group would reenter the wickiup and continue with the purification ceremony.

Following these instructions, Wild Cat placed purple sage on the rocks. He kept the door flap slightly open so that spirits, both malevolent and benevolent, could leave through the door. He told us that if the door was closed too tightly it would explode open as the spirits left. David used a pitchfork to transfer hot stones from the outside fire to a recess in the middle of the wickiup. Rolling Thunder espoused the spiritual potency of circular forms and movements in Nature, and we were blending in with these natural forms.

This evocation of our "circle consciousness" was certainly fortified by the physical reality of our sitting in a circle within a dome. When Rolling Thunder finished his reflections on the spiritual nature of the circle, Wild Cat dipped a ladle into a bucket of water in front of him and said, "Pray for your selves, brothers." This was followed by other prayers, after which he poured water onto the heated rocks several times and steam filled the wickiup. The steam immediately overtook me, sharply stinging my lungs and sinuses. I used the techniques that I was taught to fight the heat, but they did not work, and so I simply gave in to the heat. I accepted and honored the steam, and then it became tolerable. Wild Cat was drumming, but at first I suspected that I was hearing drumming in my head. Then Wild Cat instructed us to wipe the sweat from our bodies and to see this action as wiping away our impurities—emotional, spiritual, and physical. This was a difficult maneuver to undertake, but I accomplished it by focusing on my breathing, coping with the steam. I saw the light from the fire outside filtering into the wickiup from the openings of the uneven patch of hide that served as the wickiup's door. This link with the outside world helped me to endure the heat.

I could see Rolling Thunder in silhouette seated across from me. As the drumming went on and as we cleansed ourselves with the steam, Rolling Thunder's body seemed to change shape, as if it was decomposing, like sand or mud losing its sculpted shape as water washes over it. The silhouette of his human figure transformed itself into a lump of clay, mud, or sand. And then, after a short time, the form shifted again to his recognizable shape.

I refocused on breathing the steam and could feel its actual journey into my sinuses, lungs, and body. I told myself, "Breathe in, breathe out, breathe in, and breathe out." At another point I began feeling a certain oddity of the shape of the ground. I was seated on a curve, and this sensation dominated and puzzled me until I had a body awareness of the curve as the curve of the Earth. I actually felt myself sitting on the curve of the Earth. At this moment I was at one with the Earth, the very ground that Rolling Thunder had shifted into minutes earlier. Lawrence LeShan, with whom I had studied psychic healing, referred to this as entering into a "transpsychic reality," being at one with it all.

Wild Cat told us we were going to take a short break. We left the sweat lodge, cooled down with water from a hose, and returned to the wickiup, except for one member of our group, a novice spiritual warrior who was unable to sustain the heat. When RT decreed that the purification ceremony had come to an end, we dressed and regrouped by the fire, where Rolling Thunder was preparing to "doctor" Corrine. She was sitting on a chair in front of the fire, approximately twenty feet away from the sweat lodge, and Rolling Thunder stood behind her.

RT initiated the healing ceremony by placing raw meat under Corinne's feet. He instructed her to keep her feet on the meat until she was ready to leave the area. She would know when to leave and go inside the house, when she felt that the evil spirits who were responsible for her pain had left her. Wild Cat and David began drumming; the women joined the men, and we all danced the snake dance around RT, Corinne, and the fire—the very dance that we had learned the previous night.

Rolling Thunder held an eagle's feather toward the sky then lowered it over Corrine's head. I later discovered that the eagle was one of RT's "allies" and that the feather was one of his "power objects." As the feather approached her head she cringed and shrunk away from it. This happened several times, and RT interpreted this to mean that the malicious spirits knew that they were losing control over Corinne's body. Then RT started growling. He sucked a spot on Corinne's neck where she had winced visibly as the eagle feather approached it. RT spit out what looked like a black fluid. He did this several times, expectorating it into a pail. RT had given me permission to enter my own healing state, and I did what I could to facilitate the process. I was later told that this was a great honor because of the prohibition of attempting healing on another healer's land.

After a while, Corinne left the group and went inside the house. Stan accompanied her and returned to the group, telling us that her abdominal pain had disappeared. It never returned during the remaining years of her life. Corinne left the Earth in 2001 but never again experienced the pain that had troubled her for so many years. Corinne had two sons; the younger son, Michael, went on to live a happy and productive life. Her older son, Robin, took his own life. Stan and I always speculated what might have happened had he not rejected the offer to visit RT and engage in a healing ceremony.

I was invited to remain at Rolling Thunder's home for a longer visit than the few days that I had planned to stay. I left with my original group simply because I just could not adjust to the reality shift. As profoundly beautifully as the universe worked in RT's reality, it was not the universe that I was used to. I was comfortable with a type of spirituality and healing that worked gently and safely. I was content to engage in Lawrence LeShan's healing procedures, to meditate, and even to participate in the dream studies that Stan had been conducting at his laboratory in the Maimonides Medical Center in Brooklyn, where we first met. Coordinating a dance with a downpour of rain, seeing a medicine man's body change form before my eyes, and hearing about evil spirits leaving a sick person's body were outside of my repertoire of experiences. However, I wrote Rolling Thunder when I got back to Brooklyn. I thanked him for his graciousness and told him that I was lost and confused when I was with him but that at the same time my being was filled with peace and love.

In retrospect, I was amazed and literally stunned by my experiences with Rolling Thunder. My time with RT and his Carlin community brought me a deep feeling of peace. But there was a paradox. I also made a profound Earth connection that was a simultaneous overload—way more than I could take. Carlos Castaneda wrote a book titled A Separate Reality. *This had been a separate reality in spades.*

Finally, let us allow RT to speak for himself (at least insofar as Alberto was able to remember his remarks). When Alberto asked RT about sickness, he recalled that the medicine man responded:

Everything has a cause, and at the same time it is going to be the cause of something else. The medicine man knows this and takes it into account when he is deciding whether to "doctor" someone. Everything has its costs, and illness can sometimes be the necessary price that the person pays for something. This is why a medicine man can take up to three days to decide if he is going to "doctor" someone or not. If we take away an illness or a pain when we are not supposed to, the price the person pays in the future might be even greater. The sick person's spirit knows this even if, on the surface, the person is not aware of it.

I am interested in helping to alleviate pain by using herbs and the waters and all the natural things around us. Every physical object in Nature has a spiritual side; therefore, these objects can be spiritual helpers to the medicine man. The medicine man must know the laws of Nature and understand the spiritual side of things, then these objects can be helpers. This is why my medicine cannot be duplicated. One fellow I "doctored" had my herbal mixture analyzed and determined what plants were in the mixture. He thought that he had discovered one of the secrets of my medicine and put together a similar mixture. Well, that mixture did not work. He had duplicated the physical part of the mixture but did not know how to handle the spiritual portion.

When I find a plant I have never seen before I can hold it in my hand and tell what its uses are. It will communicate with me. It will sing its songs and reveal its secrets. In the winter, when there are three feet of snow on the ground and I need a certain green plant, with green leaves on it, I will find that plant even if I have never been in that place before. But a medicine man cannot do this for show. These things can only be done when they are needed.

Anne Habberton, who went on to become an advisor to international philanthropy groups, visited RT at about the same time. She wrote us a letter containing her impressions.

I was very fortunate to get to know Rolling Thunder, his wife Spotted Fawn, and their family at their home and elsewhere in the vicinity of Carlin, Nevada, for a summer and fall in the early 1970s when I was a young adult. Throughout this time I was impressed by RT's diligence and hard-working life as a healer, father, husband, brakeman on the railroad, and a medicine man. As a medicine man, he carried the burden of the larger society in regard to its relationship and responsibilities to our Earth and all her creatures and peoples. Rolling Thunder was patient, gentle, strategic, respectful, humorous, enigmatic, powerful, quiet, and serious. As a medicine man he was also a teacher and an advocate for Native American rights, a wise man who expanded my understanding of the term healer.

RT was incessant in his pursuit of healing, whether for individuals who came to him for help, or for the Western Shoshone Nation, or for all of us on the planet Earth herself. He spoke of troubled times ahead for the planet, yet he was optimistic and positive on a day-to-day basis.

I met RT with my two friends, one an author and the other a graduate student, both of whom came to RT to offer various types of support and assistance. With his agreement, they also observed and learned much that was included in their later written works. We spent time with RT and his family, both in their home and then for part of the summer RT sent us out to the nearby abandoned outpost of Palisades, on the Humboldt River, to help establish and maintain a safe place for RT's healing ceremonies. We created a camp for ourselves to live and work in, using old abandoned buildings for various work projects, writing, pottery, and the like. We made crude furniture from wood scraps. We cooked food, and I tried firing pottery in a Dutch oven and wood fire. We stored our food in coolers in shaded caves that had been used a century before by Chinese Railroad workers. RT worked as a brakeman on the Southern Pacific railroad, and when his trains came barreling thunderously through Palisades he would heave huge chunks of ice off the train and we would put it in our coolers. We held this special, beautiful place to be sacred, because RT often used it for his healing ceremonies.

At one healing ceremony RT asked those of us who were present to reflect on what we wanted to do with our lives. He asked what meaning would we give to our lives. To my great surprise out of my mouth came the answer, "I want to work with young people in New York City and help improve their lives." As it turned out, I became engaged in that exact kind of work for more than fifteen years.

Another vivid memory of RT was when we trooped out to help him clean up a sacred hot spring. We did this at night under the stars so as not to give away its location to those who might wish RT or the hot spring harm.

A humorous revelation took place one time at RT's home, the living room of which was dominated by an imposing stuffed eagle. We found out that he was using an over-the-counter medicine, Dristan, for a cold he had. We thought this was very funny, considering that he was a traditional medicine man. Yet he was never dogmatic and often was quite practical. I recall a room he had filled with herbs for making medicine and that he kindly made me a terrible-tasting dark medicinal drink for a health problem I was experiencing. The medicine had a horrible taste, but it worked.

I recall a quiet moment with RT when he was sitting out on a hill in the sagebrush discussing the value of an insect's life. He pointed to the large dung beetles busy at work in the soil and told us that they had the right to be left alone. At another time he observed with sadness how humans often step on ants and obliterate their lives without reason or thought about their actions. For RT, beetles and ants are our relatives, deserving our respect and consideration.

At summer's end, when it became too cold to stay at the camp, we rented rooms in Carlin from a retired nurse who burned coffee grounds on her electric stovetop because she loved the aroma of coffee—but as a Mormon was forbidden to drink it. When the other women who normally cooked were unable to do so for several days each month, when they were menstruating, I was called upon to help cook for RT and the many visitors who frequented his home. Although I was a vegetarian, I didn't mind helping cook huge amounts of fried chicken or calamari or whatever was on the menu. Although RT expressed respect for my "vegetable sandwiches," he made it clear he required meat in his diet to give him energy for his work. Once again, he was not dogmatic and respected my own food preferences.

Sidian's Comments

I recalled these accounts about my grandfather in 2009 when I attended a ceremony in the Brazilian rain forest where ayahuasca, a tea concocted by South American Indians centuries ago, was used as a sacrament. I had a series of colorful visions that taught me lessons that I am still trying to incorporate into my life. And I remembered what the anthropologist Jeremy Narby had written in 2001 in his remarkable book *Shamans through Time:* "Here are people without electron microscopes who choose, among 80,000 Amazonian plant species, the leaves of a bush containing a brain hormone, which they combine with a vine containing substances that inactivate an enzyme of the digestive tract, which would otherwise block the effect. And they do this to modify their consciousness. It is as if they knew about the molecular properties of plants and the art of combining them, and when one asks them how they knew these things, they say their knowledge comes directly from the plants." Rolling Thunder said much the same thing, even though both comments make little sense to twenty-first-century pharmacologists and botanists.

2

Time as a Circle

Over the years we have learned that the shaman's world appreciates the multidimensional nature of space and the undulating rhythm of time. Shamans are concerned with timing, with moving in harmony with the rising and falling of the sun and with the appearance and disappearance of the stars. Some traditional cultures have no specific word for time. The Amondawa people, who live deep in the Amazonian rain forests of Brazil, have no watches or calendars and live their lives geared to the patterns of day and night and the rainy and dry seasons. They mark the transition from childhood to adulthood by changing a person's name. For example, a child will give up his or her name to a newborn sibling and take on a new one. The Amondawa culture does have a number system, but it only goes up to four.

The previous chapter described some events that took place during the early morning, at twilight, and at night. These are three time zones about which shamans are quite sensitive, and they reserve specific rituals and ceremonies for each of these time zones. Shamans are concerned with moving in harmony with the rhythms of nature and the universe. Like some contemporary astrophysicists, shamans see time not as a straight line that can be broken down into regular intervals but as an irregular fabric that loops back on itself, sometimes in a very inconsistent way, more like a circle than like an arrow.

The circle is an important symbol in just about every shamanic tradition. In the previous chapter we made several references to circular forms in Rolling Thunder's ceremonies. The circle represents something that comes back to itself in harmony, over and over again. It represents periodic vibrations and movement. Time is the simultaneous, creative expression of all that is, that was, and that ever will be.

As day turns into night, there is a transitional state that Westerners call twilight. This marks a transition between night and day and symbolizes the transition between health and sickness, between youth and maturity, and between being a shamanic apprentice and becoming a shamanic practitioner. In the latter instance the apprentices are no longer who they were but are not yet the person they are to become. They are neither here nor there. But without entering this "twilight," individuals will not complete their initiation. Anthropologists use the term *limen* to refer to twilight states. Without crossing this limen, apprentices will not establish a balanced relationship with their multiuniverse. Entering the limen still occurs once the apprentice becomes a shaman; the practitioner enters this limen to speak to spirits or to journey to the Upper World or the Lower World. Neither of these worlds is constrained by the boundaries of space and time that characterize Middle Earth, the abode of everyone—shamans and nonshamans alike.

The Lower World often is accessed through objects in Middle Earth that go downward, such as tree stumps, caves, natural hot springs, wells, and tunnels. The shaman enters one of these openings and travels downward until reaching the intended area of the Lower World. Many shamanic traditions believe that the Lower World is the abode of their power animals and their helping spirits, many of whom may join the shaman on the journey. Their help is often valuable because tests and challenges may await the intrepid shaman who travels into these realms. Once there, the shaman may retrieve lost souls or find information or medicine that will be valuable in assisting members of the community awaiting the shaman in Middle Earth.

The shaman gains access to the Upper World through natural objects that go upward, like the branches of trees, mountaintops, cliffs, or smoke from a fire. The World Tree of some cultures has its roots in the Lower World, its trunk in Middle Earth, and its branches in the Upper World. In some traditions a rainbow bridge allows a fast journey to the Upper World if a shaman is adroit enough to catch it before it fades away. Once again, shamans may be assisted by helping spirits and power birds who live in this abode or may be assisted by suddenly appearing ladders or by the power of flight. This is the realm of "ecstasy" so often described in the literature about shamans. Practitioners may find lost souls in the Upper World or might retrieve information that will be of use to their community. Natural elements, such as water, earth, fire, wood, metal, and air, can be found in both worlds as well as in Middle Earth; they are essential elements in some shamanic medicines.

Stanley's Comments

In the English language there is an infrequently used word—*imaginal*. The imaginal world is not simply the product of one's imagination. It is a world that exists outside of the conventional world of space, time, and matter. The Upper World and the Lower World are both imaginal. They are not part of the ordinary cosmos, but shamans believe that they are just as real as Middle Earth. Shamans can be described as realists, because the worlds they inhabit and describe might not be visible to other members of their community, but they are arenas in which shamans and other medicine people obtain information and power and sometimes engage in dangerous fights and life-threatening battles on behalf of their community and its members. Rolling Thunder would often gear up for such a fight and would pummel or outwit an unknown adversary while "doctoring" a seriously ill patient.

When Western science claims to be speaking about what is real, it implies that other people's realities are merely myths, legends, superstitions, and fairy tales. This is the way in which a dominant society denies the authenticity of other people's systems of knowledge and strikes at the very heart of their cultures. As a result, what is deemed the acceptable world becomes smaller for the minority society and its members.

But in the imaginal world an action may affect people living in ordinary reality. In this era of world crises, it is essential that people learn to talk and listen together, learn to suspend their prejudices, and allow their consciousness to flow along new lines. It is in this way that the adherents of both Western and Native American realities will be able to learn from each other. This imaginal world resembles what some Jungian psychoanalysts refer to as transliminal reality, which includes phenomena that do not readily fit into the standard cause and effect of logical structures. People who have experiences in transliminal reality typically refer to these experiences as sacred and endow them with special meaning that often changes the course of their lives, even though the Western scientific worldview does not allow for their possibility.

The Native American worldview reminds many physicists of what is known as quantum mechanics, the approach to physics that posits that energy is not infinitely divisible. Instead, energy is absorbed or radiated in a discontinuous way through energy units called quanta, and they are part of the most basic element in the world. But this quantum world appears strange, because previous thinking is so ingrained in Westerners. European languages are rich in nouns and are adapted to talking about objective realities. Native American languages, and there were hundreds of them, express ways of being and living within the world, ways of bringing people together and giving a meaning to their lives—a technology of relating to the unseen powers and spirits of Nature. And these unseen entities inhabit the imaginal world, a world that may be another way of describing the quantum world. The Clovis spear point, with its groove for easy attachment to the spear shaft, has been hailed as one of the first and most far-reaching pieces of technology in the prehistoric world, and it was invented by Native Americans, not Europeans. Less attention is given to spiritual technologies, even though their underlying worldview presaged some of the postulates of quantum theory.

Furthermore, quantum mechanics stresses the irreducible link between observer and observed and the basic holism of all phenomena.

Native American traditions hold that there is no separation between individual and society, between matter and spirit, between each of us and the whole of nature. The physicist David Bohm spoke of what he called the implicate or enfolded order, an order in which the whole is enfolded within each part. This is a deeper physical reality than the surface reality (or explicate order) that is ordinarily perceived by the senses. Bohm argued that classical physics described the surface of reality, but quantum physics allows an understanding of deeper levels of the cosmos. Reality, he said, is not a collection of material objects in interaction but a process he called "holomovement," the movement of the whole.

This enfolded order may be another way of describing the imaginal world. Members of the Blackfoot tribe's Gourd Society wear a necklace of mescal beans in which each bead symbolizes the cosmos and reminds them that within each object the whole is enfolded. The Blackfoot cosmology is based on the concept that there is a spiritual power in the universe that is connected to the natural world. This power is referred to as the source of life and is intangible and elusive.

In much the same way, quantum mechanics posits that the essential stuff of the universe cannot be reduced to billiard ball–type atoms but exists as relationships and fluctuations at the boundary of so-called matter and energy. Several quantum physicists suggest that nature is not a collection of objects in interaction but a fluctuation of processes. The fluctuating quantum field has replaced the mechanistic movement of atoms and their components as the space-time embodiment of motion. In general, Native American traditions teach that the cosmos is an expression of relationships, alliances, and balances between energies, powers, and spirits. Many Native American dialects (Blackfoot, Cheyenne, and Ojibwa among them) share a verb-based family of languages that reflect direct experience.

Many quantum physicists picture the material world as being the outward manifestation of patterns, forms, balances, and relationships among the powers and entities that surround them. The various alliances, pacts, and relationships that Native Americans have entered into with these powers form an important aspect of this world. These relationships carry with them obligations and the necessity of carrying out periodic ceremonies of renewal such as the purification and sun dance ceremonies. According to the mythology of several tribes, both of these ceremonies were gifts from White Buffalo Calf Woman. According to a Sioux myth, two young hunters were on a plain when they saw a beautiful woman approaching them. One hunter immediately had lustful thoughts. White Buffalo Calf Woman did not appreciate the compliment and covered his body with a cloud; when the cloud lifted, only a skeleton remained. She told the other hunter to prepare the Sioux for her arrival. He did as he was told, and White Buffalo Calf Woman was received with great respect, especially by the young braves. After all, the tribal members did not want to end up as skeletal remains. In return for their welcome, she gave them a sacred bundle containing the first pipe and instructed them on how to use it. She also taught them seven sacred ceremonies. In addition to the sun dance and sweat lodge purification ceremonies, the tribe learned the keeping of the soul, the crying for a vision, the naming of relations, the throwing of the ball, and the preparation for womanhood ceremonies. The beautiful woman then turned herself into a white buffalo calf and strolled away. From time to time she reappears—usually in her buffalo form so as not to distract young men from her spiritual messages.

Native American creation stories often reflect a philosophical sophistication that equals or surpasses that of accounts popular in the rest of the indigenous world. The Muskogee Indians believe that the world and all it contains are the products of mind. Matter is not something that has given birth to mind but something that once was mind, something from which mind has withdrawn. Mind was visible in all living things, such as plants and animals. Medicine people were able to penetrate healing plants, animal allies, and even minerals and rocks to find that aspect of mind that could be of service to a patient.

The Omaha tribe believes that life can be found in everything, both organic and inorganic. Life manifests itself in two ways. First, all motion and all activities of mind and body are the result of this invisible life. Second, life holds structure and form together, as can be seen in mountains, rivers, deserts, plains, and forests, as well as in plants and animals. This invisible life force has considerable power and can be put to use by medicine men and medicine women. It also links the living to the dead and humans to all other aspects of Nature.

The Sioux believed that Spirit is the source of energy in all of Nature. Spirit can be seen in persons—not only humans but other "persons" as well, including animals, birds, fish, vegetation, and even stones and water. All of these persons manifest mind, reason, intelligence, and other aspects of Spirit.

The Algonquin, Sioux, and Iroquois people use a unit of ten for counting, as is done in Western cultures. But the Mayan unit of twenty is still preserved in parts of Central America and by the Inuit in Alaska.

Numerals often played an important role in creation stories. The number four, as in the Four Winds, is embodied within such images as the Medicine Wheel and sacred hoop. Numbers are represented as marks, notches, and symbols on rocks, canes, knots, or shell fragments on a wampum belt. Each number possesses a quality and a Spirit of its own. Zero was discovered by the Maya several centuries before the Arabs did, and it was seen as the symbol of the Egg Creator, out of which the cosmos was born. Quantum field theory is a branch of quantum physics and deals not only with atomic and subatomic particles but also with energy fields and the forces that hold the nucleus of the atom together; the absolute zero, the vacuum state, of the quantum world is full of energy. The center is the mirror that stands between two worlds and reflects each into the other yet belongs to neither. In discussing his early training as a medicine man, RT once recalled, "We had a seven-sided medicine house. The ceremony honoring the fire took place once every seven years and had to be started with seven types of wood native to the area." For RT, the number seven had special qualities, and he put this power to use as often as he could.

The Hopi creation story holds that at first there was only the Creator, Taiowa. All else was endless space. There was no beginning and no end, no shape, no time, no life. Then Taiowa, the infinite, created the finite, and the universe came into being. The Blackfoot Indians believe that all living creatures gain their power from the Sun and that the Sun is a living being. All indigenous people have creation myths about their tribal ancestors, and these tales provide them with an understanding of their place in the cosmos. As the famed Spanish film director Guillermo del Toro commented in a 2011 interview, art and storytelling serve primal, spiritual functions in daily life. Using himself as an example, he compared his filmmaking efforts to telling his children bedtime stories and said that he took both activities very seriously.

In Native American gatherings, a person who listens at night to the teachings of the Medicine Wheel often sees a sacred hoop in the crescent of light cast by the fire, in the circle of people around the fire, and in the smoke hole above the tepee. But the circle is always open, allowing new teachings and new knowledge to come in.

Some tribes have "keepers of knowledge" who know where all this information is stored and who are able to pass knowledge to the next generation through such oral traditions as myths, songs, games, and dances. The belts and sticks they use often serve as mnemonic devices that help the keepers of knowledge relate their long histories and creation stories. These accounts are often given at night, which holds a special power for telling stories, giving teachings, and performing rituals. The physicist David Peat relates these stories to Bohm's idea that ordinary experience is the surface manifestation of a deeper implicate, enfolded order. Tribal myths and ceremonies are ways of allowing people to enter into this larger dimension of reality, a dimension that is close to the world of quantum physics. For Bohm, science is a disciplined approach to understanding and knowledge, to the processes of coming to understanding and knowing. It provides a coherent scheme of things, thus forming a basis for action. Bohm felt that understanding was the true criterion of science.

Many Native American traditions link understanding to action. For example, many of their stories lend credence to understanding creation as a cycle. Several contemporary elders speak of a need for a great healing, calling for red and white brothers and sisters to sit in a circle together, listening to and talking with each other.

Aside from the Maya and other Central Americans, it has been assumed that writing did not exist in North America before the Europeans arrived. Once their priests encountered the Mayan libraries, they burned them to the ground, assuming that they must be the work of the devil. However, RT insisted that there was more writing than conventional scholars have identified. In addition to petroglyphs, which are ubiquitous wherever there are rock formations, there is evidence of elaborate writing systems, especially among the Ojibwa and Mi'k Maq tribes. Examples can be found recorded on birch bark, wooden panels, talking sticks, and wampum belts. RT asserted, "A great ancestor of mine, Sequoyah, never claimed that he invented the Cherokee alphabet. He belonged to the Scribe Society and only members knew about the writing at the time. The original alphabet had ninety-two letters. Sequoyah revised it so that it could be translated into English and not be destroyed, cutting it down to eighty-six letters."

Gary Sandman's Story

In chapter 1 Michael Bova discussed how his encounter with Rolling Thunder's world challenged his worldview. Several chapters in this book describe events that radically altered the worldviews of other men and women who experienced them. For example, Gary Sandman, who contributed to chapter 2, was inspired to start his vitamin company, Individualized Supplements, as a result of his friendship with RT.

In reflecting on what he observed about RT's concept of time while he (Sandman) was living at the Meta Tantay community, Sandman recalled:

When RT would talk about his famed sunrise ceremonies, he would remind us that "when Nature is in flux, there is an open doorway that will magnify your prayers. The solstice and the equinoxes are times of flux. Mornings and nighttimes, sunrise and sunset, are also times of flux." Then he would pray that those who were going somewhere that day would have a safe journey. If something was to be delivered, he prayed that it would arrive safely. And then he would ask each of us to make our own personal prayer, and that was it.

We would start our days like that, right at the crack of dawn. Then we would have breakfast, which had been prepared by the women. Once the men had eaten, we would go out into the fields and take care of the farm and the animals or continue building new structures or doing repair work, depending on what our chores were. And then the women would sit down and have their food, knowing that they had taken care of the men. And the men knew that they were taking care of the women by caring for the crops and the animals and the buildings. There was this wonderful exchange.

During one of my visits to Meta Tantay, I brought a couple of radical feminists with me who were preaching to everyone how horrible this division of labor was and how terrible women were being treated. And the women that were there would look at them and say, "You're the ones that don't seem happy, not us. Why are you trying to change us when we're very happy? We love this way of life. Why don't you try it, and maybe you'll be happy." But those words had no effect on them.

RT came over to me later on and said, "Gary, we have a problem here. You know how those two women are. They're really disrupting things, and the women they're disrupting don't agree with what they are saying. They're happy." I said, "I understand. I'll take care of it." So I approached the two women I had brought with me and said, "We're leaving Meta Tantay, and we're going to camp out in the national forest nearby." And so they settled down once they got out of there, but they were still upset, and I said, "They're happy, you're not. Why are you trying to change them?" And they just didn't understand. They simply felt that the old roles were not fair to people.

But RT had an answer to that, and he said to us, "Well, the structure of our community is that the men are the ones that take council first and make the decisions, and after the men have voted on it, that decision is then handed over to the women." His wife Spotted Fawn was in charge of bringing the women together, and they could veto the decision or not. And if they vetoed it, the men would have to do what the women had decided. So in effect there was a balance of power between men and women, a beautiful way of making decisions. It allowed the men to feel they were in charge but at the same time let the women know that they would make the final decisions. In addition to balance there was trust as well. RT would often say that whenever there was an argument between a man and a woman, the man would have to be very careful because all the woman ever had to do was put the man's saddle out on the front porch and he would have to leave the house and that was it. The woman didn't have to talk to him or explain anything. He was simply discarded. So, RT said women have that power and that men need to support that power and know that is the way it is. In fact, that was one of RT's landmark expressions. When he had expressed an insight or a natural law he often ended the discussion by saying, "And that is the way it is." At that point, there was nothing more that could be said.

Sometime later RT expanded on this theme, claiming that before the Europeans arrived Indian society never had jails, never had homes for old people, and never had hospitals because they would always take care of each other. And whoever gave birth would be taken care of by the mother of the tribe or the medicine person as needed. All the women were there to help the mother raise that child. And when a woman went on her period, her "moon time," she would go to a special tepee, where she was given three days of vacation time. She could sit back and read and go swimming or whatever else she wanted to do. During menstruation she had her own private rest days, and she could use that as her own spiritual time because women didn't need to purify themselves as often as men did. They had a purification that occurred every month for them. While they were menstruating, their meals were made for them, and they didn't have to do any work, and they were taken care of, served, and loved.

I thought, what a neat experience for someone to have: "Honey, don't do anything. Just kick back and relax." RT told my radical feminist friends about this, and they replied, "Look at it. She's trapped. She's isolated from her family. This is a horrible thing to do." But they never really got to understand the other side. The menstrual cycle is another example of how Native Americans thought of time as a circle, not as an arrow.

Sidian's Comments

Rolling Thunder was a man of tradition. He had a reverence not just for the past but also for the reasons things had come to be the way they were. That said, humanity has never experienced such a vastly accelerated time of technology and progress than now. In the life span of humanity, we've only been civilized for a fraction of that time, and, looking through the eyes of someone from one hundred years ago, we are not just living in the future but in an entirely different world.

How do we compensate for that? What old ways are too biologically ingrained to do away with, and what new ways must be taken on to come to terms with such a massively different environment? As you can see, I could make a great case for either side. What I've found seems to actually work best in life is allowing for people's individuality to take rein. Those women who believed the women in Rolling Thunder's group were being oppressed were exhibiting a strong adherence to what, in my Open Source Religion movement, we'd call a feminist belief module. This is really neither good nor bad. A belief is as productive or destructive as a person trains it to be. Those women may have been truly unhappy to join Rolling Thunder's group and operate the way it did. Then again, perhaps centuries of past tradition, biology, and psychology would eventually win out.

One has to consider self-reflecting on their beliefs from time to time and putting them under trial. As it stands, I think this story is a good example of the sort of inner struggles we can expect to have when faced with the lifestyle of a medicine man. Obviously it isn't for everyone, and some even consider it downright wrong. As you read more stories in this book you're sure to face more social and spiritual challenges. Take this time to self-reflect and become more solid in your understanding of who you are. What traditions do you keep? Which do you resist?

One of my most informative interviews was with Leslie Gray, a Native American who has a Ph.D. in clinical psychology and a California state license in psychology. But she also did a full-fledged shamanic apprenticeship and combines the two traditions when she works with patients; I refer to her as a psychologist-shaman. Gray knew RT quite well, and she reflected on his concept of the universe.

Your grandfather had a lot of rules for the young people who hung out with him, but if I had all those starry-eyed kids with loose boundaries hanging around, I'd start laying down rules too. But these rules reflected the way that RT lived in the universe. I think he felt there were laws to the universe, the laws of Nature that were central and simple. If you pollute the air you won't be able to breathe, if you don't take care of the water you won't be able to drink. There is a sense of balance in Nature, and balance was something he really understood. Sometimes there was balance with things he didn't want to be in balance with, but I don't think he had rules that he made exceptions to. I think that's part of why he had such a sense of humor.

I attended a number of his presentations where humor was a central part of the talk. I saw him once at the College of Marin, and he was about, you know, an hour late, and all these guys with "We Know How" shirts were playing drums with a heartbeat, boom-boom, boom-boom, and it created this electric atmosphere of anticipation. And finally he walks through the door and stands up there at the podium and he farts. And I laughed my head off, and most people, they were into this "be respectful to the guru" mode, and they were just sitting there very quietly as if this was a teaching or something, and I just cracked up. Rolling Thunder didn't give a damn about that, and once I even heard him say that if you keep it in you're going to get sick. So that was an unusual way to begin a talk. It is an example of what his philosophy was, and he would say, "Yes, this is the way things go, except when they don't."

Gray wrote about her psychotherapy practice in a book titled *Moonrise: The Power of Women Leading from the Heart.* In that book, she commented:

The inspiration for my life work has come from medicine people, seers, healers, and shamans—many of whom were real crackpots. That's a comfort. Their model has allowed me to operate from a place of not knowing. The direction West on the Native American medicine wheel is called the "Looks-Within Place." It is the place of dreams and daydreams. It is the dark cave. It is the place Bear goes to sleep in order to survive the harshest season. So the healing power of West is that we do not know. Surely, that is one place we can dwell in honesty. By selecting and trusting answers from the Looks-Within Place, I have personally arrived at ways to turn apparently hopeless situations around while operating from what seems to be a powerless position.

That statement reminded me of the indeterminacy principle in physics. If a physicist measures light in one way, it appears to be made up of particles, but measured another way, it is a wave. One's perspective determines what one sees and what one experiences. In her book, Gray concluded, "Many current domestic and global predicaments indeed appear unsolvable. Nevertheless, creative solutions may lie in realms where apparently contradictory elements unite. This is what Einstein meant when he said that imagination is more important than knowledge."

I would like to end this chapter by citing my grandfather's thoughts on the cosmos. Alberto Villoldo remembers sitting in RT's living room, noticing the stuffed eagle just above RT's favorite chair. RT was smoking a pipe filled with Five Brothers Tobacco, his favorite brand. RT observed, "Everything in the universe rises and falls and travels in cycles. These cycles are energy patterns created in the universe itself. And they repeat themselves in the bodies of everyone living and everything that is alive. I think that as scientists do more explorations in this area they will find that these energy patterns explain a lot. Scientists have done some experiments on the life force in plants and animals. I think this is the deepest aspect of what you call psychic phenomena. The meaning of life itself seems to be what these scientists are working on at this time, and I think it's a real good thing."

3

The Mist Wolf

In November 2007, we were invited to speak at "The Unbroken Chain," a symposium sponsored by the University of Massachusetts in the town of Amherst. This symposium brought together dozens of scholars who have studied the music, lyrics, and social impact of the Grateful Dead, the famed American rock group. Our talk at the symposium explained how RT met most of the Grateful Dead band members and the relationship RT had with the group over the years.

Harry, one of the members of the audience, told us that he had witnessed one of RT's healing sessions. The person needing help was a woman with an abdominal tumor, and she was placed on a table padded with blankets. As was his custom, RT asked for a plate of raw meat, and someone procured ground beef for him. Harry claimed that he saw smoke coming from the meat during the session and that the table started weaving. Harry also told him that the walls seemed to be wavering and that he heard strange music. Unfortunately, Harry did not have any idea whether the healing session had been successful and could not provide Stanley with the names of any other witnesses who could verify his story. However, Stephan A. Schwartz, Senior Samueli Fellow for Brain, Mind, and Healing of the Samueli Institute, sent us a detailed account of another healing session. Schwartz recalled:

We are standing in a parking lot as twilight gathers. Maybe there are twenty of us, including half a dozen physicians. Standing there, leaning in, we are watching Rolling Thunder, a Native American medicine man, attempt to heal the wound of a teenage boy lying on a massage table. It is a painful wound, torn into the muscle of his leg, and the boy is clearly in discomfort and just as obviously medicated. He got this wound through some kind of accident. And it is not healing properly, which is what has brought him to this Virginia Beach parking lot at the back of Edgar Cayce's old hospital, now the headquarters of the Association for Research and Enlightenment (ARE), the organization founded in 1931 to preserve Cayce's readings, discourses given while Cayce lay seemingly asleep but actually in a state of nonlocal awareness, in which time and space took on different meanings. It seems fitting to be standing here, a generation later, watching for signs of another nonlocal phenomenon, namely therapeutic intent expressed as physical healing.

For many reasons Edgar Cayce should be acknowledged as the father of complementary and alternative medicine. His observations about health and his therapeutics are today as fully integrated and general as no longer to be associated with him. They are part of the contemporary paradigm. But the therapeutic intent, about which Cayce spoke, the idea that the consciousness of one person can therapeutically affect the well-being of another, in 1968, is still very controversial. If this works I will see something, we all will, that shouldn't be possible—if the world is strictly physical.

A small log fire that I had built earlier at Rolling Thunder's request flickers on the ground and is just below the boy's head. I am here as a journalist. This ceremony is taking place as a part of my interview with Rolling Thunder. Some of my income comes from writing for the Virginian-Pilot about unusual people who come to Virginia Beach, which typically means coming to the ARE.

Hugh Lynn Cayce, the ARE's executive director, called late on Monday afternoon to say a shaman, a medicine man as he explained it, was coming. If I wanted to interview him I could pick him up at the Greyhound station and talk to him that afternoon. Saturday he would be doing a traditional Native American healing ritual, which I was welcome to attend. That's how I first heard about Rolling Thunder. Of course I accept, and he gives me the time. Four o'clock. I have to check the location; it seems so improbable: "The Greyhound bus station in Norfolk?" "The same," Hugh Lynn replies.

I had done a number of these interviews and was thinking of doing a book comprised of them. Although I had interviewed some other journalists and a few scientists, many of the people I had met through Hugh Lynn put themselves forward as spiritual teachers and were accepted, by at least some people, as being the genuine article. Having spent hours talking to these men and women, listening to their stories, their answers to my questions, and seeing their affect, how they dressed, how they stood, their eyes, what I can only call their beingness, I have begun to develop some discernment. It is clear to me that authenticity is in part a measure of the continuity between the public persona and private personality. To the degree they are not one and the same, that person seems diminished.

About a month before, Hugh Lynn had alerted me to the arrival of an Indian of another type, a Hindu priest from India. He arrived in a Cadillac accompanied by an entourage. In the trunk of the car were the food he would eat and the pans it would be prepared in and the dishes on which it would be served. "The master is so evolved, he is barely in touch with the physical plane anymore," an acolyte, a senyasin, explained to me as he brought out the boxes. "Wow," I thought. "This man must be in a truly exalted state of consciousness." I looked forward to hearing him speak later that night. During the event, however, he was quite disappointing. He had beautiful diction but spoke almost nothing but platitudes and slogans. By the time he was through I realized I was dealing with shtick, whether consciously contrived or not I couldn't tell. But it taught me a lesson I never forgot: if an expert is someone from more than one hundred miles away with a briefcase, a holy man may be only someone from a distant land, practicing an unfamiliar faith with a different set of altar ornaments.

This is still very much in my mind on a hot summer afternoon as I drive down to the Greyhound station. The Norfolk iteration of this cultural institution comes complete with the usual crowd: sailors joshing one another. Marines playing a game of blackjack, old black ladies sitting cooling themselves with paper church fans. And leaning against the snack counter a middle-aged Indian with an unblocked cowboy hat, an old tweed jacket, and a bolo tie with a turquoise slide. He is eating some cheddar cheese Nabs and drinking a Coke. He smokes a pipe, I can see; it is sticking out of the breast pocket of his jacket.

We introduce ourselves, and he picks up a small bag, and we walk out to the car. Twenty minutes later we are driving down Shore Drive, which parallels the coast, and he asks me to stop at a supermarket. Would I go in and buy two steaks? Sure. In those days I was a vegetarian, really a vegan, and buying steaks for a powerful shaman seems very odd. I am such a naif. Hospitality demands his request be honored, so I go into the market and buy him two of the best porterhouse cuts they have. A mile farther and Shore Drive cuts through a state park, and suddenly we are in beach wilderness such as the sixteenth-century colonists would have seen, and it runs on for several miles. We are about midway through when Rolling Thunder asks me to pull over. Reaching for his bag, he opens the door and gets out of the car, asking me when he is supposed to be at the ARE. I think he wants to take a leak. But no, he clearly intends to leave me. About 7:00 p.m., I say. He thanks me, asks me to build a small fire where he is to work, and turns and walks down the bank and into the woods. "Don't forget the steaks," he says as he strolls away. He is completely natural in all of this. It is not being done for effect, and as it is happening, it seems the most obvious and appropriate thing for him to be doing. Only as I watch him vanish into the trees does it become clear how unusual this is. Presumably he is going to sleep in the woods.

Rolling Thunder reminds me of a Polish sergeant I had. He was so thoroughly secure in his esoteric skill set that what seemed improbable he did with effortless competence. I realize they are just different kinds of warriors.

The next afternoon I go up to the ARE with the steaks in a cooler. Someone has moved a massage table out into the parking lot. Not quite sure where the fire should be, I gather wood from the forest that borders the back of the parking lot and set it up near the table, then leave for an early dinner. When I get back, just before seven, a crowd has gathered. I get the cooler out of the car and go over and light the fire.

Hugh Lynn comes over, wearing an ironed white shirt without a tie and a windbreaker. He always reminds me of a prosperous small-town banker. In fact he has the mind of a Medici and is the most interesting person I have met doing these interviews. He introduces me to two of the doctors, then goes over to the vans parked nearby and talks with two women. They are the mothers who have accompanied their sons. Inside each van I can see that each of the boys to be healed lies quietly in the back. It is twilight now, and I can see them framed in the overhead light in the vans. Another physician, almost in silhouette, moves between them.

Precisely at seven Rolling Thunder, looking exactly as he had the prior day, walks out of the woods holding his small bag. He goes up to Hugh Lynn, who, seeing him coming, calls everyone together. He says a few words of introduction, and while he does this Rolling Thunder kneels down and pulls out from the bag what I can see, from maybe three feet away, is the breast and extended wing of a crow or raven. The pinion feathers are spread. Seeing me, he thanks me for the fire and asks if I have brought the steaks. I go to the cooler and bring them over. He takes one and tears off the plastic wrap and the paper tray, handing this back to me. He walks the few feet back to the fire and drops the steak into the gravel and dirt next to the little fire ring of stones I have made. It is the strangest thing he has done yet, but like walking into the woods, it just seems the thing to do.

He gestures to Hugh Lynn, who goes over to one of the vans, and the boy within is brought out on a stretcher and placed on the massage table. Rolling Thunder talks quietly to the boy, who seems to be having trouble at first focusing on what is being said, probably because the move has caused him additional pain. But gradually he calms down and lies still, his eyes closed. His mother comes over and stands to one side. While this is going on, by unspoken consensus we observers have been slowly shuffling forward until we reach an acceptable compromise between intruding and being able to closely observe. It turns out that this is an arc about eight feet away from the boy on the table.

Rolling Thunder begins a soft, slow chant. I cannot make out the words, just the rhythm of the rising and falling sound. He begins making slow passes over the boy's form using the wing and breast of the raven, moving it just an inch or two above his body. I can see the feathers spread slightly against the air pressure as his arm sweeps along. They are long graceful strokes. Every second or third stroke he flicks the wing tip down toward the steak on the ground. As it grows darker the fire becomes more prominent, and the boy and the man drift into shadow.

It goes on monotonously. Everything else is silent. Suddenly, I notice that there is a white, mistlike form taking shape around and in front of Rolling Thunder's body. Sometimes I can see it, sometimes not. But it becomes stronger, steadier, until it is continuously present. It is almost dark now, but the fire gives enough light to see. Then it takes form, slowly at first, but as if gathering energy into itself it takes form. I can clearly see that the smokelike figure is a wolf. Rolling Thunder moves as rhythmically as a clock. Sweep. Sweep. Flick. Sweep. Sweep. Flick.

After about thirty minutes the form begins to fade, first losing shape, then becoming increasingly insubstantial. Finally, it is nothing more than a chimera, there and not there. Then it is gone. Rolling Thunder straightens up and stops. He makes *a kind of gesture, and somehow we are released and come forward. The boy is very peaceful. His mother also has come forward, and she leans over him, kissing his forehead. The wound is completely healed. It looks like your skin does when a scab falls off, leaving smooth, unlined pink skin, shiny in its newness. I am astonished. Clearly so is everyone else. I go over to Hugh Lynn. Hugh Lynn asks me, "What did you see?" I tell him, and when I say the mist took form, he says, "Was it a wolf?"*

There is a kind of break. People go to the bathroom or get a drink of water. About thirty minutes later we gather again. The second boy is brought out. I cannot see anything wrong with him. His mother, however, is very attentive, so something is wrong. Hugh Lynn says it is a broken bone that will not heal. Rolling Thunder asks for the second steak, and I go back to the cooler to get it. This one he also drops to the ground. He says nothing to me, and I know better than to say anything to him.

The chanting begins, and all appears to be headed toward what it once was. The mist, about two inches thick, begins to form. It grows stronger, stops flickering, but just as it begins to take form, it stalls. It happens once, a second time, a third. This time I look around, and my eyes are drawn to the mother. I have no idea how I know this, but I know it is the boy's mother. She is blocking this from happening.

As Rolling Thunder is beginning a fourth attempt he suddenly stops. He straightens up, turns, and walks over to Hugh Lynn. He says, "I cannot do this. The mother will not permit it. She has a mother's love, and it is very powerful."

"Yes. I noticed. I'll talk to them."

Hugh Lynn goes over and talks to the doctor for a while, then the mother and the son. I can't hear them. Then he comes over to where I am standing and says, "He was drifting away from her, now he is dependent once again. She is conflicted about giving that up."

People are drifting away. I can hear cars starting, and in the glare of their headlights, I go over and kick out the fire. Rolling Thunder is there before me. He reaches down, and I can see the steaks. Both are withered and gray. One of them hardly looks like meat at all. "You put whatever is wrong into the steak?" "That's right. The fire will purify and release it."

He throws them into the hot coals. The fat crackles and catches fire. The two of us stand there in silence. It doesn't take long, and they are gone. During those minutes I don't know what Rolling Thunder is thinking, but I am trying to reconsider how the world works.

Stanley's Comments

This account is well written and evocative. I only wish that Stephan Schwartz had recorded and published it at the time it happened, because time can play tricks with our memories. Nevertheless, I have known Stephan for a number of years and consider him to be a person of unquestioned integrity. In addition, this account squares with other accounts of RT's healing sessions told to me by other observers over the years. One of the people who Sidian interviewed was the spiritual counselor Everlight. Here is her corroboration of the story.

Sidian Morning Star Jones: Were you at the Association for Research and Enlightenment when RT came to visit?

Everlight: Yes.

Sidian Morning Star Jones: Were you there when he ordered the two raw steaks?

Everlight: Yes.

Sidian Morning Star Jones: And you saw the one steak change?

Everlight: Yes. It vaporized. Fumes seemed to come up from the steak.

Sidian Morning Star Jones: Stephan Schwartz has written up his account of this session. Do you know him?

Everlight: Yes.

Sidian Morning Star Jones: He wrote it up so beautifully.

Everlight: Whenever RT would work with the meats the only thing that would be left would be rotten because it would take on all the poisons from a patient's sickness.

Incidents of this nature are fodder for parapsychologists. The controversial field of parapsychology investigates observations, experiences, and behaviors that seem to transcend mainstream science's concepts of space, time, and energy. I use the word *seem* because future research might indicate that these reports are not as unusual as they appear right now. For me, science keeps correcting itself, adding new principles and discarding old ones. Such parapsychological terms as *telepathy, clairvoyance, retrocognition, precognition, extrasensory perception,* and *psychokinesis* are temporary labels that might yield to more sophisticated terms such as *nonlocal behavior, remote perception,* and *remote perturbation.* All of these fall under the rubric of *psi,* a word parapsychologists have used for many decades.

My personal preference is to use the terms *remote* (or *nonlocal*) *perception* and *psi beta* to refer to receptive psi, such as mind-to-mind communication (telepathy), perception of distant events (clairvoyance), knowledge of past events (retrocognition), and uncanny knowledge of future events (precognition).

I prefer the term *psi kappa* to refer to expressive psi, such as unusual influences on moving objects, on static (nonmoving) objects, and on living objects, especially organisms needing healing. All of these could be thought of as forms of psychokinesis or psi kappa.

Finally, my preference is to use the term *psi theta* in referring to phenomena associated with survival of some aspect of personality after death. Past-life reports or reincarnation are among these phenomena; after-death communication is another. So-called mediums purport to facilitate this communication with people no longer alive. Such reports as out-of-body experience and near-death experience often provide what some investigators consider evidence for psi theta.

My old friend Marcelo Truzzi, a sociologist, often remarked, "Extraordinary events require extraordinary evidence." It is not uncommon for people to have unusual experiences. But there is a chasm between an "experience," which is highly subjective, and an "event," which is more objective and can be measured, repeated, and verified by more than one person. Stephan's report could have been attested to at the time by the onlookers, but the opportunity slipped away. Even so, I would consider the anecdote a possible example of psi kappa. In this case, RT purportedly influenced diseased tissue, an influence that restored one of the two boys to health. And as noted above, one of the onlookers, Everlight, corroborates Stephan's account.

However, there is another way to look at this report. One boy wanted to get well. His mother wanted him to get well. RT's ritual may have provided the stimulus for the boy's self-healing mechanisms to kick in, releasing the bodily chemicals that are part of the immune system, that internal source of self-regulation that plays an important role in recovery from a sickness. It does not explain the mist wolf that Stephan reported; that apparition still remains *anomalous,* a word used to describe a rare, unexplained observation.

Gary Sandman spent a great deal of time with RT, and he recalls an example of possible remote perturbation. In an interview for this book, Gary recalled:

When we came back from a trip once, RT brought back a ring made for him by some Indians on the East Coast. He had a real affinity to the ring, mainly because it was made by Indians. He really loved it, but he could not find it. We looked through everything, and he said, "Well, I must have left it behind." He went into the spare bedroom and said, "I guess I'm just going to have to trade it for this one." And he took off one of his other rings and put it on the table. He said a prayer, and he left the room.

And the next morning we all peeked in there, and sure enough his East Coast ring was there. He had traded rings somehow. We don't know how he transported it, but he did the same thing another time. He had lost one of his favorite pipes, and he said, "I'll give this one up." He put another pipe on a tray, and the next morning his lost pipe was there. And we have no explanation of how it got there, because he never went back into the room. We kept an eye on him because we were interested in seeing if he could do this. And sure enough, the items that were placed there were gone, and the items that he really wanted had taken their place. So, he had some ability to use telekinesis or mental transportation to be able to move things around that way.

Another account of possible remote perturbation was given to me by Karie Garnier, a filmmaker, photographer, and writer. He met RT on August 14, 1982, on the outskirts of Falls City in the state of Washington. Rolling Thunder was holding a two-day healing circle. Karie wrote me that he was one of the people who received healing from RT and claimed that his long, life-threatening illness never returned (this account is further elaborated on in chapter 12). When Karie related the story of his healing to Vicki Gabereau on a national radio show, his compelling story generated more phone calls than any of Gabereau's previous shows.

Karie told Gabereau how three hundred people had come from around the world and gathered in a circle in the grass next to a great wooden lodge in the Washington countryside. They had congregated to hear the voice of RT, and a few were hoping to be healed.

Karie recalled, "During the weekend, Rolling Thunder would not allow any of us to take his photograph. However, on the last morning of our gathering RT promised that we could take his picture once the morning session had ended. Finally, on Sunday at twelve noon, RT announced that we could photograph him—but only until twelve thirty. He warned us, 'Any photos that you try to take of me after twelve thirty will not turn out.'"

Karie was delighted that he could finally photograph the medicine man. He told his interviewer, "I got some good shots of RT before twelve thirty. Then, as RT got up to walk away, I snapped a few more. I could hardly wait to see the results. But when my photos of Rolling Thunder were developed, the shots that I took before twelve thirty proved to be good photos. However, on the last few photos a dark gray cloud completely covered RT's face, making it impossible to see his features. This was true of every photograph taken after the twelve thirty deadline."

Over the years Karie Garnier spent a great deal of time with RT, calling him "the most amazing human being I have ever met." On his website he writes, "The great visionary was able to call down lightning and thunder. Just ask me, I was there. It was an experience I'll never forget!"

During their long friendship, Karie studied under RT, noting, "Rolling Thunder uses more than a thousand different herbs. By practicing what he learned, I was able to perform natural healing and help other people. On numerous occasions, I felt the power of Rolling Thunder's prayers."

On a visit to Rolling Thunder's home in the Nevada desert in April 1988, Karie and his Canadian friend Mike MacPherson had gathered in RT's kitchen, where he was cooking a nutritious pot of seafood. They listened as RT explained that "food and medicine are one and the same." Suddenly they heard someone outside yelling frantically, "Rolling Thunder! Come out here! Please hurry!" The man repeatedly screamed, "Come quick! Hurry, Rolling Thunder. Please hurry!"

Karie, Mike, and RT clamored outside into the backyard and saw Mario, a young friend of Rolling Thunder, struggling to hold on to a feisty young golden eagle. Mario had come from Switzerland to study with RT, and soon he would receive an unexpected lesson. While trying to hold the raptor's razor-sharp beak away from his face, Mario explained, "I was driving along the highway outside of Carlin, and half a mile down the road I could see this huge bird standing on the side of the road. I slowed down; I pulled over and stopped my car. I got out and cautiously walked up to the bird. When I was about ten feet away, I observed that it was glaring at me." Mario managed to throw a blanket around the eagle so he could bring it to RT.

RT, Karie, and Mike stepped closer to Mario and the massive bird. The eagle seemed overly alert and distressed. Its head and neck feathers were bristling. Karie recalled, "There was fire in its eyes, its beak was wide open, and it was ready to strike at us! But with his impeccable intuition, RT did what came naturally. He walked up to the eagle. He slowly opened his right hand and showed the bird his palm. He moved his opened hand to the left side of its head and stopped about a foot from its big yellow eye." Karie sensed that RT was showing the bird that he meant to do it no harm.

Karie continued, "RT then moved his opened hand, palm down, to an inch in front of the eagle's beak. The bird's eyes followed RT's hand. Very gently, RT brushed his hand across the top of the bird's head and smoothed down its ruffled head feathers. At this point RT instructed Mario, 'Now, hold the eagle's legs together with both your hands.' RT lifted the blanket off the bird and with a calm petting motion smoothed down its back feathers and tail feathers. Once again RT placed his opened hand in front of the eagle's beak. And again he petted the eagle's head and smoothed down its back and tail feathers. Rolling Thunder repeated this petting motion three times, and the eagle completely settled down.

"RT then said to me, Mike, and Mario, 'Okay, now you guys can hold him. After this he'll be tamer than a chicken.' I knew that this was an example of the medicine man's ability to communicate with—and calm— all kinds of wild creatures. I asked RT's permission to photograph him with the eagle, and he agreed. The photograph turned out quite well."

At the end of their visit, Karie shook hands with RT and thanked him for his hospitality. At this point RT paused, mused for a moment, and said, "By the way, Karie. That eagle was for you." It was as if RT knew that the photograph would have a lasting value and remind future generations of humanity's link with the rest of Nature.

During their long friendship Karie relied on RT's wisdom and consulted him many times, with RT telling Karie to "do whatever it takes" to bridge the Native and non-Native cultures. With that goal in mind, Karie completed a series of vision quests alone in the Canadian mountains. These rituals empowered Karie with the vision and the energy to "follow his heart." These experiences and Karie's close collaboration with RT led to Karie's creation of "Our Elders Speak: A Photographic Tribute," which was showcased in Vancouver at Expo '86. The collection of twenty-four life-size, black-and-white portraits of elders from the Pacific Northwest featured their wisest and most loving quotations as well as brief biographies. The inspirational show was subsequently featured at more than forty public venues across Canada.

Anomalous Phenomena during Indian Rituals

A few investigators have studied the anomalous phenomena that supposedly occur during shamanic rituals, dreams, and imagery. There are numerous anecdotes attesting to these phenomena, some of them involving remote perturbation, or psi kappa, and others involving psi beta. The Huichol shaman don Jose Rios was brought to the Esalen Institute in California during a long and severe drought when water supplies were strictly rationed. Don Jose volunteered to perform a rainmaking ceremony and began drumming while dressed in colorful regalia. He was still drumming when almost everyone else had fallen asleep. When they awakened they noticed that the drought was over and began dancing in the rain.

A practical application of purported remote perturbation is the shaking tent ceremony, performed by various tribes in the northwestern United States. A special cylindrical tent, the *djesikon,* is built for the ceremony. The specific form the tent will take has been revealed in a dream to the *djessakids,* the specially trained shaman who performs the ceremony. The ceremony typically occurs at night and begins with a sweat lodge ritual for the purification of the djessakids and his assistants. The shaman begins singing his power songs as he approaches the tent, which is already filled with members of the community. The power songs implore the shaman's helping spirits to enter the tent with him and his assistants. Sometimes the djessakids is bound securely and carried into the lodge to demonstrate that he is not using his own physical force to move the tent. In any event, the tent is said to begin shaking as soon as the shaman enters.

The shaking becomes more violent, indicating that the spirits are present. At the peak of the shaking, participants ask questions about someone's illness, about community issues, or about locating game. The spirits answer in a variety of ways. Sometimes whistling is heard, and the djessakids translates the message. Sometimes actual voices are heard, but in an unknown language that the shaman translates. Sometimes Turtle, a power animal, mediates—taking the question from the shaman to the spirits and then returning to the shaman with the answer. When the tent stops shaking, the ceremony is over, and the shaman is unbound or otherwise released to recuperate. This ceremony is performed sparingly, because the expenditure of energy is said to deplete the shaman severely.

The shaking tent ceremony takes place in the Pacific Northwest as well as in Siberia. Sometimes the tent is small enough for only one person to enter. If there are no participants inside the tent with the shaman, outsiders hear different voices and observe the tent shaking violently, even rotate on occasion. The tent becomes what chaos theorists would call a strange attractor, bringing together powerful energies from Earth and sea, wind and sky, enabling the shaman to retrieve lost souls, intercede for someone with a grave sickness, or locate a lost person. These forces of Nature interact and produce what chaos theorists would call a chaotic, nonlinear effect, one that demonstrates complexity, not simplicity. This complexity could well provide a matrix for the occurrence of remote perturbation and other parapsychological phenomena.

In another possible example of remote perturbation, Doug Boyd, in his book *Rolling Thunder,* tells about how he saw RT direct the movement of ants just by wiggling his fingers. Many readers found this an incredible account, but I was reminded of a story that Norman Cousins told me at a dinner party. Cousins, author of such well-known books as *Anatomy of an Illness* and *The Healing Heart,* told me that his neighbor's house was being overrun by ants. Just as he was about to call an eradication service, a mutual friend, Jon, asked, "Let me talk to the ants." Jon had a serious conversation with the ants, telling them that they should leave or they would be fumigated. Cousins and his neighbor listened to the conversation but did not take it seriously. However, the next day the ants had disappeared. When the trio had dinner again, Cousins dismissed it all as a coincidence. He told Jon, "The only way to convince me is to call the ants back, saying that they are now safe." Jon went into the yard, again having a serious conversation with the ants—which were now out of sight. Some twenty-four hours later, the ants were back in the house. Cousins's neighbor was now convinced and called Jon to ask him to urge the ants to leave again. But Jon had left town, and there was no way to contact him. Reluctantly, Cousins's neighbor called a fumigator, and the ants were gassed to death.

Precognition is another area of parapsychological inquiry, and RT was renowned for making prophecies of future world events. Ron Williams, a so-called psychic from the Choctaw tribe, traveled with RT from time to time. RT vowed that Williams was accurate nine out of ten times in the statements he made about members of the audience and the predictions he made about their lives. But RT also made some uncanny predictions about people he had just met.

Donna Eden, the author of several books about "energy medicine," is a celebrated healer who found herself deluged with urgent, desperate requests for her services. Sometimes when she would make an appearance, people would literally surround her, grabbing at her hands, hoping to receive a healing. But before all of that, Donna had met RT. She provided us with this account of their meeting.

I was at a conference in southern California around 1979, and Rolling Thunder was one of the keynote speakers. Before he entered the auditorium, his "spiritual warriors" lined both sides of the hall, standing protectively, eyes straight ahead, expressions quietly fierce. They were intimidating, seemed in awe of their leader, and I was repulsed. After Rolling Thunder's talk, my friend Stanley Krippner invited me to join a few others in Rolling Thunder's room at the hotel. We had to again pass through the warriors, now standing guard at the door, adding to my discomfort and sense of distrust. About half a dozen of us were with Stanley, and as the conversation got under way, there was some commotion at the window. Everyone got up to see what was happening except me and Rolling Thunder, who was sitting directly across from me. He turned to me and said, "You're having difficulty with me, aren't you?" I shook my head "yes" and added, "I have a hard time with gurus." He looked at me deeply and said with piercing eyes and perfect clarity, "I want you to know what your reaction is really about. You are, yourself, going to have to deal with this issue one day." This made no sense to me. I had no idea how that could happen. But he was right. When strangers come up to you on the street, in the supermarket, and in the park begging to be healed, you really start to take a look at the need for boundaries. I'm also as uncomfortable about being put on a pedestal as I once was judgmental toward gurus. As Einstein once said, "To punish me for my contempt for authority, fate made me an authority myself." I guess Rolling Thunder really did see what was coming for me.

The anthropologist Patric Giesler conducted several studies with members of what he termed "Afro-Brazilian shamanic cults." Both shamans and initiates attempted remote viewing to locate hidden objects as well as a task involving distant influence on ritual objects. He concluded that the shamanic practitioners did not demonstrate parapsychological effects on the laboratory tasks. Indeed, the only significant results were obtained by members of control groups, Brazilians who made no claim to be shamans.

Another anthropologist, one of my former professors at Northwestern University, William McGovern, had better luck. He once told me, "Stan, you will get a lot of negative comments when you talk about parapsychology. But I have had those types of experiences myself and have written about them." In 1927 McGovern published an account of Indians in the Amazon rain forest who regularly drank the mind-altering brew ayahuasca and who were then able to describe in great detail what was going on in several villages hundreds of kilometers away. They had never visited these villages, but McGovern knew them quite well and said the accounts tallied exactly with what he had observed. Ronald Rose, another pioneering anthropologist, tested a seventy-five-year-old Australian Aboriginal shaman using a standard deck of cards, obtaining above-chance results. Despite the sparse data and the questionable controls in the reports, this is a provocative area of shamanic lore that deserves additional investigation.

In 1975, my autobiographical book, *Song of the Siren,* was published. Two Indians wrote introductions; one was K. Ramakrishna Rao, a psychologist and parapsychologist from India. The other was written by RT, who identified himself as "Medicine Man, Western Shoshone Nation." He concluded his introduction with the statement, "It is too bad that there aren't more people who have the same viewpoints and the same object in mind that Stanley has in rediscovering these things that were well known in ancient civilizations. I think that through his efforts great progress is being made not only in bringing about better understanding among people, but also to help modern people to understand the 'other world' that they have lost. This loss has caused much of the confusion and misunderstanding among modern people today.

"I'm not only talking about this country, although we need to make a lot of changes before our land is completely destroyed and before the people are completely ruined. I'm also talking about a lot of other countries on both sides of the ocean. There is a great deal of wisdom that has been lost of the other world, of the nature of matter, and of the life force. These are the things that Stanley Krippner has been studying. I wish that more people would follow his example."

Sidian's Comments

Stories like these might have bothered me more in the past, and I would expect any skeptic to have red flags raised as well. But after reading about quantum physics, it isn't a matter of impossibility. It might be improbable, but not necessarily impossible. In quantum physics it is not unusual for a particle to jump forward or backward in time. Subatomic particles can change once they are observed by an outsider, and two particles can be separated yet react the same way, even if only one of them is altered.

Astrophysicists remind us that so-called dark matter and dark energy compose about 95 percent of the known universe, and mainstream science has little idea of how they can be studied or measured, much less explained. Its so-called scientific laws apply to about 5 percent of the universe, so scientists need to think twice before they rule out the possibility that there are psi phenomena that seem to upset the traditional laws that too many of them hold to be inviolate. Science must remain open-ended or it becomes "scientism," something just as dogmatic as fundamentalism in religion.

In *Rolling Thunder Speaks,* RT remarks, "Our religion can't be put in a book, or even an entire library, because it includes everything that has life. We don't threaten people with hells or devils. We don't say 'sin' but rather 'wrongdoing.' We don't like to think of gruesome things like people burning in hell forever and ever. That's the kind of mentality and anti-spirituality that was conjured up and brought over here because certain groups of people needed a way to control others."

4

Drumming

Drums and rattles were developed early in human history, probably in Paleolithic times. We have discovered drums that are featured in early paintings, such as the one on the wall of the shrine room in Çatalhüyük, an ancient city in Turkey. These paintings have been dated at about 5600 BCE and represent the dawn of civilization. Other artifacts found at Çatalhüyük indicate that there were special buildings reserved for spiritual activities such as rituals.

We define rituals as prescribed, stylized, step-by-step performances of a cultural worldview and its mythic themes. They attempt to promote social solidarity, provide for life transitions, and reinforce a society's values, belief systems, and rules of conduct. Rituals generally are performed in specific places at definite times by mandated persons. Although the word *ritual* often is used interchangeably with the words *rite* and *ceremony* by some writers, we find it more useful to describe rites as "minirituals" of passage from one stage of life to another (such as puberty rites and funeral rites) and ceremonies as elaborate "maxirituals" that include a series of rituals (such as coronation ceremonies and sun dance ceremonies).

Sometimes rituals become stereotyped over time, with an emphasis on form, rather than on feeling, in their performance. A ritual is alive to the extent that its performers passionately believe in its underlying worldview—whether that worldview is ritually enacted in an

59

exact manner each time it is performed or the enactment is to some extent an improvisation. The incorporation of drumming into a ritual keeps the performance alive and stokes the passion of the performers.

The drums used in rituals and ceremonies may take many forms. Some are simply dried skin or bark, but most of them are single- or double-headed frame drums. The single-headed drum is also called a tambourine and is used across much of Siberia, the eastern and western parts of North America, and the Arctic regions. They are also used in the West Indies and parts of South America. The double-headed drum is more common in the southwestern part of North America, Mexico, Central America, Nepal, and Tibet. The Laplanders decorated the animal skins on their drums with complex designs, and—like Native Americans and other groups—they danced in a circle, following the beat of the drum.

Another example of the use of drums can be found in Siberian shamanism. The shaman sings slowly as he or she strikes the drum in various places. When a helping spirit arrives, the shaman hits the drum hard and utters a few words. Then the song becomes louder and the drumming becomes more regular. As the spirits arrive, the shaman's voice becomes louder and the drumbeats become stronger, as if they would split the drum.

At this point the shaman knows the spirit world has been reached and communication with spirits is possible. However, there are many shamanic groups in Siberia and nearby areas, and not all of them use drums in the same way. The Tungus shamans use drumming to facilitate their descent into the Lower World. The Sakhalin Ainu, as well as the Hokkaido Ainu in northern Japan, use drumming for divination purposes, facilitating the ability of shamans to prophesy and predict future events. In Alaska, the Inuit shamans use drumming to ascend to the Upper World.

The drum is both functional and symbolic. The drum is connected to the Tree of Life through the wood of the frame. The drum is connected to the spirit world through the animal whose skin is used to make the drumhead. The Siberian Yakuts call the drum the shaman's horse, and the Turkish Altaics call it the whip that drives the shaman into the spirit world. In several traditions the drum is called the rainbow bridge, because it creates a connection the shaman can cross between the physical and imaginal worlds.

In numerous cultures drumming has been used by shamans. Anthropological evidence of shamanic drumming has been discovered in all the inhabited continents. In some parts of the world, rattles or other percussion instruments were used instead of drums or in addition to drums, most notably in the islands of the South Pacific. One of the largest drums in the world resides in a temple in Indonesia. It is regarded as sacred, and one must have special permission to see it.

In Indonesia shamans might be either Muslim or Hindu (the latter most typically found on the island of Bali), because shamanism is a spiritual technology, not a religion. Religions are characterized by dogmas, scriptures, and fixed places of worship, but shamanic worldviews are in constant flux and can change to meet new circumstances. Furthermore, shamanism can be practiced anywhere and is not circumscribed to a church, temple, or mosque.

Shamanism predated organized religion, and it sometimes challenges a specific faith. In Siberia, for example, shamans were persecuted by Buddhists and Christians but most vigorously by Communists, who thought they were a threat to Marxist ideology. Many shamans were killed, and others buried their drums. Upon the demise of the Soviet Union, the descendants of these shamans unburied the drums and revived the shamanic activity.

As we have mentioned before, shamanic drumming has been used to call on allies such as spirits and ancestors for help. It has been especially helpful in seeking the assistance of power animals, those mammals, birds, and reptiles that are felt to possess great power, especially for healing. Rolling Thunder worked with many animal allies, especially Eagle. In fact, he claimed that he could transform himself into an eagle when it was necessary for him to travel great distances to obtain a medicinal herb or gain information that would help one of his patients.

Rolling Thunder sometimes used drumming to facilitate the peyote ceremonies he supervised early in his career. The top, or crown, of the peyote cactus plant has been used by shamans for millennia, along with mushrooms and other mind-altering plants. The major active ingredient of peyote is mescaline, which can be produced synthetically. But Rolling Thunder urged people to use mind-altering substances rarely and with caution and to avoid chemical synthetics such as mescaline and psilocybin, the chief active ingredient of psychedelic mushrooms.

The use of drums during ceremonies was prohibited in North America by European conquerors and settlers, as were the ceremonies themselves. It was not until 1978 that the United States Congress passed the American Indian Religious Freedom Act in order to "protect and preserve the traditional rights and cultural practices of American Indians, Eskimos, Aleuts, and Native Hawaiians." (Please see plate 4 of the color insert for an example of a Native American drum.)

The disapproval of spiritual activities involving peyote, drumming, and dancing is often used to suggest that industrialized countries are myth deprived and ritual deprived. They lack culturally sanctioned altered states of consciousness that are designed to lead to personality growth and healing rather than to temporary stress reduction and stimulation. One anthropological survey found that people in 89 percent of the 488 societies studied altered their consciousness in ways that had societal approval, usually with accompanying rituals. Most industrial societies sanction the use of alcohol, tobacco, and prescription drugs but without the undergirding of ritual and myth that characterizes indigenous societies.

What special qualities do percussion instruments have that made them an almost indispensable part of shamanic practice? Psychological research indicates that drumming slows the brain waves, producing a pattern of alpha and theta brain wave activity that differs from ordinary waking consciousness. Rhythmic drumming, even when used by people other than shamans, appears to produce clarity of thinking, intense visual imagery, and enhanced energy. Ordinary consciousness is characterized by rapid beta waves and deep sleep by slower delta waves. Again, it is the limen, the twilight zone of consciousness that is marked by alpha and theta brain waves. And this pattern of consciousness can positively impact the lives of a shaman's patient.

There is rarely a period of time in which the brain exclusively produces nothing but alpha, beta, theta, or delta waves; hence, it is inaccurate to use terms such as the alpha state or the theta state. However, theta wave production has been linked to intense visual imagery, some of it quite unique and creative in nature, and alpha wave production is associated with profound relaxation. As a person drifts into sleep, the predominant beta wave activity begins to shift into a mixture of alpha and theta waves, which is why this liminal period is often marked by unusual visual imagery. Technically, this period is referred to as the hypnagogic stage of sleep, while the threshold of wakefulness is called the hypnopompic stage.

Rapid-eye-movement sleep, or the REM stage, is the period in which a person's most vivid dreams occur. REM sleep is characterized by "desynchronized" brain wave activity that contains a large proportion of beta waves, just as does ordinary wakefulness. The shift from beta wave activity to alpha and theta wave activity during drumming reflects the effectiveness of percussion rhythms to elicit the type of imagery conducive to shamanic journeying and healing. In fact, drumming seems to improve the functioning of the immune system, and Western psychotherapists have successfully used percussion rhythm in the treatment of drug addiction, alcoholism, hypertension, and autism. The anthropologist Michael Winkelman has commented that drumming activates the brain's integration of nonverbal information from the lower brain structures into the frontal cortex, producing insights that are frequently therapeutic.

An investigation of the drumming used in the ritual dances of the North American Pacific Coast Salish people to induce changes in consciousness found that the predominant brain wave pattern was in the theta wave range. Christina Pratt, author of An *Encyclopedia of Shamanism,* has surveyed the research literature on this topic, concluding that the drumming used by shamans in their rituals elicits specific neuro-physiological effects that facilitate imagery and entry into altered states.

The drum is often considered to be a power object and is sometimes seen as a living entity by shamans. Spotted Fawn told many people including Doug Boyd, the author of *Rolling Thunder,* that "the drums speak. They talk to you and they help you. They keep you there. I remember times I would start to drift away and the drums would say, pay attention, pay attention, pay attention." In some parts of the world when a drum is worn out, it is given its own burial. When honored shamans are buried, their drum is sometimes buried with them. But in other traditions it is handed down to the apprentice who the shaman has selected to receive his or her powers.

Stanley's Comments

When I was living in New York City and conducting research in dreams and dreaming at Maimonides Medical Center in Brooklyn, I would visit San Francisco once or twice a year. I would usually stay at the ranch of Mickey Hart, one of the two drummers in the Grateful Dead. Mickey was interested in hypnosis and told me that a medicine man named Rolling Thunder had taught him self-hypnosis, a skill he passed on to some of his colleagues and students.

During one my visits to his ranch I hypnotized Mickey and Bill Kreutzmann, the other drummer, at their request. They thought that playing their drums under hypnosis would help them to synchronize their improvisations during future Grateful Dead concerts.

Both drummers responded to hypnosis very well, and I also did some improvisation of my own, telling Bill that time was slowing down. "Every minute of ordinary time will seem like five minutes of hypnosis time," I told him. Their sound engineer recorded the results so Bill could hear himself playing in "slow time." But then I changed gears and told Mickey that every minute of ordinary time would seem like a few seconds of hypnosis time and that time was speeding up. Mickey quickly changed to playing in "fast time," but he had to improvise so that his drumming coordinated with Bill's. Even more remarkable to me was the way that they picked up on each other's innovation, yielding a piece of music that was pleasant and intriguing in its own right.

I also brought color into the mix, telling them that everything was turning blue. If they opened their eyes they would see that everything had a blue cast to it, and their music would reflect this world of blue. Once they had played the "blues," I had them play the "reds." Everything now was red, and the music would take on a red cast. Again, the results were remarkable—and the entire recorded session resides in Mickey Hart's archives.

Here is Mickey's recollection of those times, as reflected in a 2006 YouTube interview.

Mickey Hart: RT taught me about the sweat lodges. He taught me so much about Native American culture and history. He really turned me on to Native American music. We used to listen to early recordings of those drums and those voices when driving down the road in his van. You remember that Ford truck? We had this stereo in it, and this Indian music was bellowing out, and I had my big speakers for him. He really started me on that whole voyage that led to two CDs: *Honoring the Earth* and *The American Warriors*. RT is the one who really brought it to me. I have to admit, he gave me a lot. And he taught me about self-hypnosis.

Stanley Krippner: Yes?

Mickey Hart: He taught me how to use self-hypnosis. That played an important part. After you worked with me and Billy Kreutzmann, we would use hypnosis to practice. And so we would give ourselves suggestions and say, "We're going to practice for twelve hours, but it will seem like one. And we're not going to get tired, and we're going to stay here, and we won't have to eat much." And we would have these incredible practice sessions, and then we would make suggestions to each other and to ourselves about different ways of flowing with certain rhythms, and we would say, "You hold that rhythm, and I'll be able to hold this rhythm. It is seemingly impossible, but we can do it because it's very possible now. And it's easy really."

We would do things that you could never do in the normal state, in the waking state. And this really began our adventure in rhythmic dexterity, which turned into Grateful Dead music. There was one great experiment that you were part of with me and Billy. And you told Billy that it was a shift in time perception, and what you said to Billy was, "Okay, everything that you hear is going to come really slow to you. And you'll be able to play in and out of everything." And then you said to me, "It's going to come very fast to you, so you'll be able to play around it." And so we started perceiving each other in different ways. Whereas I felt it was coming so fast, I had to play really slowly to fit everything in, and it was the opposite for Billy.

It was an amazing experiment in altered time perception, and I remember that really well. As a matter of fact, I still have the recording. It's called "Bill's Box." I just discovered it. And it was during that experiment that we went into hypnosis and we played for maybe twenty, thirty, or forty minutes. That was a remarkable day. It taught me about the expansion and contraction of time and how you perceive time and how time is totally flexible. It made the Grateful Dead music into something different, because then we were able to flex and contract at will and not worry about it. And we could also create a new beginning and ending to things. It wasn't set in stone.

So when you start receiving things in another realm and you become comfortable with it and you can share that with someone else, then it becomes real. These experiments affected our audience in a tremendous way. It allowed our audience to be able to become deep listeners, and deep listening is when you hear below the obvious, and you hear inside of things, and you hear the spirit voice of everything. And so once they were able to let go of the metric and the thought that everything had to be perfect, they were able to fly. They moved from what we would call "clock time" to "earth time."

Our audiences were able to experience other realms of thought. And that's where all the good stuff is. Most of the good stuff you will find on the periphery of things. That's where the real rich stuff happens. It doesn't usually happen in your normal perception. When you see something you say, "That's the way it is." But then you have to look at it or hear at it. And you have to have some real ear play on it or eye play on it and just focus on it and get in on that moment and become part of it, become one with it, and then let go of everything you know and then go with what is happening in the moment.

If you can do that, there is a chance of great beauty. You can actually create something that is worthwhile as opposed to re-creating something that has already been done. So, that's what it gave the audience. It gave the audience a license to fly, a license to be able to go to these realms of perception that were not necessarily right in front of them. There were multitiered layers of perception. That's what this situation is all about. That's what the Grateful Dead music is all about. That's what trance drumming is all about. That's what the psychic experience is all about.

Sidian's Comments

In 2007 I met Mickey Hart. It was very exciting to come face-to-face with a man who had meant so much to my grandfather. Later that year Stanley joined Mickey for an interview in which they reviewed some memories of how they met.

Stanley Krippner: I remember the day in 1967 that Jean Millay heard that I was going to attend a concert by Ravi Shankar, the eminent sitar virtuoso from India, in Lincoln Center in New York City. She said, "Why don't you come over to my apartment after the concert? I'm having a party for Alla Rakha." I looked forward to meeting Alla Rakha, who accompanied Ravi Shankar on the tabla, an Indian drum, and was a talented musician in his own right. Jean Millay had been present when you and Phil Lesh paid their first visit to Alla Rakha following one of his concerts. Jean recalls wearing a sari at the time and making the introductions.

When I arrived at the party, Alla Rakha was the center of attention, having just played the tabla brilliantly during the Ravi Shankar concert. Jean took me aside and said, "We have a musician here who is a student of Alla Rakha. He is quite interested in hypnosis and would like to meet you." Mickey, you cut quite a dramatic figure with your long, black ponytail and the black-and-white harlequin suit you were wearing. And we spent an hour talking about hypnosis, because you had been using it with some of your students. Then you abruptly changed the subject and said, "By the way, do you like rock music?" And I said, "Yes. I go to rock concerts all the time." You said, "Have you ever heard of the Grateful Dead?" and I replied, "Sure. I just went to hear them two nights ago at the Fillmore East." And you beamed from ear to ear and said, "Then you've heard me play." So it was Jean Millay and Alla Rakha who brought us together. Right?

Mickey Hart: That's correct. Very much so. I originally had heard Alla Rakha on a record that Phil Lesh gave me. It was *Drums of North and South India*. I kept listening to that record, and I couldn't believe one guy was playing all that music. And so I found out that it was truly one fellow who was playing it. When he came to New York I went up to see him, and he couldn't speak English very well. But I asked him if he would teach me, and he said, "Well, come to my apartment." And I said, "Okay, fine." And I brought a metronome that had three settings. You can have three different settings simultaneously, two different groupings of rhythm and a drum pad. So I walked in, and I stayed for four days and nights. There was this outpouring, this profusion of knowledge that came out of him and of me, and of course it was overwhelming. Then I became his student. I couldn't believe what he was doing with rhythm. You and I met shortly after that, I believe.

Stanley Krippner: That's right.

Mickey Hart: When Alla Rakha died, he left me one of his high drums. Zakir Hussain, his son, has one drum, his brother has one, and I have one. And what was really amazing was that Zakir presented me with his father's shawl and his drum. It is one of my most prized possessions, a piece of him.

Stanley Krippner: Shortly after we met, you wanted to visit the dream laboratory at Maimonides Medical Center in Brooklyn. You were born at that hospital.

Mickey Hart: You remembered!

Stanley Krippner: And when people heard that you were coming to the dream lab, everybody made an excuse to take a coffee break or a bathroom break so that they could be in the lobby when you walked through the door into the building.

Mickey Hart: It was a wonderful place. I couldn't believe a place like that existed. It was in the basement, sort of like in the catacombs. It was very quiet. You rarely hear anything that quiet. Coming from such a loud, loud world, I really loved the silence. Going to the dream lab was certainly a sonic moment for me. It was heroic of you in those days, interviewing musicians and artists who had been using psychoactive drugs for personal experimentation. I remember that. I thought that was remarkable.

Stanley Krippner: Yes, I interviewed about two hundred artists and musicians who had been given psychoactive drugs by their therapists or who had taken them on their own. But that reminds me of the Port Chester, New York, gigs where the Grateful Dead played. Your audience tried to transmit a picture to Malcolm Bessent, a so-called psychic from England, who was sleeping at the dream lab.

Mickey Hart: He was sleeping at Maimonides, and we were playing for like five or six nights.

Stanley Krippner: Yes, it was six nights. We had enough nights so that we could conduct a statistical test on the results. Malcolm Bessent was in the lab, and we woke him up every time we saw rapid eye movements on the electroencephalogram. He was trying to dream about the picture that was flashed on the screen at the Grateful Dead gig.

Mickey Hart: I remember. Ronnie Mastrion was behind the soundboard, and no one knew what the pictures were. He chose one picture randomly and flashed it on the screen and asked the audience to beam the picture to the dream lab in Brooklyn.

Stanley Krippner: Exactly.

Mickey Hart: I remember us doing that. We stopped the music. We talked about the picture. Then we started playing again.

Stanley Krippner: You stopped the music while we flashed instructions on the screen. And then you started the music again as the audience began to focus on the image.

Mickey Hart: The image was on the light show screen.

Stanley Krippner: That was it. For example, we had a very beautiful picture of the seven spinal charkas and a yogi meditating.

Mickey Hart: When I saw it I said, "No way. No one is going to guess this." And sure enough, Malcolm Bessent had a dream about the spinal column. And for the whole experiment there were more hits than not, right?

Stanley Krippner: Right. The number of hits was statistically significant. Above chance. Yeah, Malcolm Bessent did incredibly well. When the audience was focusing on that painting of the chakras, he had dreams about a man who had undergone spiritual training and who had an energy box in his body, in addition to that dream about the spinal column. So when judges compared the pictures with the dreams, that one was an easy match.

Mickey Hart: That was amazing—the idea of group power and being able to translate that thought process into real information and actually send it. And then you wrote it up.

Stanley Krippner: Oh yes. We published it in a professional journal.

And then it was picked up and published in a dozen different places.

Mickey Hart: Those were interesting times.

Stanley Krippner: So then I started to visit you in California. You kept saying, "I'd really like you to meet Rolling Thunder, this Indian medicine man from Nevada. I'd really like you to meet RT."

Mickey Hart: That would have been in about 1968.

Stanley Krippner: And then you sent a private airplane to pick up RT one weekend when I was visiting you, and that's when I met the fantastic, mercurial RT.

Mickey Hart: I remember that well.

5

The Trickster

We have read about ancient mythologies around the world, and there are many characters that show up time and time again. There is the Great Earth Parent, usually a mother but sometimes a father. There is the Wise Old Person, usually a man but frequently a woman. The psychiatrist and psychologist Carl Jung called these figures "archetypes," powerful images that have become part of what he called the "collective unconscious." And one of the most interesting archetypes for us is that of the trickster or clown, the embodiment of life's unexpected surprises.

In some cultures there are both positive and negative tricksters. In the Dagara tradition of western Africa, Hyena is considered a negative trickster because he never learns the lessons of Nature and his exploits backfire on him and those around him. In that same tradition, Rabbit and Spider are considered positive tricksters because they use the powers of Nature to their fullest extent in ways that benefit all living creatures. Among the Zulus of southern Africa, Jackal and Spider are tricksters. Loki is a trickster who shows up in scores of Germanic and Nordic myths. In Greek mythology, Hermes plays the trickster role, as does his counterpart Mercury or Quicksilver in Roman myths. Maui is the prototypical trickster in Polynesian mythology, while Krishna, the Hindu deity, is well known for his benevolent tricks in Indian myths. Not only did Krishna disguise himself as a shepherd to romance country maidens, but he also used psychedelic plants to prepare the warrior Arjuna for enlightenment. In Native American lore, the trickster is a helping spirit who teaches through surprise; Coyote, Rabbit, and Raven all are tricksters, depending on the tribe under consideration.

Indian canoes, arrows, moccasins, snowshoes, knives, and so on are irregular and individually shaped. Native Americans resist having fixed boundaries and categories and forms; this is an invitation for the trickster to come in and mess up the boundaries. Native explanations of the cosmos include the roles of chance, flux, and process.

The physicist David Peat points out that Western science has its own tricksters and clowns. The most prominent is entropy or disorder. The overall entropy of a system needs to increase so that order can emerge. This is sometimes called creating order out of chaos. If science insists on generating order, this can only be done by creating disorder somewhere else. Chaos theory explores the different consequences that chance, randomness, and probability can play in the world. It negates the philosophy that the universe is a giant clock, because chance plays an important role in weather, floods, and even the growth of insect populations. The "butterfly effect" demonstrates how a tiny shift in the initial conditions of a system, such as the motion of a butterfly's wing, can have major consequences if it triggers the parts of a system that are most vulnerable to change. Medicine men and women understood this principle; all that was needed to change some potions into healing elixirs was a single drop from a freshly harvested stem of an herb.

Christina Pratt, the author of a remarkable two-volume encyclopedia on shamanism, points out that using the energies of the trickster has its hazards. However, it provides an opening for surprises, the reversal of one's fortune, and even an entry into experiences thought to be impossible. Working as an apprentice with a teacher or guru provides a student with a steady path to mastery. But when a student encounters a trickster, he or she may be derailed or may be given a shortcut that will reveal the soul's true purpose and provide ways to enjoy the fruits of one's labors. Other spiritual guides emphasize balance and wholeness, but it is the trickster who completes one's education by introducing a world filled with ambiguity and complexity. Pratt insists that the student's education is incomplete without encountering the trickster's disruption, disorder, and "crazy logic." In some tribes, a Creator God brought the world into being, but the trickster taught people how to survive in it, recognizing the ambiguity of existence and the unpredictability of their lives.

An example of crazy logic is the trickster's insistence that deceit is sometimes needed if a sick person is to respond to the shaman's healing interventions. In Stephan Schwartz's anecdote about the mist wolf (see chapter 3), RT displayed remarkable abilities that are often described as psychic because they seem to violate mainstream science's concepts of time, space, and energy. In other words, these abilities are the trickster's domain. Most scientists ridicule the possibility that some people possess these abilities. Parapsychologists, in general, hold the opposite point of view. Even so, they do not claim that telepathy, psychokinesis, and similar abilities can be evoked on demand.

This poses a problem for shamans, because their reputations, by and large, rest on their abilities to use clairvoyance, precognition, and other psychic abilities for the benefit of the community. As a result, they supplement whatever psychic capacities they may have with sleight of hand: most tribal expectations force the shaman to adopt a trickster role because legerdemain—the collection of "magic tricks" well known to stage magicians over the ages—is also the domain of the trickster. That tricksters should rule apparently contradictory domains is an example of the crazy logic they exemplify.

When shamans play the trickster role, they have several options available. One strategy is to ask one of their power animals for help; Rolling Thunder would often call on Coyote to provide this assistance. Another strategy is to use legerdemain.

Roger Walsh, in his splendid book *The World of Shamanism*, devotes an entire chapter to the shaman's "tricks of the trade." One approach is to have assistants obtain information about a patient's personal life that can be used during a healing session. For example, a shaman might remark, "Your Aunt Marie is with the Great Spirit, but she asks you to take the red-and-white blanket she gave you on your tenth birthday and sleep on it every night until you get well." Or the shaman might say, "I had a dream about your departed father, and he told me about the eagle feather that you discovered when the two of you walked into the mountain range when you were a child. You found an eagle feather, and your father told you to keep it in a safe place. Now is the time for you to put the healing power of that feather to use so that you can get well."

Another common procedure accompanies the "cupping and sucking" ritual that is a common aspect of shamanic healing rituals. A shaman simply places a dead insect or an animal bone in his or her mouth before the ritual begins. During the ritual this object seems to come out of the sick person's body, and the shaman uses it to demonstrate the success of the intervention.

Shamans also engage in mock battles with malevolent spirits in their attempts to vanquish an illness. Sometimes this warfare takes place in the Upper World or the Lower World; at other times it takes place in Middle Earth, and the patients and their families watch in awe as the shaman punches, wrestles, and ultimately vanquishes an invisible enemy.

Walsh concludes that these tricks are essential parts of the healing process and are done for the patient's benefit. However, he also notes that they bolster the reputation of the shaman, thus enhancing the patient's trust in the ritual. This trust can trigger the patient's self-healing capacities, bolstering the immune system and providing hope that they will recover. This strategy is also employed by Western physicians who use placebos as part of their ministrations on behalf of their patients. A placebo is a substance, such as a sugar pill, that has no curative effect in and of itself. A placebo can also be a procedure, such as taking a patient's weight or wearing a special medical uniform, that is performed before making an intervention.

Numerous research studies have concluded that a considerable amount of the success of both medicine and psychotherapy is due to expectancy, faith, hope, and other elements of the placebo effect. By themselves these substances and procedures are of no value. But within the context of a medical treatment, they typically facilitate a patient's recovery because a placebo reduces symptoms and facilitates healing due to one's perception of the therapeutic intervention.

It should be noted that even when patients are told by a physician that they are getting a placebo, most patients will get better. Placebos produce real physiological changes. These changes are not directly caused by a physical or psychotherapeutic intervention but arise from the patient creating meaning during his or her interaction with the physician, psychotherapist, or shaman. The placebo effect helps patients play an active role in getting better, whether or not they are aware of it.

Spiritual experiences and practices involve a number of neurological reactions that resemble placebo effects. So it is no surprise that healing shrines and spiritual healers often are successful in restoring health to someone who is sick. Spirituality is concerned with ultimate questions about the meaning of life and assumes that there is more to living than is fully or easily understood. Spiritual healing, in one form or another, appears to be driven by biological and psychological mechanisms that are similar to those involved in the placebo response. RT was aware of this connection and often said, "Sometimes I have to trick people in order to help them get well."

In addition, many of the shaman's patients know that sleight of hand is being used but assume that this is a technique that taps in to a deeper reality that can be used for their benefit. Jung's description of the trickster archetype was not fanciful. When he wrote about the collective unconscious, he was describing a basic human potential. Early humans who did not have the capability of responding to suggestion or other elements of the placebo response did not survive, and their genes dropped out of the gene pool. One could make the case that shamans and their collection of tricks actually played an important role in human evolution. It is not success that leads to useful genes; it is useful genes that lead to success. These organisms have what it takes to become ancestors, whether they are humans or fruit flies.

Stanley's Comments

On several occasions I watched RT engaging in the cupping and suck-ing movements, allegedly to remove impure material from a patient's body. Typically he would suck the part of one's skin where his eagle feather diagnosis had indicated there was an imbalance of some sort. The liquid he spit into the nearby pail was invariably dark brown, and I thought it might be tobacco juice. I also thought that this was a better ploy than the one used by shamans I have read about who bit the inside of their mouths sharply so that actual blood would seem to come from the part of the body that was cupped and sucked. In any event, RT would ask one of his assistants to take the bucket contain-ing the fluid into the woods and bury it so that it would rejoin the Earth, become "purified," and not infect either the Earth or its people.

After my wife, Lelie, and I moved to California, my visits with RT were more frequent, as Mickey's ranch was in Novato. We lived in Fairfax, which was, like his ranch, in Marin County. One day in 1985 I had a phone call from Mickey. He was very excited, saying that he had seen RT on his property, picking some herbs. RT frequently went into the wooded areas of the ranch, claiming that it was a treasure chest of medicinal herbs. My wife and I were waiting at Mickey's ranch, where Jerilyn Brandelius, a talented photographer who was Mickey's lady friend at the time, had prepared a delicious dinner. But as it grew dark, RT did not show up.

Mickey was puzzled by RT's absence, but I had an idea. I said, "Let's give RT's house a phone call in Nevada. Then we will be sure that he is in California." Mickey reassured us that he saw RT earlier in the day but did not object to the telephone call. When someone in Carlin picked up the telephone, I recognized RT's voice. My immediate hunch was to ask him what he was doing at 9:00 a.m.; if he told us that he was at Mickey's ranch picking herbs, it would verify his ability to take sha-manic out-of-body journeys. But if he said that he was sitting comfort-ably at home, that would mean that Mickey's perception was incorrect.

As soon as Mickey realized that I had RT on the line, he grabbed the phone from me and exclaimed, "Yeah, man, we want to know what you were doing at 9:00 a.m., because that is when I saw you picking herbs up in my hills." There was a moment's pause, and then I could hear RT, in his characteristic drawl, reply, "Well, now, you saw me at a crucial time. One of the folks I am 'doctoring' needed a special herb to get better, and I was all out. But I remembered that I had picked a supply of that herb during one of my visits to your ranch. So I just turned myself into an eagle, flew to your ranch, picked the leaves I needed, and brought them back. That lady is doing much better now that she has had several cups of tea made from those herbs."

So did RT make an out-of-the-body journey to Novato? Or was RT manifesting the trickster element? RT was a master of benevolent duplicity and often used it in the service of his patients.

Sidian's Comments

I first learned about the trickster when I was reading some of the books written by the philosopher Alan Watts. His autobiography, *In My Own Way,* reveals his role as a trickster. By the time he died in 1973, he had been an Anglican priest, a Buddhist scholar, a professor of philosophy, a consultant at psychiatric hospitals, and a prolific writer and lecturer. But he never took himself too seriously. He saw the illusion underlying everything, including his own brilliance and fame. His teachings on the nature of life and death, or love and sex, or transcendence and reality, or consciousness and psychedelics were all infused with humor and self-deprecating irony. For example, he wrote, "A person who truly believes in God would never try and thrust the idea on anyone else, just as when you understand mathematics, you are not a fanatical proponent of the idea that two and two are four."

Watts pointed out that the world is in flux. Nothing lasts forever. Whenever humans make their plans, the trickster comes along and plays a trick on us. For example, the celebration of chance, through gambling, becomes important. Gambling is not simply a game but also a ceremony that acknowledges the basic metaphysics of the cosmos, including the power of the trickster and other spirits.

Thoughts like these about people's beliefs and how those beliefs direct their lives were part of my inspiration for creating the Internet social network OpenSourceReligion.net, in which we recognize that every individual's "religion" is customized. For instance, some Christians also believe in karma. That's Open Source Religion. This site serves as a foundation to help people codify their own philosophies, reinterpreting or even discarding the religious dogmas from their youth. In some way I was carrying on Watts's tradition; he referred to his collection of audiotapes as composing an "electronic university." Just think what he could have done with the Internet!

You can imagine what a pleasant surprise it was to discover that RT had been part of a weeklong seminar at a university in New Mexico with Alan Watts and Stanley Krippner. When I interviewed Stanley about this event, this is what he told me:

On February 20, 1972, I arrived in Las Cruces to speak at the local branch of the University of New Mexico. Two friends of mine, Jim Hickman and Larry Amos, were students at the university and had arranged a remarkable coup. They had received acceptances to speak not only from RT but from another friend of mine, the renowned philosopher Alan Watts. The three of us did a seminar together, and each of us presented an individual seminar. RT invited students and faculty to an early morning sunrise service and was gratified by the response. Alan Watts led what he called an "alternative" church service, one that was filled with colorful cross-cultural rituals but avoided dogma and permitted each participant to worship in his or her own way. One student told me, "If I could find a church like this, I would start attending services again."

During our joint seminar, Watts remarked that he was struck by the similarity of certain Native American perspectives to those of traditional Chinese Taoism. For example, both stress the importance of balance, of community, and of closeness to nature. Watts remarked, "Just as the apple tree grows apples, the Earth grows people. You might say that the tree apples and that the Earth peoples. Human beings are a part of Nature, not superior to it."

Watts reviewed the Taoist concept of health and illness as embodied in traditional Chinese medicine. Qi, or vital energy, comes in many forms, depending on its source, location, and function. When a person is healthy, the qi is balanced, but it is imbalanced when someone becomes ill. The traditional Chinese physician diagnoses the type of qi that is out of balance, as well as the location of its obstruction or disturbance, and prescribes treatment. The therapeutic tools include acupuncture, massage, diet, and moxibustion—the burning of a special herbal concoction on selected bodily acupuncture points. All of this made sense to RT, who was an advocate of healthy food as well as massage, which he often requested from members of his retinue. When he used his eagle feather to diagnose the parts of a patient's body that needed treatment, I observed that he regularly stimulated acupuncture points, perhaps coincidentally with the Chinese network.

RT reminded the group that when Native Americans use the term all our relations, they refer to those "relations" that walk on four legs, those that fly, those that crawl, those that stand tall in the forest, and those that sit solidly in the rocky desert. I added examples from Latin American shamanism, where a similar point of view had long been a part of those traditions. A few centuries of European domination may have blunted and warped the Native belief system, but these years could not extinguish what had been around far longer. RT responded, "It is not that there is a world of stones and trees and another one of spirits, powers, and energies, but rather that they are all one, and the human way of seeing cannot grasp this unity." Alan Watts nodded his head in agreement.

Alan Watts was an early pioneer in the ecological movement, and when I spoke of the impending destruction of the Amazonian rain forest, he added examples from North America, especially the pollution of rivers, lakes, and bays. Living on a houseboat in Sausalito, California, Watts had firsthand knowledge of the exploitation of waterways and potable water sources in the United States. Years later, members of our audiences told me how much those programs had meant to them and how the new worldviews expressed by the three of us had changed their lives for the better.

Tricking the Infiltrators

But sometimes the trickster makes jokes and plays tricks just to have fun. Gary Sandman told me that when he was living at Meta Tantay,

Rolling Thunder's spiritual community, the FBI would send spies to infiltrate the camp to see if there were any criminal activities going on. Of course, there was no drug trafficking, no prostitution, and no talk of armed uprising. RT did not care much for the Bureau of Indian Affairs and some other government agencies, but his protests were peaceful, not violent.

RT frequently maintained that there are two types of Indians in all the tribes throughout the United States. There are the traditional Indians and the Bureau of Indian Affairs Indians—the "Uncle Tommyhawks" or "Tommyhawks," as RT called them. Their name refers to Uncle Toms, a derogatory nickname given to the black slaves who obediently followed their masters' commands. (Uncle Tom was a character in a novel, *Uncle Tom's Cabin* by Harriet Beecher Stowe, a book that galvanized opposition to slavery in the northern United States just prior to the U.S. Civil War between the states.)

RT claimed that Tommyhawks had become incompetent and impotent. Their lack of self-determination and self-direction was raising the rate of alcoholism, suicide, and other ills. In contrast, members of the former group still lived by the codes of conduct carried with them during all of their history: mutual self-respect, self-direction, pursuit of purpose, and their ability to walk the Good Red Road.

When the FBI infiltrators came to Carlin, RT would spot them immediately. And sometimes he made them the butt of his jokes. Gary Sandman recalls one amusing incident.

I remember one evening during a group meeting, RT said, "Today I need volunteers to go into the woods with me." And he picked the two guys he suspected of being government agents. We could tell that they were city slickers who were not comfortable going into the woods, but we also knew that they would not resist the opportunity to spend some private time with RT to see if he was breaking the law. RT told the two volunteers, "No matter what happens, and no matter what you hear out there, just stay behind me and I will keep you safe." Then RT started running through the woods, and he explained, "We are in real danger now, and we have to keep running so that nothing dangerous can keep up with us and start biting at our heels." There were fierce sounds, and the two guys were afraid something was going to bite them.

And then one of them dropped out and tried to find his way back. RT looked around and couldn't find him, so he told the other guy, "Well, we're just going to have to keep running because you don't dare stop in these woods." And the volunteer was terrified because there were all sorts of loud animal noises and screeching sounds. And then the second volunteer got lost, and RT turned around and came back to where the group was camping.

About four days later they struggled into camp. They were pale, scared, and hungry. And they said, "We're leaving you alone. Good-bye." I don't know what RT had created out there, but whatever it was, it really frightened those two guys. They were young men, half of RT's age, but they could not keep up with him because they were so horrified. And once Meta Tantay got off the ground, the government officials pretty much left RT alone, even though the camp was in a desert, not a forest.

RT was a pretty gentle dude. But if you crossed him or if you tried to trick him, he would trick you right back—and you would never know when the surprise was coming.

6

Power

The term *power* usually refers to the capacity to act and to carry on an activity to completion. Everything we have read or observed convinces us that power is central to shamanism, because the shaman is a man or woman of action. To heal people, to protect their tribe, and to safeguard their culture, shamans need all the help they can get. In addition to his pipe, RT had several power objects. He usually wore a necklace made of deer horn, sea lion teeth, shark bones, and an abalone shell. During his healing sessions, he used an eagle feather with a beaded handle. RT frequently appeared with a beaded satchel slung over his shoulder. He referred to it as his "medicine bag" but rarely revealed its contents. Those around him assumed it was filled with various power objects.

Shamans may go to power places such as caves, forest groves, or desert retreats to rejuvenate and recoup their power after a difficult ordeal. RT would often walk in the woods or seek solitude in the plains or the desert. Many shamans are described as *charismatic;* this term reflects the power that is obvious to onlookers, whether it be flamboyant and ostentatious or more subtle and humble. RT was often described in the same way by people we interviewed. His dark eyes were constantly moving and observing, but when they settled on a person, that individual often reported that RT had seen directly into his or her soul.

Stanley's Comments

Among Native Americans, knowledge is not a collection of boring facts. Knowledge is alive and dwells in specific power places. Traditional knowledge comes through watching and listening, but not in the passive way taught in Western schools or in the repetitive prayers found in most religious schools. Knowledge comes through the direct experience of songs, rituals, and ceremonies, from trees and animals, and from dreams and visions. When Indians say they have "come to knowledge" they mean that they have entered into relationships with power animals, power plants, and power objects. They have learned from birds, from herbs, from rivers, and from the winds. Sometimes this knowledge is stored on birch bark scrolls or wampum belts, in necklaces, in sacred bundles, in petroglyphs or rock drawings, and sometimes in elaborately carved talking sticks.

Connection to the Earth is one of the most powerful bonds in an Indian society, which explains the anger that Indians feel when they see the land around them being exploited and destroyed. There are spirits in a landscape, and this "spirit of place" is felt to be so strong that it enters not only the current inhabitants of a location but future occupants as well.

Some shamans point out that people live in sacred space all the time without realizing it. But once a place of power is designated, the energies of that place are maximized with rituals, ceremonies, and power objects. These places allow a direct communication between the energies of the location and the people who visit with the intention of seeking information or healing, or simply to pay respects to Mother Earth, to the spirits of the deceased, or to the past events that occurred there.

These principles were apparent in my second encounter with Rolling Thunder, which occurred in April 1970, again at Mickey Hart's Novato, California, ranch. Once again, Mickey had invited RT to his ranch during my visit, and I had invited Dr. Irving Oyle, an osteopathic physician who was a pioneer in the holistic health movement that was becoming popular in the 1970s. RT had never had a serious conversation with a physician before and reluctantly accepted Oyle's suggestion that they retire to a private room for a one-on-one conversation of their healing modalities, what RT referred to as "doctoring."

Mickey and I were rather concerned as the afternoon slipped by. There was no sign of life from the private room, and neither of us could imagine that the two practitioners would spend so much time together without speaking. Finally, our suspense was over as RT and Oyle came out of the room, arm in arm. Oyle summed up their conversation.

It didn't take long before RT and I figured out that we do pretty much the same thing. A patient comes to RT for "doctoring"; RT listens carefully and asks a few questions. Then he decides what ritual will be most appropriate and what herbs he should give his patient. More often than not, the patient follows the directions and gets well. And when a patient comes to me, I listen carefully and ask a few questions. Then I perform a ritual known as writing out a prescription. I may make some other interventions as well, as part of the ritual. More often than not, my patient follows the directions and gets well. But both of us agreed that the chances of getting well will be improved if the patient expects to get well and has trust in the person doing the "doctoring."

RT nodded in agreement, noting that the doctor's office or the medicine man's lodge could be a place of power where the energies needed for healing could be focused and galvanized. And then we all adjourned to the kitchen, where a delicious dinner was waiting for us, prepared by Jerilyn Brandelius.

Coincidentally, I was appointed to be the program director for the Third Interdisciplinary Conference on the Voluntary Control of Internal States. This conference, sponsored by the Menninger Foundation in Topeka, Kansas, brought together researchers and practitioners for five days of presentations, demonstrations, and discussions. During the 1970 conference I had noted the lack of female presenters as well as the near absence of people of color. For the 1971 conference I had decided to remedy both situations. In addition to bringing an Africa American and an Asian practitioner to the Council Grove Conference Center in rural Kansas, I decided to invite

RT to represent Native American traditions. He mulled over the invitation for a while and then accepted; after all, this would give him the opportunity to help experts from other traditions become acquainted with Native American perspectives on the healing arts.

On April 12, 1971, I left for Kansas City, where buses were waiting to take participants to the conference center. We unpacked our suitcases in the comfortable dormitories and had our first meal together. I introduced RT to the group and noted that he kept a low profile, not only during the initial meal but also for the next few days. On April 15 one of the participants, a student of mine from New York University, injured his arm during a game of touch football. When asked if he wanted us to drive him to a hospital, he responded, "Nonsense. We have a number of healers right here." He singled out Dr. William McGarey, a holistic physician known for his use of treatments advocated by the Virginia Beach seer Edgar Cayce, and RT as the two practitioners with whom he would feel most comfortable. After the physician had determined that there were no broken bones or internal injuries, RT made his preparations. He sent word to the kitchen for some raw meat, and one of the cooks brought some uncooked hamburger beef to the patio outside our meeting room. He also asked for a bucket, which was easily obtainable.

By this time the young man in need of "doctoring" had made himself comfortable on a cot. RT had prepared a small fire and placed the meat on the fire. It did not burn very well, but certainly sizzled, thus serving its purpose in the ritual. RT took an eagle feather from his medicine bag and poked the skin near the wound. When his patient winced, RT knew that he had found a point in need of balancing and purification. He put his mouth to that area of the skin and performed the cupping and sucking procedures I had read about in many articles and books about Native American healing practices. He spit a dark-looking fluid into the bucket and asked that it be taken to a vacant field and the contents buried. While a volunteer carried out this command, RT began chanting, evoking blessings and healing energy from the Great Spirit.

When RT was finished, his patient said he felt better and the physician claimed that the swelling seemed to have subsided. Andrew Weil, another physician who was later to become internationally celebrated for his books on the topic of holistic health, later wrote that he saw little difference in the wound but that the spirits of the young man were undoubtedly raised. In any event, RT's patient was in much better health the next day, a day that RT had agreed to open with a sunrise ceremony.

The morning sunrise ceremony was similar to the one in which I had participated at Mickey Hart's ranch. It was followed by RT's discussion of Native American medicine. The conference established RT as a knowledgeable and articulate spokesperson on the topic of Native American healing practices. In addition, Doug Boyd, the son of Elmer Green, the cohost of the conference, was inspired by his encounter with RT and went to visit him in July 1972. In September he received permission from RT to write a book about his experiences, titled *Rolling Thunder,* and he later gave a series of lectures, seminars, and workshops, not only in the United States but in Europe as well.

Boyd and RT attained rapport very easily. Boyd recalls being invited by RT to smoke *kinnikinnick* with him. This is a mixture of pure, untreated tobacco and various other Indian herbs. As a stuffed eagle watched the two of them at leisure, Boyd reflected that Rolling Thunder was a teacher who offered him insights that he could never achieve in the laboratory or discover in the library. Later he was invited to a peyote ceremony. As a member of the Native American Church, RT had a legal right not only to ingest peyote but also to supervise the sacred ceremony. RT toasted Boyd with a cup of the peyote tea, saying, "To Doug, who lives with us in Carlin, Nevada." It was one of the most memorable compliments that Boyd ever remembered receiving.

The *New York Times* gave an extremely favorable review to Boyd's book, pointing out that it is "about history, culture, the Earth, sky, trees, sacred herbs, vibrations, spirits, contemporary politics—and it is about these things passionately. I enjoyed reading it even more than I have enjoyed reading Carlos Castaneda, because it has real roots in a real world I can feel close to and understand."

Looking on the Internet, I discovered some astute comments from readers' reviews of the book, reviews that I feel contain considerable insights. Richard from Massachusetts wrote:

> Doug Boyd's observations were a little tendentious but I don't blame him. Rolling Thunder was and is a singular individual. And his ability to communicate with the Earth paled only to his ability to connect with other people. There's a strong environmental theme in this book. But it's much more spiritual. Although it won't try to "convert you" to anything in particular, it is an attempt to awaken its readers. The book tries to get them to connect their interests and their spirit, like RT, to the Earth. Boyd is a skilled writer. Some would say he's a little too "in love" with the subject he's writing about to be considered a scientist, social or otherwise. But it's the qualitative analysis that makes this book engaging. Boyd is a soothing author. He creates an experience so vibrant that I feel like I've actually heard RT's voice, seen his face and felt the warmth of the fire during a healing ceremony I've only actually experienced in print.

Donna from Tennessee commented:

> I have bought the Rolling Thunder book three or four times. I tend to loan it out and forget who borrowed it. In reading the book almost 30 years ago, I began to see things in a different light. I have taught my sister and my niece how to pick blackberries right off the bush with dozens of yellow jackets on them. I've learned that not everything you see is what's truly going on. What wonderful life lessons!

Diego from New York wrote:

> *Rolling Thunder* was written in a way reminiscent of the Castaneda books, but to me it was fresher, more concise, and more believable. We see Rolling Thunder, also known as John Pope, a medicine

man of the Cherokee tribe, from the perspective of Doug Boyd, a researcher from the Menninger Foundation in Topeka, Kansas, which happens to be my home town. In 1971, Boyd sought out Rolling Thunder to ask for his help in a study on mind-over-body control that began with the East Indian mystic Swami Rama. In the process, he was drawn into the world of the Native American, fighting against violations of rights and treaties, seeking harmony with others and the Earth. Rolling Thunder is a remarkable man. To him, speaking with the animals and affecting the weather is within the realm of possibility. Boyd takes us on a sober ride, describing events simply as he observed them. As any true student of self and nature knows, though, it's not the powers that matter, but rather the way of life, harmony with oneself and others, and the deeper energy in things. And from Rolling Thunder's mouth we receive some words on all of these things—on paying attention, on living in accord with surroundings, on having a good attitude no matter what happens. Not only do all of these seem more accessible than Castaneda's writings, but combined with the effort to raise awareness of the plight of reservation Indians, and the call to stop harming the Earth, it seems more relevant. The book is a series of episodes and dialogue, written in such a way that the language conveys the spirit of simplicity and doesn't get in the way. The plainness may deter some readers, though, if they are looking for action and demonstration of powers. The voice is quiet and hopeful; the book is almost a meditation.

What was RT's reaction to the book? He once told me that he never read it, even though family members had told him it "wasn't bad." His excuse was that he did not have enough time, with all the demands on him. Frankly, I think the reason was more complicated. RT had hoped to receive a percentage of the royalties from the book. Boyd did not deliver. But Boyd told me that he did not receive royalties himself and that his contract with his publisher contained many conditions and requirements that made it impossible for him to make any money from the book. In the meantime, I arranged for RT to receive a very large sum of money to write his own book. However, he turned down the publisher, saying that he preferred to wait until his memory improved so he could recall events more accurately.

In *Rolling Thunder Speaks: A Message for Turtle Island,* edited by RT's third wife, Carmen Sun Rising Pope, RT is quoted as saying that he hoped to write his own story when the time was right. After his death she was encouraged by a close friend to edit a book that pulled together transcripts of RT's lectures and informal discussions. This book was published in 1999, but a definitive biography of RT's life has yet to be written.

Shaman's Drum magazine published a lengthy review of *Rolling Thunder Speaks.*

> It covers a truly eclectic variety of topics, ranging from his childhood experiences in Oklahoma to his later encounter with various celebrities, and from his personal insights on religion to his eccentric views on politics. . . . Although I was, at times, inspired by his insights and challenged by his ideas, I grew weary of his tendency to engage in unwarranted generalizations and prejudicial invectives. . . . Despite the book's other limitations, the first chapter, "The Medicine Trail," may appeal to shamanic practitioners, as it provides RT's philosophical insights into the path of a Cherokee and pan-tribal person. For example, he describes the training and traditional tests used to prepare a medicine person. Emphasizing the importance of humility, RT explains that a medicine person doesn't do anything on his own; instead the Great Spirit works through him and through the medicines he employs.

So what did I think of the two books? I agree with the review from *Shaman's Drum;* better editing could have reduced *Rolling Thunder Speaks'* length without sacrificing any important details. However, there are enough golden nuggets to recommend it, and it demonstrates Carmen's determination to share RT's wisdom with the world. As for Boyd's book, I considered it a splendid account of a writer's experiences with a traditional Indian medicine man. The book *Rolling Thunder* does not exaggerate or sensationalize the occurrences it describes. It pays respect to Native people and strives for authenticity. Boyd describes himself as a learner, not a teacher. As a result, he does little interpretation, simply letting RT and the incidents surrounding him speak for themselves.

For example, Boyd accurately describes RT's behavior at the 1971 conference in Kansas. RT spent the first three days observing and conversing with the other participants, later saying that this is the traditional time span required for making important decisions. At the end of the three days RT told me that he was prepared to speak, and he remarked, "This is my first association on spiritual matters with white people," but added, "Some of the young, white generation out there are different from the old generation, and they like Indians."

Boyd wrote in a highly readable form. He described RT as "a gentle and compassionate healer, a crafty social strategist, a skillful debater, a thoughtful and loving father, a practical outdoorsman, and a carefree socialite." He included accounts of his interactions with family members such as Spotted Fawn and Buffalo Horse and colleagues such as Mad Bear Anderson and Grandfather Semu Huaute. Boyd ends his book with a statement by RT that "all life is a circle. The world is a circle and the atoms are circles. The circle is on the rock writings, and it goes around all things." RT called for a "circle of brotherhood" that would go around the world bringing peace. Boyd's book was published in 1974, and the world is still waiting for that circle of peace.

Grandfather Semu Huaute

Rolling Thunder acknowledged many mentors, but one man whom he held in special respect was Grandfather Semu Huaute, a Chumash-Cahuilla elder born in 1908. (Please see plate 14 of the color insert for a photograph of Grandfather Semu Huaute.) When he passed at the age of ninety-six, he left a rich legacy of healing knowledge and sacred songs, many of which urged respect for Nature and the care of the Earth. Here is one of them.

Come gather 'round and I'll sing you a song
I'll tell you a story of people who are strong
We live with Nature in harmony
Obeying the laws that were taught to me
Greeting each stranger with an open hand
Sheltered and fed him and called him friend.
Ey-ay-oh-ay!

Once I was wild as an eagle in the sky
Free to love and to live and to die
We roamed this land from the mountains to the sea
Brother to the elk, the bear, the deer
Of the rivers, the lakes, and the redwood trees.
Ey-ay-oh-ay!

I had no jails or prison farm
No barbed wire to do me harm
I paid no one to rule over me
No one owned the shade of the tree
I swam the ocean with the mighty shark
Played with the dolphins when the moon was dark.
Ey-ay-oh-ay!

So come be as wild as an eagle in the sky
Free to love and to live and to die
We roamed this land from the mountains to the sea
Brother to the elk, the bear, the deer
Of the rivers, the lakes, and the redwood trees
We'll live together in harmony.
Ey-ay-oh-ay!

According to RT, each song has its own individual being apart from human minds and voices. He often remarked, "The song sings the singer." In addition, RT had a great respect for drums. He remarked, "The drum can talk, and I've heard it talk in meetings and ceremonies.

I've seen the Earth shake in meetings and ceremonies and heard a voice come out to give me teachings and instructions. There is a lot of power in our drums. Sometimes we drum the evil spirits right out of people who persist in clinging to them so that they can come back together feeling good. Our songs have power, and they are a good way to drive out the evil spirits. We have songs to drive out evil spirits and whatever it is that makes us afraid."

Sidian's Comments

When the topic of RT's power is discussed, my mind drifts back over the years. One of my most vivid memories about my grandfather when I was very young is seeing him with his tomahawk. He only used it for ceremonial purposes, but I don't recall a time when it was not visible around his waist. On the surface his tomahawk was a simple instrument—carved wood and a rough stone tied to it with a tight cord. Nonetheless, it was both elegant and magisterial in its appearance. It felt imbued with a special power, a quality that was almost visible. There were times when I could not keep my eyes off it, and I am sure that my grandfather noticed my attention to it.

One day when I was about eight years old, he handed the tomahawk to me. I was surprised, but I also felt honored and privileged. I can still remember the unique authority of the tomahawk. In fact, when I held it, it was quite overwhelming in a way that I have never felt from any other material object, so I handed the tomahawk back to my grandfather. But my grandfather smiled, and the look in his eye told me that he understood my experience and why it was necessary to return the tomahawk to him.

Gary Sandman told me a story that demonstrates how RT sometimes combined his power with his trickster quality in order to drive a point home. Gary recalled:

We were in Santa Barbara about to give a talk, but we were about to hold the sunrise ceremony first. We were out in this big, open field, about the size of a football field. RT is at one end, and I'm at the other. I'm facing this wall that a couple of people are leaning against. They are talking to me about what it's like to be with RT and are just asking general questions. So my back is to RT, and I'm facing the wall where these two people are facing me. And out of nowhere, I feel this bolt of pain go through my back, out of my chest, hit the wall in front of me, bounce off it, hit my chest, and spin me around. And as I turn around, I'm going, "What the heck was that?" I see RT a hundred yards away flipping his little eagle feather, and he's going, "Come here." I said, "Okay, I got the message." Interestingly, my back was toward him, so it wasn't something that I might have imagined.

So when I get to him he said, "Good. It's time to start the circle. Stop talking to everybody. Get over here." That was his way of calling us in. So he did the morning circle and gave a talk later that day. And this woman approached him and said, "I need your help. I'm not well." We didn't hear what she talked about, but we knew she was ailing and was asking RT for help. So he said yes, even though he had not taken his customary three days to decide. And he gathered us together and said, "All right, I need you all to make a circle. And it's very important that you watch what you're thinking because that's what I need you to be doing. I need you to think positively to give me the energy so I can do this healing."

There was this one guy who had an attitude that RT was a big fake. So RT said, "I really need you all to watch your thoughts." And this guy muttered, "That's a bunch of crap. This guy doesn't even look like an Indian. And he wants me to watch my thoughts." RT, not looking at him, addressed the group and said, "Now, it's very serious when I ask that you direct your thoughts to help me to help this woman. So I'm really asking all of you to control your thinking and really be positive with this." So this guy said, "Yeah, this is a bunch of crap. What does he think I'm thinking? What does he know?" Then RT said, "Now, this is the last time I'm warning y'all, because it's important that I have your cooperation in this because it's really important that we do the right thing for this woman." The guy murmured, "That's a bunch of crap." And then RT stroked his eagle feather, and the guy was knocked unconscious, flat out in the dirt. And we all just kind of looked and thought it would be best if we kept holding on to our positive thoughts.

RT started the ceremony. As soon as it was done, the guy woke up and said, "What happened?" And we said, "Oh, nothing much." And he just kind of wandered off by himself. But RT often used the eagle feather with energy behind it *as a sacred instrument to communicate with people. And he also used it as a healing tool. It was real power. It wasn't something that you would see anywhere else. It was something that was absolutely real and not phony by any means.*

And RT would talk about power and responsibility in a very interesting way. He did not talk about having power over somebody else, but about having the power to be who you are and to hold your ground. So, if you knew what you believed, and if you knew what your path was, and if you kept your integrity, you would know where your power was.

7

Truckin' with the Grateful Dead

In the middle 1960s a gigantic wave of cultural and political change, originating in San Francisco, California, swept over much of the United States. The Grateful Dead rock band was an important part of this movement and spawned a subculture known as the Deadheads, loyal fans who followed them from concert to concert, bought their records, and emulated what they considered to be their lifestyle. Although the band ascribed to the descriptor of "sex, drugs, rock and roll," we know that the band members were skilled musicians. Some of them had classical music backgrounds, and the entire band would sometimes obtain tickets for the famed San Francisco Opera, one time sitting in on all four operas of Richard Wagner's Ring cycle.

The Grateful Dead began performing in 1965, were the featured band at author Ken Kesey's "Acid Test" parties in California, and participated in various festivals that year. The events and festivals were known for the presence of LSD, a powerful psychoactive drug that had been used to study such psychological phenomena as perception and hallucinations, as well as being used in psychotherapy. Once the recreational use of LSD spread, the U.S. government closed down the research studies and imposed draconian fines on manufacturers of the substance.

Jerry Garcia, the best-known member of the group, once told Stanley how the name originated, a description that occurs in several published accounts including *Song of the Siren*. "Back in the late days of the Acid Tests, we were looking for a name. We'd abandoned 'The Warlocks'; it didn't fit anymore. One day we were all over at Phil Lesh's house getting high. He had a big Oxford dictionary, opened it, and there was 'grateful dead,' those words juxtaposed. It was one of those moments, you know, like everything else on the page went blank, diffuse, just sort of oozed away, and there was GRATEFUL DEAD, big black letters edged all around in gold, blasting out at me, such a stunning combination. So I said, 'How about Grateful Dead?' And that was it."

The group lived in Los Angeles for several months with Augustus Owsley Stanley III, the supplier of the black market's highest quality LSD. The group returned to San Francisco in the middle of 1966 and lived in a musical commune for a period of time between 1967 and 1969. The band released several records during that time, parts of which were designed to be heard while the listener was in an altered state of mind. In 1969, following a raid by police officers, the group abandoned its San Francisco house and moved to separate houses in the countryside. But it was while they were in San Francisco that they had their first encounters with RT.

In songs like "Casey Jones," "Dark Star," and "Truckin'," the Grateful Dead's "acid rock" music displayed its roots in jazz, country and western music, rhythm and blues, and folk music. But they also borrowed musical idioms and instruments from Native American, Latin American, classical, and electronic music. It was rock and roll, but the rocks originated in the Earth, and the roll was reminiscent of Rolling Thunder's thunder.

One of RT's friends in the community of rock music was Barry Melton, a lawyer who has a long history of advocacy for Native Americans and other ethnic groups. But Melton is better known as the cofounder and original lead guitarist of the rock band Country Joe and the Fish. He appears on all the Country Joe and the Fish recordings and wrote many of the songs that the band recorded. Melton described RT as "a regular guy, without airs or pretense. But I was really impressed by his extensive knowledge about world medicine."

Melton discovered that RT had studied not only the Cherokee and Shoshone medicine traditions but those of the Paiute and Sioux as well. Melton met RT through Mickey Hart and later helped RT with some legal services. He was present when Mickey was cutting his solo album, *Rolling Thunder,* on which RT starts the album with a traditional prayer to the Four Directions. The prayer was simple yet direct.

> *To the East where the Sun rises.*
> *To the North where the cold comes from.*
> *To the South where the light comes from.*
> *To the West where the Sun sets.*
> *To the Father Sun.*
> *To the Mother Earth.*

RT had great respect for the Hopis and often cited the ancient Hopi prophecy: "The day will come when the children of the white man will begin to dress like Indians, when they will begin to wear long hair, beads, and headbands. That will be the generation from which will come the first true non-Indian friends." RT felt that the Hopis were the principle custodians of the traditional American Indian spiritual doctrines and considered David Monongye, one of his revered teachers, to be the custodian of other Hopi prophecies and secrets. If RT had taken David Monongye to a Grateful Dead concert, a glimpse at the audience of long-haired, beaded fans might have served as an ample fulfillment of the prophecy.

Stanley's Comments

The richly textured and multicultural nature of the Grateful Dead's music and lyrics stimulated a group of scholars to create the Grateful Dead Caucus, which meets yearly in conjunction with the Southwest Popular American Culture Association. This transdisciplinary group is composed of ethnomusicologists, psychologists, anthropologists, sociologists, historians, physicians, and students of business theory, communications theory, critical studies, and library science, among other disciplines.

The group considers me its godfather because I wrote the first scholarly article about the band, in 1973. This was a report on the experiment in telepathic dreams discussed in chapter 4 (in which the band played in Port Chester, New York, and the audience was directed to use whatever telepathic powers they could muster to influence the dreams of a psychic who was sleeping at Maimonides Medical Center in Brooklyn). I conducted experiments in dream telepathy at that medical center for ten years before accepting a teaching position at Saybrook University in San Francisco. The experiment was fairly successful and was published in the *Journal of the American Society of Psychosomatic Dentistry and Medicine*.

Also in 1973, I was in New York City for a parapsychological convention at the same time that RT was giving a workshop there. We arranged to meet for lunch, and I brought some friends with me. They included Celinda Madera, a parapsychologist from Puerto Rico, Robert McGarey, the son of Dr. William McGarey, the physician who had worked with RT at the Council Grove healing session, and Michael Bova, the art therapist and "psychic healer" who had joined me in my first sweat lodge ceremony on RT's land. RT brought one of his sons, Buffalo Horse, with him.

Buffalo Horse told me that he had been spending the summer in the Haight Ashbury district of San Francisco in the hippie era of the 1960s. He happened to be a neighbor of the Grateful Dead when they were living together, commune style, in an old mansion, and introduced them to his father. So it was Buffalo Horse who made the connection between Mickey Hart and RT. Mickey Hart was not an original member of the band, but he brought knowledge of non-Western music with him to enrich the group's already eclectic heritage.

Through my connections with friends in academia and holistic healing, RT had obtained invitations to lecture at the State University of West Georgia and the Association for Research and Enlightenment in Virginia Beach, the repository of the psychic readings given by Edgar Cayce when he was in a self-induced altered state.

In addition, I was able to bring RT to the annual meeting of the Association for Humanistic Psychology when it met in Reno, Nevada, in September 1973. I was presiding over a special showing of a documentary, *Psychics, Saints, and Scientists,* in which I made a cameo appearance. When Mickey heard that RT was going to attend, he drove over the border from California, and the conference participants were delighted to have a surprise celebrity guest.

Both RT and Mickey discussed their own parapsychological experiences with the group, much to the delight of the audience. But Mickey had an additional surprise. He presented me with a copy of his first solo album, *Rolling Thunder.* RT had already received his copy of the LP in the postal mail.

In his 1975 introduction to my book *Song of the Siren,* RT recalled how we met. And he also demonstrated the ability to change one's mind, an attribute I have observed in my contact with other shamans over the years.

There was a time when I was quite suspicious of scientists. I'll admit this. Like when I met Stanley Krippner for the first time at Mickey Hart's place. Mickey is one of the Grateful Dead and has been associated with rock music and the rock people. I've known those people for many years. And it was through the efforts of Mickey Hart that I met Stanley. For some reason, they wanted to bring us together. I never push to meet anyone, and I admit that at that time I was in no hurry to meet anybody. They had wanted me to meet a lot of different people and I had been disappointed a few times in some religious leaders they wanted me to meet. So when they came and told me he wanted me to meet a man named Stanley Krippner, at first I was skeptical. And I was even a little suspicious when I first met him. And I know we both tested each other.

From my pagan or primitive point of view, I wondered if a person with scientific training could be sincere in studying the other world. That was the reason for my skepticism. It wasn't a personal thing, I admit, because I couldn't find any fault with Stanley personally. As a matter of fact, I liked him from the beginning when I first met him. But I think it was the scientific terms—the high language and words that I didn't always understand.

I know that Stanley felt a bit skeptical too, and he knew many of my thoughts the same as I knew many of his thoughts. And I knew, even though he didn't say so, that he thought he was meeting with a pagan and a savage. And most people would think that these two—the savage and the scientist—couldn't be one and the same and probably couldn't get along together.

But I've found since that time that many of the findings of parapsychologists reflect the teachings that many of our people have known from old civilizations, ancient times, and even other worlds. Much knowledge has been handed down to us about such things as how the pyramids were built, how to reverse the law of gravity through magic and through mathematics, how to communicate with other people in dreams, how to use the electrical force that you find in all living things, and many other things that are assumed to be lost. But they are only lost temporarily, until the people are able to handle this wisdom without destroying themselves and without destroying the world.

RT would often refer to himself as a "savage." In one of his lectures, he commented, "Yes, I'm a savage. I like children, I like animals and birds, and at my age I still like women." Further, "I'm not a Red Apple—Indian on the outside but a white man on the inside. The Red Apples claim to have been educated, but they were really brainwashed to be ashamed of being Indians, so they forgot the old ways and the real values."

Sidian's Comments

I learned more about RT's connection with Mickey Hart through Cookie, Mickey's lady friend in the late 1960s.

Sidian Morning Star Jones: How did you meet RT?

Cookie: Mickey and I lived on a ranch in Novato, California, and RT would come to visit us. One time, some of his young braves came to stay with us because they were being persecuted by townspeople in

Carlin, Nevada. We had fifty-two acres of land, so there was plenty of room. But we didn't know how we would feed them. They went out hunting and brought back game. And they planted extra vegetables in our garden. So it worked out.

Sidian Morning Star Jones: They knew how to take care of things.

Cookie: They certainly did. And that's when I met your uncles and your grandmother Spotted Fawn. RT really enjoyed our ranch. He would take me into the forest in back of our ranch to an area we called "Little Mountain Ranch." And he would teach me about the plants we would find there and which ones would make good medicines. If someone in the house had a cold or a rash or a stomach ache, or if they were constipated, he would find something in the forest and put it to use.

Sidian Morning Star Jones: How would he help someone?

Cookie: If someone was sick he would sniff the person who was ill, and then he would take a piece of raw meat or chicken and put it in a fire. He would cup his hands around part of that person's body and would spit some horrible looking black stuff onto the meat. He claimed it was the poison from this person. Then we could see him get pale and weak. But it always worked.

Sidian Morning Star Jones: That is amazing.

Cookie: The night before RT was going to do a major healing ceremony, he would ask Mickey to find him a young woman because that would renew his spirit. My name came up, and my daughter's name came up, and some other family members' names came up. But Mickey wasn't into sharing his family in that way. RT told him in all seriousness that he would be happy to give him Spotted Fawn for a night, but Mickey had other ideas. He found one of the groupies who were always hanging around the ranch. And she was happy to help out RT and renew his energy.

Sidian Morning Star Jones: No wonder he liked coming to your ranch.

Cookie: We also had sunrise and sunset ceremonies. The sunset ceremonies were more solemn. They had to do with trying to deal with stuff that was more difficult to accept. There would be a fire for both ceremonies, and he would call upon the Four Directions. And during the day, he taught us about smoking kinnikinnick.

Sidian Morning Star Jones: What is that?

Cookie: It is the bark of a tree that you mix with herbs and smoke in a pipe. And we would sit for hours, smoking and talking. But sometimes RT would use a form of hypnosis to take us on internal trips.

Sidian Morning Star Jones: Where did you go on these trips?

Cookie: Sometimes I would see totem animals. One of them was a wolf, and RT told me that it was my power animal.

Sidian Morning Star Jones: Tell me about the wolf.

Cookie: Mickey went out and got me a real wolf. He was three weeks old, and I named him Buck. His mother was sick, and so they had to put her to sleep. So Buck thought that I was his mother. And a mother wolf would eat some food and regurgitate it for her babies to eat. Of course, I couldn't regurgitate when Buck started to nibble at my mouth. But I kept a little hamburger on my plate, and sometimes Buck would wake me up in the middle of the night, and I would feed him this hamburger. I fed him milk from a bottle for a while.

Sidian Morning Star Jones: Did Mickey put up with this?

Cookie: Oh yes. Mickey was really supportive. He read that wolves were very territorial. And so he took Buck outside when he was about seven months old. And he told Buck that this was his territory. And Buck started to pee all around the house like he was staking out his territory. One month the Grateful Dead went to Egypt to play at the Great Pyramid. I left Buck with a friend who took good care of him. But one day Buck wandered into a sheep farmer's ranch. And the farmer thought Buck was after the sheep so he shot him.

Sidian Morning Star Jones: Was he trying to catch a sheep?

Cookie: No, but the farmer didn't realize that Buck was domesticated. But Buck was part of our family for nearly three years.

Sidian Morning Star Jones: I'm sorry to hear that. You must have been devastated. Did you take RT to any of the recording sessions?

Cookie: Oh yes. And he really enjoyed them. And once we had a big party for the Tower of Power rock band when my daughter Debbie turned twenty-one. There were about five hundred people there, and someone had caught a wild boar. We dug a pit, and everyone feasted on that boar. We called it a "pig out." And the band played because their new record had just come out. Later, Mickey called his first album *Rolling Thunder,* and I have the original album cover. I designed the collage on the back of that album.

Sidian Morning Star Jones: Sounds like you had a great time.

Cookie: It wasn't all so great. My daughter Teri was riding her bicycle on the highway and was killed by a drunk driver when she was fourteen. I had her cremated, and RT came to conduct a ceremony. After he left, I just couldn't cope with my daughter's death. I got addicted to heroin because it helped to take away the pain.

Sidian Morning Star Jones: Did RT try to help you?

Cookie: Yes, he tried to help, but I was very rude to him. I would spit out whatever he tried to feed me. I would tell him to go and mind his own business. When you are hooked on hard drugs, that's the way you reject help. But RT understood that it was my addiction that was speaking and not me. He never got angry at me. When I recovered, I decided to make amends with him. When the Smithsonian Institution built the Museum for the American Indian, I sent money to inscribe RT's name as one of the first one hundred people honored on the wall. I got back a beautiful certificate. RT had passed on by then, but I wanted to honor someone who had really done a lot for me and for my family.

Another person Stanley and I interviewed was Franklin Fried, a photo journalist who had studied drumming with Arthur Jones, Mickey Hart's former teacher in high school.

Franklin Fried: Arthur Jones was Mickey Hart's band instructor in high school. He later became the director of all music departments in the school district that I went to as well. I liked the Grateful Dead since I was six years old. I was a big fan of the Dead when I was growing up. My favorite record was called *Rolling Thunder*. It was Mickey Hart's first solo record. It started out with RT doing the morning sunrise ceremony chant, and I loved it. I finally got to see them live around 1978. The day after the concert I went to the hotel where they were staying. I heard that Mickey went to my high school, and of course I wanted to meet him and Jerry Garcia and all the rest of the band. I waited in the lobby for a long time. Then Mickey came down, and I said, "Oh, you went to Lawrence High School?" He said, "Yes." I said, "And you studied with Arthur Jones?" And he said, "Let's talk." So after we talked about Mr. Jones, he gave me a note saying that there will be twelve tickets for me and my friends at their Madison Square Garden show and a backstage pass. He told me he would see me there, and that is the show where I met Stanley Krippner backstage. So, here I am sitting next to Stanley Krippner, and we started talking, and we hit it off. About a year later Stanley said, "Why don't you check out Rolling Thunder?" and Mickey said, "Yeah, why don't you check it out? Meet RT, and go to Meta Tantay." So in 1980, I took a Trailways bus from New York City to Carlin, Nevada.

That was a long trip, three days, and at the time I had braces on my teeth, so it was hard for me to eat anything at the rest stops. I traveled across the country having no idea what to expect and them having no idea what to expect from me. I ended up at the Carlin Café; it was like a truck stop. I walked in there, and we didn't have cell phones then so I had to use a pay phone to call RT's house in Carlin. So I called the house, and they said, "Somebody will be coming to pick you up." Well, when I first walked into the Carlin Café, all heads turned because I had long hair and I was wearing a Grateful Dead shirt with the skull logo on it. All the heads turned, all the miners and cowboys and rednecks. And here I am, an eighteen-year-old, long-haired, Jewish kid from New York. I made my call, and I went outside because I didn't think I was wanted inside. A pickup truck came zooming up, and a fellow was looking out the window, and he asked, "Are you Frank Fried?" And I said, "Yes, I am." And his face dropped because Stanley didn't tell them how old I was. Stanley just said, "Oh, he's a jazz drummer," because I was studying jazz drumming at the time with Arthur Jones. Well, they said, "We were expecting a forty-year-old man." And here I am eighteen years old with braces on my teeth, wearing a Grateful Dead shirt and long hair. But they took me into town to RT's house, and I sat down in the sunroom, the room RT's son, Buffalo Horse, built. So, I'm sitting there and notice a pay phone in the house. I found out later that they had to put the pay phone in or their guests would be making long-distance calls all over the world without paying for them.

They said that RT would be out in a little while, and I guess they had a discussion about me and what to do with me. Then they asked me if my mom and dad knew where I was. I said, "Yes, of course." So then RT came out and looked at me and said, "Oh, we've met before." And I said, "I've never met you before." "Well," he said, "did you have a dream last night?" and I said, "Yes, I had a dream about an eagle." And he said, "Well, that was me visiting you." So then RT said, "Today's my birthday." And I said, "No, I didn't realize that." He said, "We don't celebrate political or religious holidays here, but we do celebrate birthdays. Are you coming to my party?" And I said, "Of course." RT said, "You'll go to Meta Tantay in a little while, and we'll drive you out there." So I went out there, and of course they were shocked to see me because I was a stranger. But they showed me a place where I was going to stay, and it was one of the old trailers. There were wickiups and trailers and tepees. The wickiups were domes made out of Mylar plastic. Christo, the Bulgarian environmental artist, and his wife, Jeanne-Claude, had built a fancy fence in Sonoma County, California, and it got international publicity. One of RT's friends asked Christo if a band of Native Americans could have the material when they took the fence down. They told him about Meta Tantay and the wickiup domes, and Christo said it sounded like a good way to recycle the Mylar plastic. The plastic was silver, and the domes were stunning.

Sidian Morning Star Jones: I remember seeing one of those domes when I went up there as a kid.

Franklin Fried: That's when I think I met you, when you were a little kid. So I was in a beat-up old trailer that must have been from the 1950s, and I put my gear in there and talked to a couple of people and found out that it was the men's trailer. Later that evening the party for RT was happening in the barn. There was a woman who lived in Meta Tantay, and she was a beautiful belly dancer. What was her name?

Stanley Krippner: She went by the name of Mushroom, for obvious reasons. I knew her in San Francisco and told her about Meta Tantay.

Franklin Fried: Everybody was at the party who lived there, and all sorts of other people came to this party from all over the country. And actually before I walked into the barn, they said, "Whatever you do, don't approach Buffalo Horse. Let him talk to you." So, inside the barn, I sat right next to Buffalo Horse, and we started talking, and we became good friends. So while all this is going on they told RT to close his eyes. They had a birthday present for him, a surprise. So he closed his eyes, and they walked in a cow. They put the cow right up to his face. And RT opened his eyes and said, "Oh, that's for me?" So he was very happy about getting the cow, and the cow's milk was for everybody at Meta Tantay of course.

There were a whole bunch of things happening at the time, acid included. It's as if many things came together, and this often happens in the history of creativity. There is a slew of events that tend to converge, and you get a whole new consciousness. Back then we got rock music, women's rights, black rights, civil rights, gay rights. It was all opening up, all an antithesis to the 1950s. This was a fertile period for consciousness studies too. It gave birth to many movements centering around meditation, psychedelics, and communal living.

But RT reminded us that Native Americans speak of obligations rather than rights. When a group has found it hard to gain their rights, they have an obligation to use that power to help other groups that are still oppressed.

I went back to New York at the end of the summer. But I saw RT again when he came to Madison Square Garden to participate in Bob Dylan's Rolling Thunder Review. RT told me, "You know we were driving to the park, that big green space you have in New York." And they were driving in the park in a place you weren't supposed to drive, so the cops pulled them over, and there RT was in full regalia. He was even wearing his Cherokee turban and his eagle feathers. He was wearing his ribbon shirt, and everyone else in the car was all decked out too. So the cop was very surprised to see these Native Americans who looked lost, and they said, "We're going to a concert. How do we get to Madison Square Garden?" So the cops told them which way to go. I think the cops were a little freaked out by the outfits. They had never seen anything like that.

Sidian Morning Star Jones: What was the most important teaching you learned from RT?

Franklin Fried: I remember him saying, "You can't just sit down and talk about the truth. It doesn't work that way. You have to live it and be part of it, and then you might get to know it.

Sidian Morning Star Jones: And what was the most dramatic healing that you remember?

Franklin Fried: Mickey was in a car crash and was in bad shape. His ear got torn off. He had to have plastic surgery to restore his ear. RT paid a special trip just to spend several days with Mickey. He brought medicinal herbs and made teas for him. He also did drumming and chanting. Mickey came through it in good shape.

Sidian Morning Star Jones: What other rock stars was RT close to?

Franklin Fried: Especially John Cipollina of the Quicksilver Messenger Service and Clarence Clemons, the saxophone player who later was a member of Bruce Springsteen's E-Street Band.

8

The Sweat Lodge Ceremony

We have noted that the sweat lodge ceremony is one of the most widespread traditions for purification of spirit, mind, and body among Native people in North and Central America. To sweat in this manner is regarded as a sacred act, and the ceremony is usually performed in a spiritual context. The shamans in many tribes used the ceremony, also called a "sweat," as a healing procedure. For example, Maidu shamans in California used their sweats to heal chills or fevers; herbal medicine was placed in the water that turned to steam on the hot rocks, allowing them to inhale the medicine. In treating muscle strain, the injured area was covered with warm mud and the patient spent the night in the sweat lodge.

The sweat lodge ceremony is also performed for other purposes, such as to induce a vision, to prepare for a hunt, or to commemorate the arrival of puberty. It has also been used as a preparation for warfare or to celebrate the killing of an enemy. An individual might sweat before participating in a sun dance ceremony, before embarking on a vision quest, or simply as preventive medicine.

In 2011, Fawn Journeyhawk, a Native American medicine woman, told Stanley that the sweat lodge ceremony allows people to search for solutions for their problems by getting in touch with their spirituality. For her, the sweat lodge strengthens connections between people, bringing them together in an atmosphere based on love and concern.

There are many different ways to construct the lodge, and this varies from culture to culture. There are also several ways to bring heat into the lodge. In one way, stones are heated in a fire pit outside the lodge and then are brought in. Water is then poured on the hot rocks, producing steam. In the second type, the fire is built in the lodge to heat the rocks and then the fire is removed. The third type employs a duct that conveys heat from an outside fire into the lodge. This procedure is primarily used in Central America.

In much of North America the lodge is a wickiup constructed on a frame of flexible poles that are bent and tied together to form a dome seating about ten people. The frame can be covered with animal skins, blankets, canvas, or bark from trees. In the far northern part of the continent, the ceremony may be conducted in a structure made of cedar planks. In the Southeast, lodges were often dug into the earth or into the side of a hill.

Once the participants begin to sweat, prayers are offered and songs are sung. This part of the ceremony varies from tribe to tribe, as do the contents of the lodge. Some lodges contain an altar on which a sacred pipe rests. In others, a ring of small stones forms a circle around the area where the hot rocks are placed. Sometimes sage or other sacred plants are placed on the hot rocks. At other times there are four breaks between "rounds," during which time participants can leave the lodge and spray each other with cold water. The rounds may last from fifteen to forty-five minutes, with the entire ceremony taking from between one to three hours. The ceremonial leader usually has an assistant who may bring in rocks from the outdoor fire pit, at which time each new rock is welcomed.

The Lakota Sioux tribe believes that the sweat lodge ceremony was taught to their ancestors by White Buffalo Calf Woman. She told them that if the ceremony is done properly all the powers of the universe are brought into play and will aid the participants. She is a manifestation of Wakan Tanka, the Great Mystery, and brings gifts to humans, the sweat lodge ceremony being one of them.

Wakan Tanka is often equated with the Christian God the Father.

However, the anthropologist William Lyon has noted that the Lakota Sioux did not have the concept of a single supreme god until their contact with the Europeans. Previously, there were several powerful spirits. A shaman was referred to as a *wakan*-man, or "mysterious man," who had a secret system for understanding the Great Mysterious.

The first round often begins with a calling to an animal spirit or a welcoming song or prayer. The songs are generally simple and repetitive so that newcomers can learn them quickly and join in. Drumming is used in some of the ceremonies; if so, it is repetitive and fairly loud. At the end of each round, the door flap is lifted and the steam rushes out. The fourth round is the time during which participants may experience the most profound shifts in their awareness. The ceremonial leader may attribute this to their spirit leaving their body. Visions are common, as are voices from unknown sources. At the conclusion of the final round, the leader congratulates participants for their success in completing the ceremony. Group members may share experiences at this time and may adjourn for refreshments.

Participants' accounts often include reports marked by colorful visual imagery, intense emotion, recall of important life experiences, insights into their personal path, freedom from physical or mental pain, and an overall feeling of cleanliness and purification.

Stanley's Comments

My first visit to RT's home in Nevada was also the time of my first sweat lodge experience. As part of the healing ceremony that was to follow, RT led us into the wickiup that had been built directly in back of his house. It had been constructed of saplings bent and tied together, over which animal hides had been draped. A shallow pit had been dug in the center and filled with red-hot rocks taken from a nearby fire pit. One of RT's assistants took a ladle, dipped it into a pail of water, and poured the water onto the rocks. As the water contacted the rocks, an explosive hiss was followed by a wave of intense heat that enveloped our naked bodies.

We took turns adding water, and the heat increased until I thought that my skin was on fire. With every breath, the fire extended itself into my lungs. Finally, I realized that I could not fight the heat. I became one with the heat, the fire, and the air and allowed every breath I took to enhance the feeling of oneness. The feeling of unity extended to the group and even to the entire universe. As the sweat poured from my body, I felt purged of anxiety, depression, and all the petty concerns that would have prevented me from participating in the healing ceremony that was to follow. I have participated in several sweats since 1974, but my inaugural experience was unforgettable. RT once observed:

We have two sweat lodges, one for the men and one for the women. We don't go in together. Some Indians nowadays have mixed sweats, but we do ours the old way, the original way. We don't go into sweat lodges with a dirty body or a dirty mind. I take a bath before I go into a sweat lodge to get the most out of it. A lot of good spiritual power is generated there. I've heard the universe sing, even after our singing stopped. That's how powerful some of our ceremonies and sweat lodges are.

From a Native American perspective, the importance of these ceremonies is renewal, because nothing persists, all is flux, and a society will pass away unless it is willing to renew itself.

Sidian's Comments

Michael Neils invited Stanley and me to a sweat lodge ceremony when we were in Phoenix, Arizona. I wasn't prepared for the intensity of the heat, but I pulled through and felt very revitalized after it was over. What I hadn't realized until we stepped out of the tent was that, by Michael's count, it had been one of the most heat-intensive sweat lodges he'd ever done. Michael started visiting Indian tribes when he was nine years old. With the help of a family friend, he found a tribe of Cree Indians in Montana, and three years later, a family adopted him. He returned every summer, and when he was fourteen the tribe allowed him to participate in a three-day sun dance. He told me that for their ceremonies, both men and women could dance and nobody got pierced.

Michael told me about an early encounter with RT at the Westerbeke Ranch in Sonoma County, California. He and RT were walking in the woods, and Michael observed that the Cree had given him (Michael) the name of He Who Climbs High Mountains. Michael asked RT if he had a Cherokee or Shoshone name as well. RT stopped walking and said, "Let's see what Nature has to say about that. Look down on the ground and you will see a large stone. Pick it up and turn it over." Michael followed the instructions and found a large, flat stone between his feet. He picked it up. Without inspecting the stone, RT said, "Now turn it over, and you will have another Indian name; the initials will be on the other side of the stone, the side closer to the Earth." Michael turned the stone over and discerned the initials "T. C." etched into the rock by millennia of weathering. RT said, "There you have it. Thunder Cloud is your other Indian name. And it suits you well."

A few weeks later the building where Michael was staying was burglarized, and many of his possessions were stolen. But his medicine bag was untouched. And, of course, the flat stone was safely ensconced in Michael's medicine pouch.

Stanley also has an Indian name, Wicasa Wasste (pronounced wi-cá-sha wa-shte'), which can be translated as "good man" or, as Stan prefers, "mensch," a Yiddish term. He was given this name by Edwin Stronglegs Richardson, the first Native American to receive a Ph.D. in clinical psychology. I stopped hoping I'd be given an Indian name long ago and have since taken on the name Sidian, a tribute to the volcanic glass used by the Indians, and the middle name Morning Star, my mother's Indian name.

9

Shamanic Dreamwork

Both of us have had a long-standing interest in dreams and have read about the near-universality of rapid eye movement sleep among mammals. This commonality indicates that dreaming probably was an evolutionary adaptation needed to consolidate what was learned during the waking hours. This task is accomplished by reviewing new learning during sleep. Dreams also download the emotions and feelings accumulated during the day, and probably rehearse future activities. Shamanic visionary experiences engage a capacity for self-exploration based on the same systems that underlie dream experiences. Besides the representation of oneself, both wakefulness and dreaming involve creating a scenario for the examination of the dreamer's options. Previous scenarios are replayed, and unresolved emotional issues are played out and incorporated into behavior patterns. All of these functions play a role in shamanism. In addition, some medicine men and women are called to their profession through dreams.

In fact, shamans receive their "call to shamanize" in a number of ways. Some of them are born into a family of shamans and were born into their profession. Others received the call through recovering from a serious illness; they are often called wounded healers, because the cure for their wound was to shamanize. Still others are called in visions and dreams. Among the Inuit, a dream about the spirit world constitutes a call to shamanize. Dreams of deceased relatives mark one's call among the Wintu and Shasta tribes of California.

Among the Southern Valley Yakuts of California, a shaman's power may come from a vision quest, a trip that is taken alone in search of one's life path. Some young Yakuts who go on this vision quest are called to shamanize either in daytime visions or nighttime dreams. In the Diegueno and Luiseno tribes, future shamans can be selected at as early as nine years of age on the basis of their dreams. In most of these tribes the dream character that initiates the call might be a bird or an animal, such as Bear, Deer, Eagle, or Owl. For most Native Americans dreams and visions are similar. They are their own reality. RT once commented, "We listen to everyone's dreams, even those of the very young. We listen to dreams for guidance."

Rolling Thunder's call came during the night. He did not remember the dream, but he awakened in the morning feeling as if he had been transformed overnight. He felt a sense of power that was completely new to him, and he knew that he must use this power for the service of others. He later remarked, "This power just comes to you, which you have to honor, respect, and use, otherwise it can make you sick. Once you accept your call, you never stop learning." Rolling Thunder reported having periodic dreams, visions, and conversations with animals and plants, all of whom became his teachers.

The shaman's "soul flights" resemble what Western psychologists refer to as out-of-body experiences and near-death experiences. They reflect innate psychophysiological processes and a nonverbal symbolic capacity such as those found in dreaming. There is often a complex synesthesia, a blending of visual, auditory, and kinesthetic sensory modalities. This synthesis often provides a special form of self-awareness experienced as being apart from the physical body. This cross-modal translation is the basis for symbolic thought. The resulting images form a preverbal signal system that integrates unconscious, emotional, and bodily information at cognitive levels.

Humans have innate mental hardware for detecting intrusive forces, whether they are human or nonhuman. This self-protective mechanism was a result of human evolution but can become too much of a good thing. When it is overactive, it constructs forces when none are actually present. This is often the case in the detection of spirits. But there are also evolutionary advantages in a system that detects unknown forces. Whether one is prey or hunter, an overactive detection system is an aid for survival.

Assumptions about unseen humanlike actors are even more adaptive, endowing spirits with characteristics such as psychological dispositions and emotions. This detection mechanism protected early humans against sudden weather changes, dangerous serpents, insects, and animals, and even against natural disasters such as earthquakes. These forces became known as spirits, and the frequent inference of spirit forces is called animism. This belief system finds spirits in trees, rocks, rivers, and other forms of Nature. The tendency to ascribe humanlike characteristics to natural forms is derived from dreams, daydreams, out-of-body experiences, and near-death experiences. Over time these spirits took on a reality of their own, becoming part of the imaginal world, the world of archetypes, of thoughtforms, and of other collective phenomena on the limen, or border, of consensual reality and fantasy. The shamans who took journeys into these invisible realms discovered that they seemed to be inhabited. Some of the inhabitants were friendly and others were hostile; in any event, the shamans needed to know the difference.

Animism involves anthropomorphism, the attribution of humanlike characteristics to spirits and other nonhuman entities. Anthropomorphism is adaptive because it imposes order on the unknown through the projection of human models on the environment. Spirits are a basic aspect of the human tendency to project meaning onto poorly understood aspects of the environment when the intent of the surrounding ambiance is unknown.

Anthropomorphism projects meaning and intentionality onto nonhuman elements of the natural world. This projection is adaptive because it helps humans operate effectively in a social context, making sense of others' behavior and explaining why they act in certain ways. Assumptions that spirits know more than humans do is adaptive because the concept has an empirical basis in the unconscious processes that people engage in through divination or foretelling the future. Alan Watts observed that the I Ching and other methods of divining often worked because an individual has given up on using his or her rational resources to solve a problem, allowing access to his or her unconscious processes. More often than not the new solution is successful, but the I Ching, tarot cards, or a collection of shells and bones gets credited for the success. Actually, they serve as the vehicle by which unconscious knowledge is accessed.

For too many years Westerners have scoffed at belief systems involving animism, anthropomorphism, and the belief in spirits. These ways of thinking and believing helped early humans to survive in unpredictable environments; they were successful often enough to reinforce the future use of prayer, sacrifice, divination, and other methods of contacting the spirit world. But this world was not mere fantasy. It was imaginal; it was rooted in human psychoneurology and psychophysiology to such a great extent that it could be experienced, manipulated, and even depended on in times of uncertainty and crisis.

Stanley's Comments

One day I talked with a young man, Anthony, who had been bothered by a repetitive dream for years. He was convinced that only Rolling Thunder could provide the interpretation for this dream. Fortunately, I made arrangements for Anthony to spend a summer at Meta Tantay. In exchange for some work Anthony did at Meta Tantay, RT listened carefully to Anthony's dream: "I saw a white buffalo. The white buffalo was fighting with a black buffalo, but neither could win. Suddenly both buffalos disappeared, and there was a gray buffalo standing firm and strong."

Rolling Thunder replied, "Just close your eyes, Anthony, and we will try to find out. Now ask what part of you could be symbolized by the white buffalo. Then ask what part of you could be represented by the black buffalo." Anthony carried out the exercise and allowed his imagination to run free. Eventually he replied, "The white buffalo stands for the part of me that does all the right things, makes all the right moves, and makes my parents proud. The black buffalo is that part of me that gets into trouble, that does not follow the rules, and that gets criticized by my parents. But sometimes I think that the bad part of me is more interesting and more creative than the good part of myself. This is why the white buffalo cannot win the fight. And when the best part of both buffalos merge, they become gray. And this is the type of person I would like to become."

Rolling Thunder smiled and said, "Anthony, you have just interpreted your own dream. The answer makes sense. And it also tells you that you can trust your own judgment and don't have to rely on other people for all the answers."

Rolling Thunder did not dismiss the dream scenario as fantasy, as would many Westerners who dismiss the meaning that can be found in dreams. Instead, he treated the buffalos as players in the imaginal realm, using a method of dreamworking that is popular among many Western psychologists. In this procedure dreamers are asked to project themselves into a dream character and to think, feel, and act as if they were that dream character. This enactment can be done silently, with a guide, or with a group. Sometimes other members of the group play the roles of dream characters. Two of the types of Western psychotherapy that specialize in these procedures are known as Gestalt psychotherapy and psychodrama, but similar procedures were used by North American shamans centuries ago.

In 1996, April Thompson, a political science student, and I read everything we could find about Indian dreamwork on the North American continent before it had been invaded by Europeans. We found sixteen tribes whose methods of working with dreams had been recorded, and we published our findings in *Dreaming*, a journal affiliated with the American Psychological Association. Some of these tribes have begun to work with their dreams again, using the traditional procedures that shamans used centuries ago. We asked the same questions about these procedures that have been used to describe contemporary Western dreamworking systems, such as Gestalt psychotherapy, psychodrama, Freudian psychoanalysis, Jungian archetypal psychology, and others. These questions are:

1. What is the function of dreaming?
2. What motivates people to recall their dreams?
3. What is the source of dreams?
4. What is the language of dreams?
5. Are dream meanings universal?
6. How is one's life situation reflected in dreams?
7. What procedures are used to work with dreams?
8. What is the role of the dreamworker?
9. What role does dreamworking play in the culture?
10. How are visionary dreams viewed?

The tribes we studies included the Alaskan Eskimo, the Blackfoot, the Crow, the Dakota Sioux, the Hopi, the Klamath, the Kwakiutl, the Mandan, the Maricopa, the Menominee, the Mohave, the Navaho, the northern Iroquois, the Ojibwa, the Yuma, and the Zuni. Of course most of these tribes refer to themselves by their traditional names, not the names given them by Europeans. For example, the Yuma refer to themselves as the Marica.

Western anthropologists use the term *Alaskan Eskimo* when referring to the Inuit people. The language is a member of the Eskimo-Aleut linguistic group. They live in the Alaskan Arctic area, but their culture stretches for some six thousand miles across the shores of the Arctic Ocean from Siberia to Greenland. Of course there are many regional variations, but there are remarkable similarities that have persisted over the millennia. Anthropologists estimate that the earliest members of this tribe arrived in North America by way of the Bering Strait in 3000 BCE or earlier. The Eskimo livelihood centers on sea animals such as whales, walruses, and seals, which are hunted for clothes, food, and fuel. Their characteristic igloos, harpoons, and kayaks are only part of an artistic heritage that includes storytelling and shamanic rituals. Many of their shamans discount the arrival from Siberia, claiming that their people were "always here." This can be seen as a metaphor or a statement consistent with local mythology, but it is similar to the claims made by several shamans from other tribes.

The Alaskan Eskimo Model of Dreaming

The Alaskan Eskimo model of dreaming varies somewhat from region to region, but most shamans would answer the key questions in the following way.

What is the function of dreaming? Dreams review the past, they represent the present, and they can predict the future.

What motivates people to recall their dreams? Dreams are a source of knowledge, especially about the spirit world. They are also a source of power and tell the dreamer how to use that power.

What is the source of dreams? Dreams come from the soul. The soul wanders during sleep. Usually, the soul can find its way back to the dreamer's body, but sometimes it gets trapped in some part of the spirit world. If the soul gets trapped, the *angakok* (shaman) must perform a special ritual to retrieve the dreamer's soul.

What is the language of dreams? Dreams often use symbols. This explains why the dreamer may not behave in dreams the way he or she behaves in everyday life. Dreamers may perform activities that they would like to perform while awake but cannot for one reason or another. Other people in dreams may act or look very differently than in everyday life. This type of dream may symbolize an unknown or hidden part of that person. Or the dream character may be a symbol of someone else or of some present or future activity. The angakok is trained to recognize symbols in dreams and to explain them to the dreamer.

Are dream meanings universal? There are some dreams that mean the same for everyone. For example, a dream about the moon indicates that there will be a death in the household. But a dream in which there are loud noises can have the same meaning. Many other dream images are relevant only to the dreamer.

How is one's life situation reflected in dreams? Dreams can reflect important aspects of the past, present, or future. But dreams may also predict illness. If someone's soul is trapped in a dream, the soul must be retrieved. But the dreamer must remain on guard against getting sick in daily life.

What procedures are used to work with dreams? If a dreamer is trying to contact a spirit, the dreamer simply keeps trying until he or she is successful. This may be the spirit of an ancestor from whom the dreamer needs to obtain advice. Or it may be a spirit that is needed to ensure success while fishing or hunting. In this case intention is important. The dreamer needs to focus on this intention before going to sleep. If the dreamer finds the spirit, the dream is shared with members of the community. However, negative dreams such as those predicting death are not shared.

What is the role of the dreamworker? The angakok often makes journeys to the spirit world to find helpful spirits. Once the spirits are found, the angakok promises them that the knowledge and power that they give will be used for benevolent purposes. The angakok also vows loyalty to the helpful dream spirits. The angakok helps members of the community to interpret their dreams. If a dream is not remembered completely, the angakok will help the dreamer to complete the dream by suggesting an appropriate ending. The angakok is so familiar with dreams that this ending is rendered accurately.

What role does dreaming play in the culture? Dreams are not a central part of the Alaskan Eskimo culture. However, the culture stresses intention and voluntary control of one's awareness. Examples would be the ability to withstand the extreme cold or the intense pain that often results from the environment. These skills often are reflected in dreams. And this is why soul retrieval is an urgent task if someone loses control during a dream.

How are visionary dreams viewed? Some dreams that do not seem to reflect the dreamer's past, present, or future may reveal the dreamer's former life. The angakok is able to identify those dreams. Visionary dreams about the future are taken seriously, especially if they are omens of illness or death.

The Navaho Model of Dreaming

A contrasting dream model can be found in the Navaho tribe, the largest Native American society in the United States. The word *Navaho* is derived from a Spanish term meaning "people with big fields," but in their own language they call themselves the Diné people. They are members of the southern Athapaskan linguistic group.

What is the function of dreaming? Among the Navaho dreams are felt to give guidance to the dreamer. As a result they are closely connected with Navaho religion, medicine, ritual, and social life. For example, traditional Navaho burial rituals were thought to have been given to tribal elders in their dreams. Unlike the Alaskan Eskimos, for whom dreams are peripheral to the culture, dreams are a central part of Navaho life, and their guidance is clearer if the dreamer's waking thoughts do not obstruct the message.

What motivates people to recall their dreams? Navaho people pay close attention to their dreams because of the guidance they provide. Some dreams are thought to predict illness, and a few dreams are felt to play a causal role in the onset of an illness. As a result, dreams are labeled good or bad, depending on their aftereffects.

What is the source of dreams? In dreams, the "inside spirit" of the dreamer is activated. When the dreamer is asleep, this inside spirit travels, bringing back messages from deities, deceased people, and animal spirits, among others. Sorcerers are able to create bad dreams that will endanger the health of the dreamer.

What is the language of dreams? Dreams are thought to convey information brought back from the spirit world. The language is geared to the needs of the dreamer, and so each dream is a personalized message.

Are dream meanings universal? Because dreams are personalized messages, there are few universal dream symbols. However, extremely important dreams use symbols that have the same meaning for everyone, especially if they are bad dreams. Dreams about dead livestock, for example, predict illness. A dream about teeth being extracted indicates misfortune. Dreams about family members getting sick are especially ominous; they do not always predict illness but indicate forthcoming trouble. Dreams about certain animals, reptiles, and birds have standard interpretations. For example, dreams of buzzards, hawks, and snakes presage death. But the dream is always individualized to the life of the dreamer, even if a dream image has a standard meaning.

How is one's life situation reflected in dreams? Navaho dreams reflect cultural mythology, but the form of the dream is highly personal. If a dream indicates that a ritual is needed, the dreamer has a great deal of personal choice in deciding what song or "chantway" is most appropriate. Dreams of mentally deranged individuals vary so widely from typical Navaho dreams that they can be used to diagnose mental illness. Dreams of young people often contain information about their life path but are often disregarded, because they have not learned to turn to their dreams for inspiration or direction.

What procedures are used to work with dreams? Most dreams can be explained by elders, family members, or by dreamers themselves. More important dreams require the advice of a shaman, or *hataalii*. Dreams about death require that the hataalii chant the "Chantway of Terrestrial Beauty." Dreams of dangerous objects such as lightning or poisonous snakes require the performance of the "Shooting Chantway." The "Star Chantway" is required following dreams about flying, falling, being stranded on a rock, being caught in waves or a whirlwind, or defending oneself against an enemy. The same chantway is mandatory if there have been dreams about bees, thunder, cacti, or coyotes. Performing the "Night Way" is part of an extensive ceremony, often lasting up to nine days. The "Enemy Way" is used to counteract witchcraft and malevolent spells; some shamans have used it to treat veterans returning from combat with post-traumatic stress disorder.

People who have lost contact with their culture and who want to return are urged to pay special attention to their dreams, which will suggest ways of restoration as well as the appropriate chantway that they need. If dreamers have good dreams that they want to come true, a medicine person may be requested to sing for them. Many chantways are performed in a medicine circle especially constructed for the dreamer. This ritual is attended by family and community members, who offer their support, especially if the chantway is geared toward healing. Although the medicine circle may take hours to construct, it is totally destroyed once the ritual has been completed.

What is the role of the dreamworker? The hataalii presides over dreamwork that requires chantways or medicine circles. The chantways need to be impeccably performed. If the hataalii makes a mistake, the chantway must be sung from the beginning. Its performance has been compared to singing all the roles of an opera, and some chantways take several hours to perform. Other dreams can be interpreted by elders or medicine people who do not have shamanic status. These dreams include good dreams, those about minor illnesses or misfortunes, and those about forthcoming opportunities. Family members and the dreamers themselves can interpret many of these dreams.

What role does dreamworking play in the culture? Navahos take dreams seriously. Telling another person a dream is not a casual activity but is done after careful consideration. Navaho dreams reflect the cultural mythology, but with many variations depending on the life situation of the dreamer.

How are visionary dreams viewed? Many dreams are felt to predict the future, especially bad dreams and those sent by sorcerers. However, there are ways in which an unpleasant future event can be modified by the hataalii and the proper rituals. Some dreams give specific instructions; if dreamers have dreams about planting crops such as pumpkins, squash, or corn, those dreamers will probably plant them during the appropriate time of the crop cycle. Corn often appears in dreams, because it is the manifestation of something deeper, something that transcends the individual plant and links all Corn together. People can enter into a relationship with this spirit, this active power that takes the form of the corn plant.

If a dream setting is a specific place, the dreamer will make every effort to make a trip to that location. Dreams about the Land of the Dead are not necessarily bad dreams, unless a deceased person shakes hands with the dreamer. If so, the tribal hataalii must perform a ritual as soon as possible, or the dreamer might die.

A Synthesized Dream Model

In our 1996 article April Thompson and I presented a synthesis of the common elements we found when studying Native American dream models. There were considerable differences, of course, but there were some striking similarities.

What is the function of dreaming? Dreams are sources of power, especially for hunting, healing, and defense of the tribe.

What motivates people to recall their dreams? Dreams provide dreamers with sources of power and knowledge that they can get nowhere else.

What is the source of dreams? The spirit world is the source of dreams. Dreams describe the reality of the spirit world and are sometimes more real than the everyday world.

What is the language of dreams? Dreams convey their meaning through stories and images that reflect events in the dreamer's past, present, and future or in the spirit world.

Are dream meanings universal? Some dreams have the same meaning for every member of the group, but other dreams convey personal meanings. In either case, the same story or image may have several potential meanings depending on the context.

How is one's life situation reflected in dreams? Dreams often serve a problem-solving function, reflecting the dreamer's present, past, or future. Dreams may direct someone to carry out an action prescribed in the dream. Some dreams convey warnings of activities or people to avoid.

What procedures are used to work with dreams? Working with dreams can be carried out by acting out the dream, by sharing the dream with others, or by consulting a shaman, an elder, or another person who specializes in dreamwork.

What is the role of the dreamworker? The social role of the dreamworker is one of respect. Working with dreams is an important social function.

What role does dreamworking play in the culture? Dreamworking is a valuable activity, because it provides beneficial knowledge and power to community members and especially to shamans, who often use dreams to diagnose illness or solve a society's problems.

How are visionary dreams viewed? Dreams can reflect distant events, experiences from a former lifetime, or future happenings. Visionary dreams contain knowledge and power that is beneficial for the entire community, while ordinary dreams are only relevant to the dreamer.

There are several accounts of Native American dreams and visions that demonstrate several aspects of this model. In 1799, Handsome Lake—a Seneca youth living with the Quakers—had a vision while he was critically ill. The Quakers took this vision seriously, because they had a spiritual tradition that honored dreams and visionary experiences. They helped Handsome Lake arrange a feast that had been dictated to him in his vision, one that included the killing of a white dog. On the day of what was known as the White Dog Feast, Handsome Lake began to recover. From that time on he became a spiritual leader who attempted to rescue his people from alcoholism and the destructive behaviors that had resulted from their departure from the Red

Road, in other words from following their traditional lifestyle.

Born in 1863, Black Elk, a medicine man of the Oglala Sioux Nation, claimed to have foreseen the Battle of Little Big Horn and, in retribution, the massacre of his people at the Battle of Wounded Knee. When he became a young man, Black Elk participated in both events. Earlier, as a child, he dreamed of two Grandfathers calling him. They brought him to the Council of Grandfathers, who taught him many profound lessons and provided many remarkable visions. The council also showed Black Elk a broken hoop that was in need of repair. Black Elk found himself on top of a tall rock mountain and was guided back home by an eagle. He shared this dream with his tribe and resolved to try to mend the broken hoop of the Sioux traditions, becoming a powerful spiritual leader. A book about his life, *Black Elk Speaks,* made such an impression on the psychoanalyst Carl Jung that he arranged for a German translation. Jung felt that his concepts of archetypes and the imaginal world were confirmed by Black Elk's stories about his life.

The sacred words from the dream are important, because for Indians words are living things, actual physical powers. The vibrations of words are energies that act within the setting in which they are uttered, whether it be a hogan, a valley, or a riverbank. Anthropologists have observed that a shaman's vocabulary contains more words than those of his or her peers. The average number of words used by Native Americans in their daily activities is about 1,500, but a shaman typically uses several thousand.

The English language brings the speaker back to a world of objects. But physicist David Bohm rejected this notion of the universe; his vision was a cosmos of processes and activities in constant holomovement. I once attended a lecture by Bohm and recall him mentioning that quantum physics emphasizes that the context in which events occur is of key importance. I relate this statement to RT's emphasis on context, especially the need to conduct healing at the right time, in the right place, and with the right attitude.

Sidian's Comments

James Swan, an anthropologist and psychologist, remembers hearing my grandfather tell him two dreams that he had as a young man. In one of them he saw a huge golden door open in front of him. Slowly, he saw a majestic figure dance through the shining gold portal. He immediately recognized it as Quetzalcoatl, the feathered serpent deity and Aztec ruler. Quetzalcoatl danced right into RT's body and merged with him in a blaze of golden light. RT woke up crying, feeling as if he had been on fire. For the next three days, anyone who touched him received an electric shock. RT later realized that this dream was a very special gift, one that would endow him with extra healing power.

In the other dream RT had a face-to-face encounter with the devil. This dream frightened RT until he realized that the devil represented his trickster side, one that he would develop to help people get better when he worked on them. And sometimes he *would* have to trick people in order for them to get well. The Quetzalcoatl dream came first and revealed RT's heroic side to him. The trickster dream came later, when RT knew that he could accept and integrate this shadow element of his psyche without losing his spiritual grace.

I used to avoid working with my dreams, because so many of them were violent and forced me into situations where I'd have to converse with dead people. But my study of dreams taught me that most people remember more unpleasant than pleasant dreams. There is a reason for this, according to psychologists who have studied the role that dreams played in human evolution. One of the functions of dreams is to process daily events. Important lessons are remembered and find their way into our storehouse of memories. Plans for the future are rehearsed; this is a way that memories are applied. Emotional experiences are downloaded. During the day we might not have had time to fully express our anger, our grief, our disappointment, or other emotions that have surfaced. During our dreams we can concoct experiences in which these same emotions are present, albeit in different settings and with different people. This is our dreams' ingenious way of replaying those emotions in ways that help process them through our brain and our body. Then we can awaken the next day refreshed, without an emotional hangover. Sometimes, of course, it takes several days and several nights for the emotions from daily experience to work their way through dreams. And sometimes the emotion will show up several days after the event instead of on that very same night.

In the course of human evolution people who did not have this ability might have awakened feeling just as angry or morose or resentful as they did the day before. They might even have started fighting with people around them, people who had nothing to do with the unhappy event of the previous day. These hapless men and women often became social outcasts and were sent away from the tribe. They might even have been killed in fights that they instigated themselves. In either case, their genes dropped out of the gene pool and were not passed on to future tribal members.

Some years ago many scientists did not think that dreams played an important role in human evolution. They were seen as accidental by-products of sleep, by-products that might be useful in psychotherapy but not for a person's biological health. And some scientists did not even think that dreams were useful in psychotherapy—they were random images that had no meaning or usefulness.

Things have changed a great deal since then. Several studies indicate that when dreams are used in psychotherapy, the patient moves through therapy more quickly and has a greater level of satisfaction with the therapist and the therapeutic process. And evolutional psychologists have become aware of the role that dreams and dreaming played in the development of the brain and in the way that people were able to handle emotional experiences without upsetting or disturbing the social network of which they were a part. Many people have told me about how my grandfather helped them to understand their dreams. And he was doing this when mainstream science was debunking dreams and their importance. Once more, RT was a visionary thinker who was truly ahead of his time.

10

Dreamwalking the Shamanic Way

During our interviews we discovered that one of the most unusual series of stories about RT describes his purported ability to walk into someone's dream in order to provide guidance or instruction. This is referred to as dreamwalking and appears in several accounts of shamanic activity. For example, Franklin Fried recalled, "Sometimes when I would stay at RT's house, RT would take a nap. And I would take a nap at the same time in a little trailer outside. Sometimes if I didn't feel good, he would come through my dreams and heal me in my dream."

This is not the only type of unusual dream that is associated with shamanism. In 2002, Stanley and two colleagues, Fariba Bogzaran and Andre Percia de Carvalho, published a book, *Extraordinary Dreams and How to Work with Them.* They described several unusual dreams, many of which are common in shamanic societies but the reality of which are denied by mainstream Western science.

For example, lucid dreams occur when a dreamer is aware that he or she is dreaming. In many cases the dreamer is able to exert some degree of control over the dream. The existence of this type of dream was denied by most academic dream researchers until other researchers began studying it in sleep laboratories. Dreamers were asked to flex their arm muscles or to move their eyes in an angular fashion once the dream became lucid. Many people were able to do this, and now the investigation of lucid dreams has entered mainstream dream research.

Many years earlier Carlos Castaneda suggested looking at one's hands before falling asleep so that when one viewed those hands during a dream, some dreamers could become aware that they were dreaming. Many people tried this technique and succeeded, but their testimony was disregarded until the doubts were laid to rest by laboratory investigations. Now it has been discovered that most people have had at least one lucid dream in their lives and that one out of five Americans report having at least one lucid dream a month. Many of these dreamers were reluctant to share these dreams, because they seemed to be so bizarre. But now there are frequent panels on lucid dreaming at the annual meeting of the International Association for the Study of Dreams and similar venues.

However, this extraordinary type of dream has a long history. In traditional Tibetan culture a practice known as dream yoga has been taught to adepts for centuries. Tibetan lamas start with ordinary dreams, the first level of practice, which is felt to reflect ordinary experiences and the dreamer's emotional reactions to them. These dreams may be forgotten, or the dreamer might remember only a few details about them. The second level of dreaming represents dreams that are clearer and more detailed, with awareness that one is having a dream. Sometimes these dreams will transport the dreamer away from customary time and space and even introduce the dreamer to spiritual teachers in other dimensions of reality. The third level is called clear light dreaming and is free from emotions, thoughts, and images. At this point the dreamer is lucid and is aware of an expansion of consciousness.

To reach the level of clear light dreaming a dreamer needs to recognize that one is dreaming, purify and develop the dream spiritually, recognize the illusory quality of dream content, and practice getting beyond dream content to sheer awareness. In other words, this is a form of yoga practice within the dream itself, hence the term *dream yoga*. It follows a different direction from Western lucid dreaming, and so the two terms should not be confused. But both of them reflect the self-regulation of consciousness.

There are many other types of extraordinary dreams reported by shamans, although a large number of other people will occasionally experience them as well.

An Eskimo medicine man named Igjugarjuk received his call through a series of dreams. In these dreams strange, unknown beings came and spoke to him, and when he awakened he recalled his dreams so well that he could tell his friends every detail.

Soon it became evident to them that Igjugarjuk was destined to become an angakok. He was given an instructor, who put Igjugarjuk through difficult tests. In one of them he was placed in a tiny snow hut with barely enough room for him to sit cross-legged. He was given nothing to eat and nothing to drink and was told to think of the Great Spirit and of the helping spirit who would appear to him in a dream. After five days he was brought a glass of water and after fifteen days a small piece of meat. Toward the end of thirty days a female ally, or helper, came to him in a dream. She seemed to hover in the air above him. He knew that she was his helping spirit.

The anthropologist Barbara Tedlock has reminded dreamworkers that in Native American societies dream reality and waking reality are overlapping experiences, not compartmentalized worlds. The role of dreams in these societies is to provide an arena in which human beings can enter into intimate contact with spiritual worlds and their inhabitants. Tedlock added that for Native American dreamers the goal is the enhancement of self-knowledge as well as to make a connection to the spiritual world. And one goal complements the other. When Tedlock was a child she had a dream in which her deceased grandmother visited her and sang a song, "Thunder Birds on heaps of clouds startle me." Her grandmother then seemed to awaken Tedlock and walked her toward the door. The night sky was red, and Tedlock realized that she was still dreaming. They walked a long ways until they found a nest filled with serpent bones and bits of eggshells. Her grandmother poked around until she found a red feather. She told her granddaughter, "This was the home of a Thunder Bird."

Tedlock never forgot that dream and, as a result, entered into a shamanic apprenticeship to complement her studies as a cultural anthropologist. Sidian and Stanley attended one of Tedlock's workshops and were impressed with how well she had integrated the two traditions. They also engaged in several conversations with Leslie Gray, a licensed clinical psychologist who had undergone an apprenticeship with shamans.

In 2007 Sidian and Stanley received the Woodfish Prize from the Woodfish Foundation, which is devoted to integrating traditional knowledge and Western knowledge. They cited Tedlock and Gray as pioneers whose academic credentials are impeccable. But equally impeccable are their shamanic credentials. And the combination of the two disciplines has prepared them for birthing a new science, a new psychotherapy, and a new mode of inquiry that does justice to the shamanic worldview and its many dimensions.

Stanley's Comments

In 1986 I received a report from a college student, Perry, who had never met Rolling Thunder but was convinced that RT could help him. Perry reported:

I wrote a letter to Rolling Thunder several years ago. In the letter I asked him about a bird with which I was enamored. This bird, the ivory-billed woodpecker, was last seen two decades ago and was considered extinct by some ornithologists. Some weeks later I had a dream and spoke to Rolling Thunder. It seemed like he spoke in Spanish and said that some of the birds still lived in Cuba or in Mexico. The dream was very vivid. I told Rolling Thunder that I wanted to talk longer with him, but he said that he was tired, traveled a lot, and had even more traveling to do. As he left me, I had a sense of excitement that I have rarely experienced. A few weeks ago, several ivory-billed woodpeckers were seen in Cuba. I was really excited when the news confirmed the answer that Rolling Thunder had given me in the dream.

The Taoist scholar and martial arts instructor Kenneth Cohen recalled a dream in which RT appeared.

In the dream, we were Apache brothers. I was about to leave for a trip, and my brother told me, "We will never meet again in this life. But in the future you will see me again. I will be older, and I will look different. But in the future you will see me again. You will remember this experience in a dream, but you will know that it is not a dream. It is real. I will now teach you some words in our ancient language. When you see me again, repeat the words to me, and I will remember you from the past."

When I awoke, I remembered those words and later told the dream to RT, as well as the words. He nodded and exclaimed, "Ho." That was an acknowledgment of the validity of the dream. Later I discovered that RT had a long-standing interest in the Apache and with their great warrior and spiritual leader, Geronimo. RT believed that he rode with Geronimo in a past life and later told me that he and I were members of the same Apache band. He also told me that the dream was a sign that he was to teach me Native American medicine. This was my introduction to his teachings, and RT observed, "I can teach you because I know you won't steal my medicine and sell it." And I never have.

One of my students at Saybrook University, Faith Suaso, conducted what is called a participant observation research study with a Native American medicine woman from the Blackfoot tribe known simply as Dreamwalker. For seventeen years Faith participated in Dreamwalker's classes, rituals, and group discussions. She engaged in "spirit walks" with Dreamwalker in the White Mountain range of Arizona. She served as Dreamwalker's apprentice for the last three years of her study, assisting with classes and participating in healing sessions. Faith was surprised at how often Dreamwalker would use dreams for teaching purposes, believing that they were the basic method used to obtain guidance regarding one's life path and to develop one's spiritual power.

Classes often involved the sharing of Dreamwalker's dreams about a student. She also helped her students interpret their dreams, and this provided information about the most challenging aspects in a person's life. Students were encouraged to record their dreams and use them as a way to determine a course of action for personal development. This routine was a preliminary step to recalling visitations by Dreamwalker while they were dreaming.

As students progressed in their training they often reported that they saw Dreamwalker in their dreams and would describe the experiences they had. These experiences often would consist of some form of teaching or the testing of acquired skills. Dreamwalker relied on students recognizing and recalling specific images that she claimed to have embedded into their dreams to determine their level of awareness and as an indication of what information to share with that student. This process was used to establish a hierarchy of training that these students could only enter when they could acknowledge the appropriate images they had received while dreaming.

Dreamwalker reported that her first experience with dreamwalking occurred when she was quite young. At this time she was experiencing nightmares that involved a monster that was trying to hurt her. On one occasion, Dreamwalker's grandmother appeared in the dream and instructed her how to handle the situation. Dreamwalker followed the instructions and was able to gain power over the monster, eventually sending it away.

From that time on, Dreamwalker often met her grandmother while dreaming and received instruction. As a young adult she received instructions while dreaming on the preparation procedures for the sun dance. Dreamwalker continued to receive guidance from her grandmother, even after her grandmother's death. There are other nonphysical guides who appear in Dreamwalker's dreams, some of whom are deceased and some of whom never lived on Earth.

Before we continue our discussion of Dreamwalker, let's look at the sun dance a little more closely. The sun dance is a sacred ceremony that celebrates the powers of the Sun spirit. The Blackfoot name for it is *ok'an* and means "coming together." The ceremony is considered an act of sacrifice that renews participants' relationship with Nature. Among the Blackfoot it occurs in the summertime after the serviceberry ripens. These berries are needed for sacramental purposes and are an integral part of the ceremony.

The major sacrament of the Blackfoot sun dance is the buffalo tongue, which is cut into thin strips and dried for the ceremony, when it is eaten to sustain the dancers. Unlike the sun dance of the Sioux, the Blackfoot do not pierce their flesh; instead, they engage in a complicated rhythm of fasting, prayer, contemplation, and dancing.

Not all tribes insist that women be pierced during the sun dance, concluding that the blood they shed during menstruation is enough of a sacrifice. In tribes that endorse piercing, a sharp bone with cords attached to it is used to cut into the dancer's left and right chest. When the dancer falls due to exhaustion, the cords break, and the dancer will often have a visionary experience.

The Blackfoot sun dance is also the time when the sacred medicine bundles, which contain sacred objects and are considered to be potent power objects themselves, are transferred from one owner to the next. The transfer process can last a long time because the new owner needs to learn the proper care and use of each bundle. It is during the sun dance that new bundle owners are expected to show competence in the accuracy of each ritual associated with the sun dance ceremony. The ceremony is organized by the local medicine society, which consists of men who own medicine bundles. The bundles contain sacred materials such as medicine pipes, traditional medicines, and skins of birds and animals. The Beaver bundle is the oldest and one of the most powerful of the bundles; it is called the "daddy" of the other bundles.

The sun dance also serves a social function by bringing the various Blackfoot groups (known as bands) together. This gathering allows members of the Blackfoot tribe to meet other bands, share stories, exchange ancient fables, and meet potential spouses. Each Blackfoot tribe consists of many bands that are highly autonomous. Individual members are identified by their band membership rather than the tribal unit. When a band performs this ceremony, it believes it is performing for the entire world. It is a call for the renewal of relationships with the spirits, the powers, and the energies that animate the cosmos. It is alien to most Indian societies for one person to lay down rules, give orders, direct the lives of others, or claim that one person speaks for the tribe as a whole. This philosophy is reflected in governance, in ceremonies, and even in daily conversation.

The sun dance reinforces the beliefs of the Blackfoot and how essential they are to daily challenges. It provides a glimpse into the interconnecting relationship between the men and women of each band and tribe during this sacred time. One Native name for the Blackfoot tribe is Niitsitapii, which translates as "the real people." Another Native name is Siksika, which translates as "blackfoot," probably referring to the custom of staining their moccasins with ashes. At the present time there are three distinct tribal divisions of the Blackfoot in southern Canada and in Montana. These three groups are independent, linked in a confederacy. They share a common language, culture, and history. Their contact with Europeans led to a decimation of the tribe through disease as well as through starvation when settlers drove buffalo from their traditional ranges.

Faith interviewed a dozen of Dreamwalker's longtime apprentices and discovered that the apprentices manifested unusual abilities as children and that their parents accepted these skills and did not discourage them. However, their childhood and teenage years were marked by a surprisingly large number of personal traumas, such as severe illnesses, motor vehicle accidents, and the loss of loved ones.

Specific techniques the apprentices claimed to have learned from Dreamwalker included creating an intention that she would enter their dreams. Apprentices also engaged in preparatory rituals and observed changes in their bodily sensations prior to sleeping and dreaming. All of the apprentices claimed that Dreamwalker *had* appeared in their dreams, as noted by their awareness of Dreamwalker while dreaming, their recall of the lesson being taught, and their ability to find a beneficial result of that lesson. Apprentices claimed they would also dream about other members of the class and that they engaged in group learning sessions taught by Dreamwalker while dreaming.

It is difficult to determine how many of these reported effects resulted from expectation and compliance. However, the benefits obtained attest to the persistence of students who continued to attend Dreamwalker's classes over the years. They also are in accord with the Blackfoot view of dreaming. This model holds that dreams serve problem-solving functions and provide specific information on the composition of sacred songs and rituals and that dream recall is a route to personal power and the maintenance of health. Sometimes a specific remedy for an illness will appear in a dream, and the dreamer will embark on a quest to discover and use it. The source of some dreams is believed to be dream spirits, and it is believed that life events are an important part of dreaming. The Blackfoot have long believed that instructions for the prevention of pregnancy can be obtained in one's dreams!

Stanley's Comments

Faith Suaso has done pioneering work in investigating Dreamwalker and describing her connection with Blackfoot dream traditions. She observed there are a few universal symbols in Blackfoot dreams. For example, an old man and old woman symbolize the Sun and the Moon. Healing dreams are often enacted during wakefulness as a treatment for an illness. Spiritual dreams are differentiated from personal dreams and are the gift of dream spirits, including dream animals.

Horses figure prominently in dreams because the Blackfoot have a long tradition of using, trading, and even stealing horses. They first saw horses in about 1730 and soon became expert riders. Small horses existed in prehistoric North America but disappeared. The Spanish soldiers brought horses back to the continent, and the animals slowly worked their way north, where the Shoshone took a special interest in them even before the Blackfoot Indians were aware of their uses for both peace and wartime.

Blackfoot family members are encouraged to share dreams and may even have the same dream at the same time. Therefore, Dreamwalker's classes fit within the traditional model of Blackfoot dreams. However, there is a notable exception. Blackfoot dreamers are discouraged from sharing dreams unless a dreamer would like to sell a dream. If a dream is particularly favorable, the dreamer is allowed to sell it to a tribal member who has a more urgent need for it than the dreamer.

The sophistication of the Blackfoot worldview inspired the physicist David Peat to write a book, *Blackfoot Physics*. In this book he notes that Blackfoot dream imagery is seen as a reflection of a reality that is far broader and wider than the Western worldview. Dreams are not confined to the present but can range backward and forward in time. This enables members of the Blackfoot tribe to live their lives in a wider reality of deeper significance than that of most people, including Westerners, whose reality is more constrained. Peat made the cogent observation that these tribal members partake of reality in a much fuller way, a way that transcends the ordinary limits of matter, space, time, and causality.

Dreamwalker's students, few of whom are Native American, have been given an opportunity to move beyond their cultural constraints and enter into a world that is broader and deeper than the reality in which they were raised and acculturated. Needless to say, this is the world in which Rolling Thunder lived, and this explains why so many people attended his lectures, participated in his workshops, and came to live at his spiritual community, Meta Tantay.

Sidian's Comments

In 1982, RT began to "doctor" Molly, a woman in her forties who had been diagnosed with multiple sclerosis, a degenerative disease that affects the central nervous system. It is usually accompanied by partial numbing or paralysis of one or more limbs. James Swan, an anthropologist and psychologist, had been treating this woman for depression, but with little success. One day she remarked that she was part Cherokee, and about the same time Swan agreed to arrange a workshop for RT in the area. He asked her if she would consider seeing a Native American medicine man for a consultation, and she agreed. Following Swan's advice, she bought some Five Brothers tobacco and sent it to RT at his Carlin, Nevada, home.

Three days later she told Swan a dream, one which she described as the most vivid dream she had ever had. Standing at the foot of her bed she saw two figures; one was a man wearing a dark cloak, and the other figure resembled a huge, pink caterpillar. She felt so infused with energy that she could not get back to sleep for the entire night.

The following afternoon Molly had a dream while napping. This time she and RT were in a supermarket together. He unrolled a carpet on the floor of the supermarket. They both got on the carpet and flew around the world. Upon returning, RT gave her a kiss. She awakened filled with energy and somewhat embarrassed, because she still felt the pressure of his lips from the kiss. She then discovered that she could get up and move around her house with more ease than she had known in years.

As RT's workshop drew near, Molly had enough energy to help organize the event. She and a friend met RT and did all of the cooking for him and his retinue. RT was grateful but told her that he could not start "doctoring" her in person until he got permission from the Great Spirit. One evening, RT said he would like to talk with Molly but that she would have to meet him upstairs. It took all of Molly's energy to climb the stairs, but she succeeded on her hands and knees, refusing help from anyone. The meeting lasted an hour, with RT asking questions that amounted to a very thorough case history. When he had finished asking questions, RT gave Molly some advice about her diet and said he would let her know if he would be able to work with her.

Two evenings later RT summoned her again. Once more Molly climbed the stairs on her hands and knees without anyone's help. This time a chiropractor was present and had set up a massage table. He and Swan helped Molly get on the table and watched while RT went to work. For nearly an hour RT performed a series of subtle physical manipulations on her body, testing her range of flexibility and performing the type of treatment that might be given by a physical therapist. Molly seemed to fall asleep, and RT asked the two men to leave the room and wait downstairs. Swan and the chiropractor joined a group of people downstairs who had come for the workshop. Most of the group members fell asleep, and the last thing they recalled was a misty cloud that seemed to enter the room.

When RT came downstairs there was a tear in his eye, and he muttered, "She's had a tough time of it," and walked out the door into a wooded area to get instructions from the Great Spirit. His weekend workshop started the next day. Once it was over, he announced that he had received permission from the Great Spirit to conduct a healing ceremony for Molly; RT said he would need some help, and several dozen people agreed to stay. RT thanked the group and said that this support was needed. "Medicine people do not conduct rituals just for entertainment," he said. "There is a right time and a right place for everything." He then went into a private room to prepare himself.

Two of his spiritual warriors, Alan Fat Bear and Cloud Lightning, placed a large drum in a cleared area in the forest. They asked Swan and the others to form a circle and taught the group a simple Shoshone Indian chant, "Hey, hey, hey, unduwah." This chant would unite the group and help them focus on the healing session.

RT emerged from his room wearing a bright blue and gold shirt, khaki pants, and boots. Over the shirt was a black vest decorated with beads. He was wearing his traditional dark-blue turban, to which several eagle feathers had been fastened. On the front of the turban a large turquoise stone had been fastened, set in a silver seven-pointed star pin. The seven points of the star referred to the stars in the Pleiades constellation, known to Westerners as the Seven Sisters. To RT, this constellation was the ancestral home of the Native Americans.

RT had painted white symbols on his cheeks, two circles representing Grandfather Sun and Grandmother Moon. RT used a white chalklike substance to paint the same symbols on the cheeks of several volunteer helpers. He also painted a symbol on their foreheads that he described as representing the Cherokee Tree of Life. It consisted of a central trunk with branches directed upward on each side. A full badger skin was hanging from RT's waist. Several eagle feathers protruded from the badger's mouth, and the skin had been fashioned into what RT called his "medicine bag."

RT entered the circle and chuckled, "Don't let me frighten you." These were appropriate words, because most members of the group had never seen an Indian medicine man in full regalia. RT taught the group a simple dance that he called the Cherokee two-step. Soon group members were holding hands, chanting the Shoshone chant, and dancing the Cherokee dance. Most of the group members did not realize that RT claimed to have been born into the Cherokee tribe but had been adopted by Shoshone parents. Both of his tribes were represented, allowing him to draw on his personal roots. RT instructed the drumming to stop and began to pray to the Great Spirit, the Earth Mother, the Four Directions, and the healing spirits. He lit his corncob pipe, filled with raw tobacco, and blew a puff of smoke after each of his prayers. The silence was broken only by the sound of the wind and by the call of a raven, one of the most powerful bird allies in Native American lore.

RT then asked Alan Fat Bear and Cloud Lightning to resume the drumming. Once again Swan and his group began to chant and dance. RT looked skyward and then at each member of the group. They noticed that RT had changed. His expression was cold, and his eyes were piercing. It reminded me of the gaze on an eagle, one of RT's power birds.

RT began to dance in the circle, slowly at first and then with outstretched arms that resembled wings. He moved around in circles, reminding me of an eagle floating on a warm summer breeze. Gradually his pace changed into a frenzied move, as if he were an eagle plummeting down to Earth. Then he yelled a loud "Whoop!" The group immediately stopped dancing and chanting.

RT's composure changed again. He smiled and said, "You didn't tell me that you were all Indians." The group laughed and welcomed the shift from the serious ritual to a more informal type of encounter. RT led them deeper into the woods, where they found a large circle that had been cleared without their knowledge. There were giant cedar trees on the outskirts of the circle, and Alan Fat Bear and Cloud Lightning moved the drum to the new circle and resumed playing, each striking a different side of the drum.

A third spiritual warrior, Mike Thor, entered the group holding a mixture of sweet grass and cedar. He circled each person with the smoke from the mixture and told them that they were being purified for the healing session. He directed the smoke with an eagle feather, first to their hearts and then over the top of their heads.

RT had been carrying a blanket and a weather-beaten suitcase. He placed the blanket on the ground and created an altar from the contents of the suitcase, namely a buffalo tail whisk, a band of eager feathers, and several crystals. Mike Thor brought RT a jug of water, which was said to have come from a nearby sacred spring. He placed an empty mug near the water jug.

Finally, Molly arrived, accompanied by two women. She was wearing her underpants, covered by a colorful blanket. RT directed the women to help her lie down on the ceremonial blanket and asked them to wrap the smaller blanket around her. RT took the buffalo tail whisk and walked around Molly several times, moving the whisk through the air as if he was cleaning the area. He put the whisk down and picked up the eagle feather wand, again moving it gracefully through the air with long strokes. He moved the wand into each of the Four Directions, as if he was asking for their help.

RT put down the wand and stood with his right hand directed toward the sky. Then he brought his left hand to his mouth and spat on it, letting out another whoop. During this entire procedure the group was chanting and the spiritual warriors were drumming. But they were no longer moving; they were transfixed by the ritual that was unfolding before them.

RT knelt beside Molly and slid his hands under the blanket, resting them on her naked back. In a few moments he withdrew, stood up, whooped again, and repeated the procedure of raising his right hand skyward and spitting on his left hand. This time several group members detected a bright purple mist glowing around RT's hands. They did not say a word but compared their impressions afterward. The glow appeared to be an aura coming from each hand. It became very intense and then disappeared as RT slid his hands under the blanket, again placing them on Molly's back.

Again, RT's composure changed. He removed his hands and knelt down on all fours as if he were an animal. He began to whine, growl, and sniff Molly. It seemed to Swan that he had become a badger, the animal from whose skin the medicine bag had been made. The medicine bag was nowhere in sight, but RT had now taken on characteristics of a badger. He crawled under the blanket, continued to whine and sniff, and then began sucking on Molly's lower back, making growling sounds.

RT suddenly withdrew from Molly and spit a dark-green fluid into the empty mug. He washed his mouth with the spring water and repeated the procedure. Every time he sucked Molly's back, he growled furiously and then spit the viscous fluid into the mug. Finally, he spit up water that was clear, and at that very moment a huge black and orange wasp flew into the circle, heading directly toward Rolling Thunder. The wasp circled RT three times and then headed back into the forest while the members of the group ducked for cover.

RT stood up and circled Molly, again waving the whisk around her body. Her two female assistants brought a chair into the circle and helped Molly into it. Her face was radiant. Molly shouted, "I am alive!" She stood up from her chair, took her cane, and started to walk around the circle. Then she threw down her cane and walked without assistance for the first time in years. Group members were in tears. They hugged Molly as she walked around the circle.

In the middle of this celebration, RT struck a note of caution. He observed, "This woman has been healed today. But she has not been cured. If she leads a good life, walking the Good Red Road, and takes care of what she eats, she will continue to feel better. She needs to be doctored a few more times by me or by somebody like me. If she does this, she will live a long, full life and will walk again. This is the Great Spirit's way. I only act as an agent for the Great Spirit here. The healing comes from the spirit world. I am just the helper. Ho!" And with his last shout, RT and his spiritual warriors collected their paraphernalia and went back to their rooms to rest.

The members of the group began to discuss what they had experienced. Six members of the group told Swan that they also had seen the purple glow. They told him this in six separate conversations, and they could not possibly have overheard each other. Later, when Swan spoke with Molly, she recalled her time under the blanket, first entering a deep trance and then seeming to leave her body while looking down at herself. But what she saw was an Indian princess. The princess decided to "go on the warpath," and it was then that Molly threw down her cane and walked independently. She demonstrated to Swan how she could walk without a cane and also told him that she had discovered a new source of strength.

Later that day, Molly needed to use her cane again. But she was not discouraged, because she could still walk much more easily than she did before the treatment. And RT had told her that she had been "healed" but not "cured." Swan spoke with Molly on the telephone one week later, and she was still optimistic. She said she had her "ups and downs" but felt stronger and more energetic than she had in years.

Molly moved and Swan lost touch with her, but several years later he was able to contact her once more through a friend. Molly was not able to walk independently, but she told Swan that she was able to swim three times a week and ride a horse twice a week. She also told him that "the Indian part of me has taken over" and that she was spending more time with "Nature, animals, rocks, and the Great Spirit." She never saw RT again but said she had been treated by some alternative healers who shared RT's philosophy. She no longer felt the need to be completely "cured" because being "healed" had changed her outlook on life. Swan recalled that the life expectancy of people after receiving a diagnosis of multiple sclerosis is about ten years, and Molly had certainly beaten the odds.

The day after Molly's healing session, Swan had dinner with a physician and told him about the session. The physician remarked, "Perhaps we can say that Rolling Thunder's charisma and manner were somehow able to inspire this woman to get well in a way that couldn't otherwise be accessed. If so, the fact that he was successful in changing her physical symptoms when all else had failed seems to suggest that his understanding of psychology demonstrates an expertise from which we could benefit greatly."

Swan agreed with his physician friend to some extent. But he also felt that there were several things that could not be explained so easily. The vivid dreams that Molly had before meeting RT seemed more than coincidental. The trance that Molly entered seemed to affect everyone. And what about the purple glow? Not only did Swan witness it, but six other people independently said that they had seen the glow as well. Swan remarked, "I have observed RT's healing ceremonies several times, and I have seen him transform many times. He could be a wise and warm father. He often joked and played. But sometimes he startled and frightened us. Other times he seemed to change his appearance, taking on the form of animals. He seemed able to manifest energies, induce trances, extract poisons out of a patient's body, and affect the dreams of others."

There was one additional puzzle. If RT had worked with Molly in her dream, why did he have to get permission from the Great Spirit when she was awake? When Swan asked about this contradiction, RT replied, "The dream world allows for short cuts that the waking world does not."

11

Rolling Thunder, Social Activist

From his study of Native American history, Stanley knew that in the 1860s a local Roman Catholic bishop told his Northwest Indian congregation to give up all traditional dancing, to stop consulting shamans, to cease "potlatching" giveaway rituals, and to abstain from drinking and gambling. Spirit dancing was explicitly outlawed in the Washington Territory of the United States by decree of the superintendent of Indian Affairs in 1871. In British Columbia, Canada, spirit dancing was suppressed by the 1884 Potlach Law, and the ban was not lifted until 1951. School indoctrination in both countries was used to coerce young Indians into believing that these rituals were vestiges of a bygone era of superstition and barbarism, and in 1914 a local Indian government official declared the dances to be "obsolete."

The U.S. and Canadian governments instituted policies and laws to force Indians onto reservations while, at the same time, encouraging them to become assimilated into the mainstream culture. The high rate of suicide among Native Americans may be due to this suppression of their culture and spiritual practices. Another result was the incidence of alcoholism; it is ironic that the sacred substance used in the Roman Catholic Mass to represent the blood of Christ has caused so much devastation among Indians, while the Native Americans' sacred herb tobacco has caused major health problems for numerous Christians.

However, there was a revival of traditional dancing in the 1960s, and in January 1971 the anthropologist Wolfgang Jilek counted about eight hundred people from virtually all of the West Coast Salish regions to be active participants in spirit dancing or observers when a new longhouse at Tzeachten, British Columbia, was opened. Traditional masks and costumes were publicly displayed for the first time in several decades, marking the abatement of suppression by legal and ecclesiastical authorities. Jilek interviewed one initiate who reported:

The spirits use the old dancers to work on you because they've got the power, and they bite on your side to put their power inside you. . . . I passed out about three times while they worked on me, and they kept doing that to me every morning and every night. It was the third day that I saw how my face was to be painted, it was in my sleep, in a dream, that I saw the way I was supposed to dance; I saw myself and I heard my song. Then they put the hat and uniform on me and then the spirits take your stick. When you start to sing the stick just moves to the beat of your song and that's how they get to drum for you. Sometimes you see something there, the one that watches you all the time. We call it your "power animal." Your "power animal" is like a good babysitter, always watching you and doing its best to take care of you.

The repression of Native rituals demonstrates how powerful social authorities and institutions take it upon themselves to socially construct rules of conduct that are "legitimate" while prohibiting alternative rules that are "illegitimate." The suspension of these prohibitions was due to the accumulation and use of power—legal, political, economic, and perhaps spiritual power by Native people.

Casino Jack

In 1988 the U.S. Congress passed the Indian Gaming Regulation Act, allowing Native Americans to set up gambling casinos on their reservations. The tribes were allowed to keep about half of the earnings, and within a few years thousands of new jobs were created. Within a few years almost half of the 561 tribes registered with the U.S. government had established casinos in half of the fifty states in the United States.

Some of Sidian's relatives have worked in these casinos, so he has seen the benefits of this legislation firsthand.

However, these casinos also attracted criminal elements, and none was more notorious than Jack Abramoff, whose scams were the topic of a documentary film named *Casino Jack*. Federal investigators finally were able to document the trail of deception and manipulation that Abramoff, a business executive and lobbyist, had expertly exploited. In 2008 Abramoff and fourteen others were sentenced to jail. Their crimes involved defrauding gambling casinos run by Native Americans and corrupting public officials. Abramoff stole tens of millions of dollars from six American Indian tribes eager to open new casinos or to protect those that already existed. Much of this money went into the private coffers of Abramoff and his associates, but additional millions were diverted to Republican Party organizations. This $84 million scam transferred wealth from Indians who received monthly dividends from their tribe's casinos to millionaires and lobbyists in Washington, D.C.

For example, Abramoff and his associates took advantage of the Tigua Ysleta del Sur tribe, most of who lived on a small, poor reservation near El Paso, Texas. A casino had opened in 1988, lifting the Tiguas out of the poverty in which they had lived for generations. However, the legality of the casino was in question, and Abramoff asked a competing tribe, the Coushattas, to pay him millions of dollars to guarantee that the Tigua casino be closed. To accomplish this, Abramoff spent some of this money to organize a group of members of the clergy and their friends to create an antigambling movement among local citizens to close the casino. Once the casino was closed, Abramoff offered his services to the Tiguas, promising to move a bill through the U.S. Congress that would make gambling on the Tigua reservation legal. The bill never passed, but Abramoff and his associates kept close to $5 million given them by the Tiguas.

But Abramoff was not finished exploiting the Tiguas. In 2003 he approached the Tigua tribal council with a novel proposition: free life insurance for all the elders of the tribe. Abramoff promised to pay the premiums, but there was one condition. The death benefits would not be paid to the families but to a private school owned by Abramoff, which would use the money to pay what the tribe owed Abramoff for lobbying on the tribe's behalf in Washington, D.C. The scheme fell through, because the Tiguas turned it down. Rolling Thunder, who had spent much of his time and energy exposing powerful groups who attempted to take advantage of Native Americans, would have been proud.

The Leonard Peltier Case

During one of his last public talks, Rolling Thunder remarked, "It's not only our duty as medicine people to keep our people well and healthy, but also it is our duty that if we see someone in prison unjustly to go in and get them out. I've gotten a number of people out of prison. I expect I am going to have to look into it again as soon as I can walk again and get around. I know Leonard Peltier is still in prison. We want him out. Nothing good is going to happen for any of these authorities who continue their pogrom, their wrongdoing against Native American Indians."

Sometimes RT would tell incredible stories that really stretched the limits of his credibility. For example, he told Gary Sandman that when Leonard Peltier was held in a Canadian prison, he was delegated by a group of medicine people to see him. At the time Peltier's own lawyer and his family couldn't get in to see him. RT said that he went to Canada with a convoy of Indians, but in the parking lot he told them that he would go into the prison by himself. He took out all his identification and left it with his friends. The only items he took with him were two eagle feathers, his own and one for Peltier.

RT said that when he got to the front gate it was open and the guard was looking the other way, so he walked in. He went through half a dozen iron gates with a guard at every one of them. He walked by a number of guards, administrators, and wardens. He just held his eagle feather and looked at the guard, who would then unlock the gate.

He walked right into the central part of the jail with no problem. The guard at that gate had a rifle over his shoulder and a pistol on his hip, but he unlocked the gate. RT claimed that he went on to where they had Peltier and found him in something like an animal cage. He went inside and talked to Peltier for a few minutes. He explained how to survive the ordeal and gave him the eagle feather. Then he went out with no problems at all. Later there was a demonstration for Peltier that RT attended. He recalled that there were seven eagles that came down and circled as the demonstration was going on.

RT's comments regarding Leonard Peltier reflected an ongoing campaign to review the conviction of this Native American social activist. In 1968 the American Indian Movement was founded to promote traditional Native American culture. It accused the U.S. government of breaking a long list of treaties, one of which resulted in the loss of most of their land in the state of South Dakota. In 1973 the group took over an area called Wounded Knee, a famous battle site between Indians and the U.S. military, a battle that resulted in the massacre of hundreds of Sioux men, women, and children. This takeover resulted in military action by the U.S. government, which sent troops and tanks to end the protest.

In 1969 there had been a more peaceful takeover of Alcatraz Island in California. Indian militants occupied the former prison for nineteen months, winning several concessions from the United States federal government. Land was returned to three tribes, and President Richard Nixon voided the regulations that had stopped the recognition of Indian nations. Nixon substituted a policy of self-determination that gave more power to tribal authorities. Rolling Thunder took time off from his lecture schedule to visit both Wounded Knee and Alcatraz, boosting the moral of the militants and sympathizing with their cause. He observed, "Yes, I'm a militant. So was the great healer, the one called Jesus Christ. I'm a militant even though I no longer carry a gun."

However, the occupation was not the end of the protest in South Dakota. Soon thereafter, in 1973, the nearby Pine Ridge Indian

Reservation, which was close to the site of the original battle of Wounded Knee in 1890, was taken over in 1973 by tribal leaders who followed the dictates of the U.S. government. The resulting conflict triggered crackdowns and murders that remain unsolved to this day. The American Indian Movement asked for volunteers to protect Native Americans who lived on the reservation, and Leonard Peltier responded to the call. He was thirty years of age at the time and had been accused of the attempted murder of a police officer in a nearby state.

In 1975 two officials from the FBI were looking for an Indian who had been accused of armed assault. They followed a red and white van that they believed was his escape vehicle. They were wrong. The van contained Leonard Peltier and two friends. However, Peltier thought the agents were looking for him, because of his earlier accusation, and stopped the van.

What happened next is a confused narrative for which there are several versions. There is general agreement that Peltier and his two friends jumped out of the vehicle and shots were fired. Rifle fire came from nearby houses as well, and the agents were caught in the crossfire. Peltier admitted taking part in the shooting, but in self-defense. In any event, both agents died, as well as an Indian who had come to support his comrades.

Peltier escaped to Canada, but his two companions were put on trial. After five days the jury declared that it was "hopelessly deadlocked." The judge ordered them to keep working, and they eventually arrived at a not guilty verdict. The U.S. law enforcement officers did not give up and renewed their search for Peltier, who was arrested in Canada by Canadian police and deported to the United States in 1976. The following year a jury convicted him of first-degree murder of the two government agents, and he was sentenced to life in prison.

There have been many attempts to overturn Peltier's conviction or to gain him a new trial. RT and Grandfather Semu Huaute, a renowned Chumash-Cahuilla medicine man, both wrote letters to Attorney General Janet Reno in 1995. In 1979 the U.S. Supreme Court refused to review the case, but in 2003 the Tenth Circuit Court of Appeals condemned much of the U.S. government's handling of the case, claiming that it withheld evidence and intimidated witnesses. Nevertheless, the Supreme Court rejected Peltier's appeal, and in 2005 he was moved to a federal penitentiary in Pennsylvania. His supporters claim that Peltier has been harassed and beaten in the penitentiary, despite his poor health and advancing age.

Stanley's Comments

In 1995, I was one of several people to whom Grandfather Semu wrote, asking for donations to finance a trip to visit Leonard Peltier. I sent what I could afford as I knew that Semu's presence would bring comfort to Peltier. Personally, I felt that the facts were insufficient to establish Peltier's guilt or innocence. At the same time I was convinced that the case had been poorly managed by federal authorities and that a change in his sentence was overdue. Later that same year I was invited to São Paulo, Brazil, to speak at an ecology conference. Grandfather Semu was a featured guest, along with the celebrated Brazilian musician Gilberto Gil and various environmental activists.

When I arrived I discovered that Semu was resting in a private room while dozens of journalists and conference speakers were insisting that they needed to speak with him. His spokesperson said that he would only see one person and announced my name. I was surprised but went to Semu's room and told him that there were many important people that he could have allowed to interview him. But he reminded me of my small donation for his trip and said that it had given him the final amount of money he needed to visit Peltier. He gave me a report on Peltier's deteriorating condition, informing me that he had been subjected to several days of isolation—a measure we both thought was unnecessary and punitive, whether or not he was guilty or innocent. I also brought him up to date on RT's political activities and treasured my time alone with this noted elder.

The conference organizers wanted Semu to open the conference at 8:00 a.m. the following day, but they had not told him that events in Brazil generally start a little late. So the next morning I arrived at 8:15 and found Semu and his wife, Eneke-Alish, standing outside the locked door, sweating in the tropical sun. There was no place to sit in the shade, and I knew the exposure could be devastating for a man in his nineties. I used my rudimentary knowledge of Portuguese to get the door opened, and Semu rested until the participants finally arrived. He joked with me, saying, "Brazilian time must be similar to Indian time," referring to the Native American custom of starting an event when all conditions are favorable, whether or not it conforms to a prearranged schedule.

Semu conducted several ceremonies during the conference, events that left him exhausted. I told the Brazilian organizers to use my honorarium to give him a first-class seat on an airplane to his next stop in Brasilia, the nation's capital city. Sometime later a grateful Eneke-Alish wrote me that the first-class trip provided the rest that her husband needed for his Brasilia meeting with chiefs, elders, and medicine people from the Amazon rain forest. She also told me that the visit concluded with a huge celebratory feast that included family members of the distinguished participants. By that time Semu was in top form and left a lasting impression that I heard about on subsequent visits to Brazil.

National Politics

Mad Bear Anderson, one of RT's teachers, was a leader, or *sachem,* of the Iroquois Confederacy and was a medicine man in the Bear Clan of the Tuscarora Nation of that confederacy. He visited native people all over the world and passed on much of what he learned to RT before he died in 1985. RT referred to him often in his discussions of social activism.

RT enjoyed discussing history and politics. He claimed that he could recall his two most recent past lives. His most recent past life, he told us, was when he was a young scout for Cochise, the famed

Indian warrior. When talking about politics he said he didn't have much use for most politicians, but "Ted Kennedy has done more to help the Indians than anyone else in Congress." He also admired California governor Jerry Brown. In one of his lectures, RT recalled:

I met with Jerry Brown once. I believe he was sincere, and I have noticed that he seems to be a pretty good man. At least he didn't allow them to extradite Dennis Banks back to South Dakota, where they wanted to kill him. Governor Brown refused to sign the extradition, and he did so against major opposition as well as against judges and courts that are supposed to deal in justice. I know many people didn't agree with Governor Brown, but I said for many years before I met him that he was a good politician. He impressed me so much that I gave him an eagle feather that I "doctored" to hang in his office so that he would not forget us.

Dennis Banks cofounded the American Indian Movement, participated in the occupation of Alcatraz Island, and was part of the Wounded Knee protest, the 1972 occupation of the U.S. Department of the Interior and the Bureau of Indian Affairs, and similar activities, one of which resulted in a call for his arrest. Once Brown left office, Banks found temporary refuge in New York, then went underground for a while, but eventually served eighteen months in jail. Once out of prison, he organized sacred foot races that have become international events, led successful reburials of the remains of ancient Indians, helped pass state laws against desecration of sacred Indian sites, served as a drug and alcohol counselor for Native American youth, and organized colleges that served young people who wanted to study Indian customs.

RT also had contact with Russell Means, an early member of the American Indian Movement who played a leading role in the occupation of Alcatraz, Wounded Knee, and the building housing the Bureau of Indian Affairs in Washington, D.C. Means resigned from the American Indian Movement in 1988, saying it had achieved its goals. A few years later the organization split into several competing groups and never regained its visibility or influence. Means preferred the term *American Indian* to *Native American,* saying that *Indian* could be reconceptualized as coming from the Italian term *in Dio,* or "with God," rather than referring to the Indian subcontinent that Columbus thought he had reached.

RT liked Jerry Brown but did not think so highly of another governor of California. In his words, "Right after Governor Ronald Reagan started the welfare cuts, I met an old lady who was crying. She had been putting three daughters through college and high school at the time and was in one of those programs that had been cut. She had no food in the house, and our young men went out and brought her back groceries. And the next time I saw that lady she wasn't crying. She had a job in the American Indian Movement office."

In *Blackfoot Physics,* David Peat points out that at the time of European contact about one-fifth of the Earth's population was living in conditions that today would be viewed as ideal. People worked two or three days a week to provide themselves with food, shelter, and basic life necessities. The rest of the time was spent playing, gossiping, visiting, worshipping, engaging in artistic activities, and having sex. But the European contact brought with it diseases that killed most of the Indians and left the others a legacy of heart disease, breakdowns of the immune system, addictions, allergies, cancer, suicides, and mental illnesses. In 2011 the U.S. Centers for Disease Control and Prevention estimated that about half of all American adults will suffer some kind of mental illness during their lifetime. Mental illness was defined as a "mental disorder that substantially interferes with or limits one or more major life activities." If contact with the Europeans led to civilization, it may be no exaggeration to say that the United States, including its Indian population, has been civilized to death.

As RT put it in one of his lectures, "From the first time the Europeans set foot on this land they took our children to be brainwashed in their schools. Education was left to the missionaries, who were mostly fanatical Christians who called Indians heathens. For many years, our young people did not keep up with the culture. It was a shame, because we have a complex culture that came from this land, and there is no other than can fit this land or replace it. My folks sent me to white schools so that I wouldn't be brainwashed in reservation schools. They wanted me to get a good education so that someday I could talk for my people. I went to the first year of high school, and then I dropped out. I knew that the real knowledge was not in the schools. I built my own house and lived in it for a year to develop a sense of independence and to get to know myself and my path."

A few U.S. presidents have recognized the contributions of the Indians and how they were deprived of their land and their rights. The first American president, George Washington, told Congress, "Indians were the prior occupants of the continent and to dispossess them would be a gross violation of the fundamental laws of Nature and of that distributive justice that is the glory of the nation." President Washington warned Congress that no harm could be done to Indian treaties without undermining American democracy.

Nevertheless, America's treaties with Native Americans, some of which predated the U.S. Constitution, were violated or ignored time and time again as settlers moved toward the West. When the state of Georgia demanded that the entire Cherokee Nation be removed from its territory, President John Quincy Adams, a staunch opponent of Indian removal declared that Georgia had put the country "in the most imminent danger of dissolution. The Ship of State is about to flounder."

In desperation the U.S. federal government turned to the U.S. Supreme Court. In 1832 Chief Justice John Marshall offered a series of judgments that angered advocates of states' rights but affirmed that Indian tribes "are domestically dependent nations" entitled to all the principles of sovereignty with the exception of making treaties with foreign governments. He also ruled that treaties involved a granting of rights from the Indians to the U.S. government, not from the U.S. government to the Indians, and that all rights not granted by the Indians were presumed to be reserved by the Indians. These two landmark decisions became known as the "federal trust doctrine" and the "reserved rights doctrine."

However, individual states as well as private corporations often ignored these doctrines, most notably between 1831 and 1839, when Georgia defied the ruling and, with the support of President Andrew Jackson, removed thousands of Cherokee, Choctaw, Creek, Chickasaw, and Seminole Indians from their homelands in what became known as the Trail of Tears. This notorious journey was spurred by the increase of settlers in Georgia after the rumor spread that gold had been discovered in the North Georgia Mountains. By this time, the Cherokee Nation had its own alphabet, perfected by the famed Indian scholar Sequoyah, as well as schools, roads, and even Christian churches. None of this mattered.

In 1830 the U.S. Congress passed the Indian Removal Act; among those members of Congress voting against it was the legendary American frontiersman Davy Crockett. After being declared invalid by the U.S. Supreme Court, the act's provisions were imposed on the tribe; it was defended by a small but powerful group of Cherokees, who RT referred to as "Tommyhawks" (defined earlier on page 81 of this book).

The bill then went to the U.S. Senate; such prominent senators as Daniel Webster and Henry Clay opposed it, but it passed by a single vote and was signed by President Andrew Jackson, who had fought the Seminole tribe in Florida earlier in his career. In 1839 the uprooted men, women, and children were forced to walk a thousand miles through the wilderness, foraging for food along the way, to their new home in Oklahoma—a desolate territory at that time. More than four thousand Indians died, and those who survived arrived in the middle of a brutal winter. By 1840 most members of the tribes in the southern United States had been subdued, annihilated, or forcibly removed to land west of the Mississippi. Only a small number of Native Americans remained in their ancient homelands; there are Choctaws and Chickasaws in Mississippi, Seminoles in Florida, Creeks in Alabama, and Cherokees in North Carolina and other states.

Many members of Congress were infuriated and asked for an investigation. The inquiry was conducted by Ethan Allen Hitchcock, and it revealed what Hitchcock called "a cold-blooded cynical disregard for human suffering and the destruction of human life." Hitchcock's final report was filed with President John Tyler's cabinet member in charge of national defense, the secretary of war. When Congress demanded a copy, the request was turned down by the secretary, and no trace of this report has ever been found.

One of the soldiers on duty during the displacement was Private John Burnett. He wrote, "I saw the helpless Cherokees arrested and dragged from their homes, and driven at the bayonet point into the stockades. And in the chill of a drizzling rain on an October morning I saw them loaded like cattle or sheep into 645 wagons and started toward the West. The sufferings of the Cherokees were awful. The trail of the exiles was a trail of death."

There were more Indian removal acts, and soon one hundred million acres of land once protected by treaties had been wrested from Indian control. In 1934, President Franklin Delano Roosevelt and Congress finally put an end to the land grabs. Federal courts began relying on Chief Justice Marshall's century-old legal precedents in a series of decisions that reminded lawmakers of the binding obligations to the tribes. But there was no way to return the land that had been stolen, and the remnants of the once great Indian nations were too poor to afford suitable lawyers.

The turning point for Native Americans occurred in July 1970, when President Richard Nixon delivered the first speech by a U.S. president on behalf of the Indians. Nixon told Congress that federal Indian policy was a disgrace to the nation's character. "The American Indians," he said, "have been oppressed and brutalized, deprived of their ancestral lands, and denied the opportunity to control their own destiny." Nixon, who credited his high school football coach, a Cherokee, for teaching him leadership skills, noted, "The story of the Indian is a record of endurance and survival, of adaptation and creativity in the face of overwhelming obstacles." Henceforth, he concluded, federal Indian policy should "operate on the premise that Indian tribes are permanent, sovereign governmental institutions in this society." Nixon's staff started writing what became the American Indian Self-Determination and Education Assistance Act, which gave tribes more direct control over federal programs that affected their members. By the time Congress passed the law in 1975, Nixon had left office in disgrace, but for some 1.5 million Native American citizens of the United States, the Nixon initiative had far-reaching and positive effects.

Considerable publicity had been given to the American Indian Movement's violent siege of the town of Wounded Knee, South Dakota, in 1973. But at the same time, thousands of young Indian men and women began attending colleges and universities. In 1968 there were only some five hundred Indian students in institutions of higher education, but a decade later that number had jumped tenfold. Rolling Thunder was correct in pointing out the duplicity and hypocrisy of U.S. governmental actions over the course of history. However, there were a number of U.S. presidents and other officials who came to the aid of Native Americans, and tribes began to acquire political power.

RT played an important role in supporting this struggle. Even though Native Americans account for only 1 percent of the U.S. population, their tribes hold 40 percent of the nation's coal reserves, billions of cubic feet of natural gas, and 20 percent of the nation's freshwater. These are resources that have begun to end the cycle of poverty, alcoholism, drug addiction, sexual and emotional abuse within families, and the other ills that are a hangover from the European Conquest.

The United States is not the only country that has ignored or downgraded Native American culture. In British Columbia, Canada, the 1884 Potlatch Law was still in effect in the late 1940s. Once the law was revoked, potlatch giveaways became important events for West Coast Native Americans (or *First Nation People,* a term often used in Canada). In 2011 I was invited to a four-day memorial potlatch honoring the late Chief Pat Alfred of the Namgis tribe, part of the Kwakwawa'wakw Nation. It was a moving experience to observe the rituals, dances, and dramatizations, and to listen to the tributes to the late, beloved chief. The masks of that area are masterpieces of art and design, featuring prominently in rituals marking "the gathering of the animals." Was I given a gift? Indeed I was, and the hand-painted drum depicting the spirits of the sea is one of my most prized possessions (please see plate 4 of the color insert).

The Sonoma State Lectures

On February 3, 1973, I arrived in San Francisco and was met at the airport by some of my friends. We drove to Novato and Mickey Hart's ranch, where I had been invited to spend the night. RT and Buffalo Horse had arranged to be there at the same time and I had invited them to speak at my class at Sonoma State College (now Sonoma State University) on the sixth. At this time I was visiting professor of psychology at Sonoma State and was teaching a course that focused on shamanism and other indigenous spiritual practices. When RT and Buffalo Horse arrived for their part of the lecture, they were joined by OhShinna Fastwolf, a well-known Native American storyteller and so-called keeper of secrets, being familiar with many of the Native American prophecies.

Jerilyn Brandelius and Barry Melton were members of the large audience, which had been scheduled for an auditorium rather than my customary lecture hall. Even so, there was standing room only. As RT, Buffalo Horse, and OhShinna recounted the sad tale of colonization, members of the audience were enraptured. Although many of them had heard these stories before—stories of how the European invaders had taken Indian land by treaty or by force and how, for example, strychnine-laced dead cattle were set out in hopes of poisoning Indians— several members of the audience began to cry, while others asked penetrating questions.

Whether by deliberate means or by simple contact, contagious diseases ran rampant in Native American settlements; a conservative estimate is that some two million Indians suffered premature deaths as the result of the European invasion, more from disease than from combat. A similar number died in South America, reducing the indigenous population to a fraction of what it was before what many historians refer to as "the Conquest."

Buffalo Horse listed the many ways that Native people had been mistreated over the centuries. They were displaced from their traditional lands. Their sacred sites were excavated, and their sacred objects were placed in private collections and museums. Their dead were exhumed from their traditional burial sites to make room for ranching and industry. Their artwork, which was never seen as separate from their culture, was commercially reproduced and modified for Western tastes. Traditional ceremonies and stories were depicted in novels, movies, and on television—usually inaccurately. Their way of life was disrupted, and they were forced to accept religious institutions whose dogmas were often in conflict with Native American values. Buffalo Horse's obvious anger was shared, not rejected, by most members of the large audience.

RT also expressed fury when describing the horrors of colonization. Although Doug Boyd had noted that he had never seen RT show the slightest hint of anguish, despair, or depression, RT indeed showed anger when it was appropriate, especially during a series of lectures wherein he had recounted his people's distressing past.

OhShinna spoke about leadership in Native American communities.

My mother is Mohawk, and the Mohawk tribe is a matriarchy. But in the Indian world almost all the major decisions are made by the women and then carried into council by the men, who act like they're the ones who made the decisions. In essence it's the grandmothers, mothers, sisters, and wives who are making them. There are no decisions made without the influence of the clan mothers. Power can be taken from any chief or medicine person through the clan mothers. They're the only ones who can "dehorn" a chief, as we put it. Chief is the wrong word; it's a leader. Chief puts it out of touch with the people. It's like calling someone a guru. You put them onto this pedestal, and then they lost touch with people. The leaders are the mirror image of the people, of their will and wishes, and they become leaders through the will of the people and through their ability to assume leadership. It's far different from the image of a "chief" that you see in movies and on television.

RT concluded his talk by saying, "I can show you ways to walk softly upon Mother Earth. And if you will learn these ways, you will begin to both heal the planet and heal yourselves." The trio received a standing ovation.

Sidian's Comments

When I started to read Alan Watts's books I discovered that he had an early passion for respecting and saving Nature. In his autobiography, Watts cited President Dwight Eisenhower's warning that "the industrial military complex" was a danger not only to world peace but also to the natural ecology. Watts wrote that Eisenhower was aware of the danger to life resulting from the liaison between corporations and the armed forces of the United States, a marriage that endangered life on Earth. This liaison evoked "a marching and mechanical rhythm," as Watts put it, which jolts, fractures, and interrupts everything organic, oceanic, and vegetative, a rhythm that is beaten out by people who do not realize that Earth is for all of its creatures and not merely for human beings.

I also read that Eisenhower was fond of quoting the Norwegian playwright Henrik Ibsen's statement, "I hold that man is in the right who is most clearly in league with the future." Again I thought of Alan Watts, who forecast future natural disasters if humans did not concern themselves with the fate of the Earth.

There are powerful insights in how to live in the natural relationship with the cycles of Nature and the natural world. Watts found these insights in Taoist philosophy, and I have been told that my grandfather admired Taoism. He called himself a "pagan" and was not sympathetic to organized religion. After all, it was Christianity that not only condoned the Conquest but also tried to convert Indians to the invaders' way of thinking. However, Kenneth Cohen, who visited Meta Tantay frequently, was allowed to give courses on Taoism. RT felt that the Taoists believed in the balance of humanity and Nature just as the Native Americans did. In one of his interviews,

RT observed, "It is amazing to notice the similarities between those Chinese Taoists and our own American Indian traditions. Thunder People are people of truth, and those teachings are the same among traditional people all over the world. For lack of a better name, I call people who want to hear the truth the Thunder People. If there are enough Thunder People, civilization does not have to go down."

Cohen later reminisced about Meta Tantay, writing:

I was fortunate to be able to meet with RT privately during my first visit to Meta Tantay. Normally, a visit with RT could take weeks to arrange. People came to the land to experience a spiritual way of life, not to meet a master or a guru. On my way to the meeting, I stopped at the outhouse. While I was sitting on the toilet seat, a sudden gust of wind blew the outside latch shut. Trapped, I started banging on the door, hoping that someone would hear me and rescue me. No one did. I had no choice but to continue shouting until, about half an hour later, I simply gave up. Suddenly, another gust of wind blew open the latch. As I stepped out into the bright sun, whom should I see passing by the outhouse but Rolling Thunder. Smiling, he said, "You must be Ken." Perhaps the spirits of Meta Tantay had used humor to teach me an important lesson: I had to deal with my own shit before I could learn anything new. And if I refused to face my problems, the Great Mystery would see to it that I did. Once you are committed to the Red Road of Native American spirituality, lessons will come your way.

I have read that no Native American language has a word for art because creative activities permeated all of a tribe's activities. Nor do these languages have a word for religion because beliefs and activities that Westerners consider to be religious are an inseparable part of an Indian's daily life. Religious institutions can be thought of as cultural venues that codify, structure, and interpret people's search for meaning by providing ceremonies, rituals, and explanations that provide a framework that is accepted by members of that institution, whether it be centered in a church, temple, or mosque.

Joseph Epps Brown, a distinguished scholar of religions, has described the way that Native Americans' spiritual resources have been diminished by a civilization that is "out of balance" because it has lost those values. This is ironic. But Brown added that Americans would gain a great deal if they would understand the ways in which Indians relate to Nature. If so, the Native American heritage would gain its rightful place among the great spiritual traditions of the world. By following what they understand to be the laws of Nature, Indians bypass the abstract religious doctrines that have been the basis for conflicts, massacres, and wars by dogmatic religious groups.

Brown, Alfred Koreber, and others classified the Native American tribes living in the United States into six major groups: the Arctic, the Eastern Subarctic, the Eastern Woodlands, the Plains, the Prairie, and the Southwest. RT claimed to have been born into the Paint Clan of the Cherokees, a clan of medicine people. His early life was spent in the Plains and Prairie areas among tribal people known to attribute spiritual power to each form and element of the natural world. He used the term *Great Spirit* as a type of shorthand, but Native tribes would not have limited the creative force with a noun. A better translation of *Wakan Tanka,* the Lakota term, or *Wakonda,* the Osage term, would be the Great Mysterious, an adjective that does not place limits on what it is describing.

Mickey Hart lent me several tapes of RT's lectures. One of them provided me with an insight into the way that my grandfather viewed the world of social activism. He said:

A long time ago we were at war down in Texas, Oklahoma, Arkansas, and Louisiana, and we needed more horses. After all, the white people who came into the plains took most of our land and many of our possessions, and they started to kidnap our children and put them in white schools. So when our people would ride, they would sing. We had songs, riding songs we'd call them. Nowadays we ride in our cars and we sing. Sometimes we would be walking along, a long ways out there, and we'd sing, and it made the journey easier. Sometimes we'd be there before we'd know it. We don't get tired when we travel in that kind of a way. There's a lot of power in those songs because they started out as battle songs.

Well, as we'd ride along we'd have good luck with our cars, and we wouldn't be tired. In other words we'd treat our cars just like the old timers took care of their horses. There's a little difference there, but still it works. Now you young hot-rodders ought to think that over because it does work. And singing works with yourself too. It keeps you from being tired or going to sleep when you are driving so that you can travel a long way.

Some Indians travel across this whole country. A lot of Indians are moving now and going to visit their brothers and sisters in different tribes, in different places. We are doing all we can to save this planet. I was with one group who went to the United Nations, or "the waters of the East," according to our prophecies. We attended the Spiritual Unity Conference there in 1975, and before we left a group of medicine people decided that Grandfather David Monongye, a Hopi elder and keeper of the prophecies, should go and deliver a message. Mad Bear Anderson and I went to New York City to accompany him. And those people at the United Nations heard spiritual people from all over the world; the Christians, the Jews, the Muslims, the Taoists, the Buddhists, they all got to speak. But when it got to the Indians and the Tibetan Buddhists, we were the only two groups who didn't get to speak. They had run out of time.

Now I can tell you something, the little that we had to add, the American Indians and the Tibetan Buddhists, should have been listened to. It might have been the little bit that could have made peace if they had wanted to do so. But I don't think they wanted to hear it at all, so the people running the meeting managed to run out of time before the American Indians' spiritual representative and the Tibetan Buddhist monks could talk.

Now isn't that strange? Why didn't they want to hear us? How could it be that way? Did they consider us dangerous? Or were we a danger to something else they wanted to do? None of the other religions talked about saving Mother Earth. That would have been dangerous to the big corporations. And maybe the Chinese politicians didn't want the Tibetans to speak. Anyway I didn't mean to get away from talking about riding songs. That's the way we are. We talk in circles, and we dance in circles.

And I've got a lot of bad habits. I am highly suspicious of people who are perfect. They might turn out to be dictators, or government agents, or they might be moneymakers. But I do have a lot of bad habits. I smoke strong tobacco. I get wound up and talk all night, like we do on the reservation. Indians get together, especially to talk about old times. And worst of all I still like women. My wife,

Spotted Fawn, called me last night. I told her I was okay and that I was behaving myself. And she told me she missed me, and I hadn't thought she would. After all we had only been gone a few days. It's good to know anyways. It's good to know when someone misses you and that they're waiting for you to come home.

An Interview with Michael Neils

One of the people whom I interviewed for this book was Michael Neils, C.E.O. of Arize Technologies and President of Solar Generation, whom we discussed earlier. Michael has been interested in Native Americans all his life and, at the age of nine, met a member of the Cree tribe through family friends. He was invited to spend his summer vacation with the Cree in the state of Montana and gleefully accepted. He repeated these summer visits, eventually being permitted to participate in the annual three-day sun dance ceremony. He was adopted into the family of a tribal member and, as mentioned earlier, was given an Indian name that translates as He Who Climbs High Mountains because of his skill as a mountain climber. When I interviewed him, I asked him how he met RT.

Michael Neils: I met RT through Stan Krippner at the Westerbeke Ranch in Sonoma County, California. This would have been in the fall of 1973. Stan had been invited to stay there when he was giving courses at Sonoma State College, and he knew I needed a place to stay, so got permission for me to move there too.

Sidian Morning Star Jones: You're really good with those dates.

Michael Neils: We had only been there a couple of weeks when RT showed up.

Sidian Morning Star Jones: What was RT there for?

Michael Neils: He was there to see Stan. And RT got permission from the Westerbeke family to set up a reburial on the property. A number of Native Americans had been dug up near there, and their bodies were stored in the Anthropology Department's museum at Sonoma State.

Plate 1 (right).
Rolling Thunder
at home in Carlin,
Nevada

Plate 2 (below).
Rolling Thunder,
Stanley Krippner,
and friends. Stanley
Krippner is kneeling,
second from left;
Rolling Thunder is
standing
fourth from right.

Plate 3. Tepees in the snow at Meta Tantay, Rolling Thunder's spiritual institution in Nevada. Courtesy of Karie Garnier.

Plate 4 (above). Native American drum

Plate 5 (below). Michael Neils, friend to Rolling Thunder, in a sweat lodge. Courtesy of Michael Neils.

Plate 6 (above). Rolling Thunder's dictate.
Plate 7 (below). Dwellings at Meta Tantay.

Plate 8 (above). Rolling Thunder and spiritual warriors. Courtesy of Eolah Bates.

Plate 9 (left). Mickey Hart and Rolling Thunder

Plate 10 (above). Native American psychologist Dr. Leslie Gray
Plate 11 (below). Russell Jones, Stanley Krippner, Spotted Fawn, Morning Star Jones

Plate 12 (above). Rolling Thunder imparts wisdom. Courtesy of Karie Garnier.

Plate 13 (right). Rolling Thunder's medicine trailer. Courtesy of Michael Bova.

Plate 14 (above). Grandfather Semu Huaute, Chumash medicine man and friend of Rolling Thunder. Courtesy of Eneke-Alish Huaute.

Plate 15 (above right). Nevada Landscape. Courtesy of Michael Bova.

Michael Neils (con't.): I can remember RT saying, "People dig in our graves instead of asking us what they want to know. We would never dig for other people's bones because it's an amateurish, ghoulish way of going about getting information." That statement made good sense to me.

Sidian Morning Star Jones: People had been dug up and put in a museum?

Michael Neils: Yeah, there had been a Native burial site on the property. Archaeologists and anthropologists from Sonoma State had excavated it and had taken a number of the remains. We led a campaign to get these returned and reinterred.

Sidian Morning Star Jones: How were you able to get the remains back?

Michael Neils: We just told them we were going to take them and rebury them.

Sidian Morning Star Jones: Really? Did they put up a fight?

Michael Neils: There was no resistance. The professors in charge of the museum actually welcomed it. Sonoma State was a great place.

Sidian Morning Star Jones: The professors decided that so quickly?

Michael Neils: Yeah. They decided that they had learned everything that they could from the remains. And so now was the time to rebury the remains. And it was back in 1973; they were definitely ahead of the national curve. Now there is a national movement in the United States to reinter bones of Native people, but Sonoma State was one of the first.

Sidian Morning Star Jones: Was RT involved in that?

Michael Neils: Oh yes. He was very directly involved. Very few institutions were reinterring at that point, and he was very eloquent in reminding the museum officials that those bones were the remains of human beings. He asked them what they would think if a century from now the bones of their family members were put on public display. RT stopped by the Westerbeke Ranch numerous times during that winter. Once the remains were reburied, he came with many other medicine people to visit Stan and me and to gather medicines. He gathered red oak bark and willow bark and many different plant medicines. There was a hill in Sonoma County that was very rich in biodiversity, and a lot of incredible medicine plants grew there.

Sidian Morning Star Jones: Was that something that you helped him do?

Michael Neils: Yeah. He would always come and get me, and I would go along.

Sidian Morning Star Jones: And what else did you do when RT visited?

Michael Neils: I would help out with some sacred ceremonies that he put on at the ranch. But we also collected a lot of food, truckloads of food from the ranch. We would go around picking up leftover apples, grapes, and pears and other fruits. We picked up the fruit after the main harvesters had gone through the orchards.

An Interview with Patricia Westerbeke

I also interviewed Patricia Westerbeke, the owner of the ranch, about this project.

Patricia Westerbeke: We sponsored an archaeology project for the Marin Country Day School, and we followed the guidelines from an anthropological field guide. We'd cut out a square piece of earth, and we sifted everything. Not everything got through to the flat piece of plywood. We found bones and stones that apparently had been used for scraping hides. The Archaeology Department at Sonoma State University came over and classified everything and

put them in different bags. And then I don't think they ever looked at them again but put them in a basket in the bottom of some warehouse.

Sidian Morning Star Jones: Yeah. All that work for nothing.

Patricia Westerbeke: And Rolling Thunder heard about this, and he suggested that they stop doing this. So he came over, and we filled up a big hole with the bones from the museum, and he blessed the bones and the field from which they had been taken. We never really dug up a whole body, but RT didn't like any disruption of the dead, and so we had this ceremony of blessing the land and closing it up and not doing this anymore.

Sidian Morning Star Jones: So you filled up the hole. How big was it?

Patricia Westerbeke: Oh, it was about six feet deep and about eight by five.

Sidian Morning Star Jones: Yeah, it must have taken some work.

Patricia Westerbeke: Well, we all were very careful. We tried to do this according to what the archaeologists and anthropologists had told us to do. And there were some interesting things there like these little balls that were used as weights for fishing nets, and we found some nice arrowheads. Now the arrowheads in Sonoma were different from those near Mount St. Helena farther north where there was an obsidian outcrop. And the group would bring the rough obsidian back to the camp and do the work there. Is that where you got your name, Sidian?

Sidian Morning Star Jones: Yes, I took it from "obsidian," because I knew obsidian was one of the materials used by Native Americans for their arrowheads and other weapons. And like my grandfather, I am on the warpath for truth. Obsidian is difficult to work with, precise, and potentially quite dangerous.

Patricia Westerbeke: It's like glass.

Sidian Morning Star Jones: Obsidian scalpels are actually sharper than their steel equivalents.

Patricia Westerbeke: It splinters into fractures.

Sidian Morning Star Jones: You have to be very careful, because even simply touching it can cause bleeding. It's the risk you take when honing an instrument of such precision.

Saving the Pinyon Nut Trees

All native people at one time or another have had a Tree of Life. In Europe it was the oak tree. For the Iroquois it was the maple tree. Where RT lived, it was the pinyon tree. This also served as an important food source for the local Indians.

Several people told me about my grandfather's social activism in a project close to home. In the late 1960s local authorities began clearing the land so it could be used for grazing livestock. The problem was that this land belonged to the Indians. The authorities assured the Indians that clearing the land made it more accessible for the wild deer to run freely. They also claimed that only "decaying forests" were being cleared. And the Indians whom RT called Tommyhawks went along with these excuses.

My uncle Buffalo Horse worked with RT on that project. He also helped the crew for the television show *60 Minutes* make a feature story about it. And he helped another crew make a documentary, *The Broken Treaty of Battle Mountain,* directed by Joel Friedman. Buffalo Horse told me:

The ranchers wanted to clear the land and get rid of the pinyon nut trees. They took two big Caterpillar tractors and put chains between them, and when the chains rolled along they would tear up the land. The trees would literally explode. They could clear twenty acres in about an hour. They would destroy so many of those trees that they lined up down the road as far as the eye could see. And nobody was allowed to pick nuts from the trees or use them as firewood. They would just burn them. This was an insult, because pinyon nuts are sacred to our people. And you could live on pinyon nuts forever if you had nothing else to eat. A pinyon nut tree is literally the Tree of Life.

As my uncle noted, the clearing was accomplished by dragging heavy boat anchor chains between two tractors. These chains took everything in their path, including pinyon nut trees and juniper bushes, both of which were considered sacred by the local tribes. The real reason for the clearing, of course, was to expand the number of cattle and sheep who could graze the land. The process was quite efficient, ripping off twenty acres of trees and bushes in two hours. In the meantime the local government charged the Indians taxes for any pinyon nuts they harvested. At the same time the U.S. Bureau of Land Management provided low-cost access of these lands to wealthy ranchers. Doug Boyd, the author of *Rolling Thunder,* played an important role in this struggle, writing letters to key people that pointed out how the old treaties were being violated by the chaining operation. He pointed out how fifty thousand acres of forestland had been destroyed in Nevada alone.

It was said that Rolling Thunder gathered some of his spiritual warriors and other tribal members together and, in the middle of the night, took photographs of the tractors. They were careful not to get caught, and their strategy helped to stop the process, at least in that part of Nevada. In the meantime, the Western Shoshone Nation hired knowledgeable lawyers to fight the action as well as the illegal grazing of livestock on Western Shoshone land. This onslaught of daytime and nighttime activities stirred up considerable anger among the local populace, and the ranchers suffered from the negative publicity. In 1972 the U.S. Bureau of Land Management stopped the chaining process as well as its support for the illegal grazing activities. This type of social activism would have been unheard of several decades earlier, but it took awhile for Indians to find smart lawyers who knew about the Supreme Court's concepts of the federal trust doctrine and the reserved rights doctrine. And it also took awhile for lawyers to have the courage to represent Native Americans in court.

Everyone in RT's group knew that the Bureau of Land Management was destroying thousands of acres of living, growing trees to serve the mercenary interests of a few individuals who had become politically powerful because of their wealth. In order for the bureau to do this, they broke a number of treaties and lied to the American public. Destroying thousands of acres of pinyon nut trees involved ignoring ecology, destroying a natural food source, and harming wildlife.

Anne Habberton recalled:

With RT we visited the elderly Shoshone chief Temoke in Ruby Valley. RT explained later to us that Chief Temoke, although at some point in our visit he had seemingly fallen asleep in his chair, was actually traveling on another plane, working on the pinyon nut tree problem during his sleep.

We accompanied RT on several excursions regarding the issue of the Bureau of Land Management's "chaining"—destroying with tractors and giant chains—the indigenous tribes' pinyon nut orchards that were growing naturally. Their motive was to allow white ranchers to plant grasses for their cattle on these Indian lands that had been leased to the ranchers. We observed this true rape of Mother Earth and her pinyon pines. RT conducted a ceremony, held a press conference, and worked hard to try to stop this travesty. It was a very sad and moving experience to witness this tragic destruction of a traditional food source by our government for the purpose of growing crops that were not indigenous to the area.

To RT, the destruction of the pinyon nut trees was part of a larger problem, the deteriorating spiritual condition of America. Most of the chaining took place on Indian territory, but there were instant profits to be made, even if the land became a dust bowl. RT kept maps charting the destruction of the trees. He also kept records of the treaties with the Shoshone people that had been broken, many of them with the complicity of the Tommyhawks.

Chief Frank Temoke of the Western Shoshone Nation named RT spokesperson and legal advisor, and this gave RT an opportunity to attend several meetings regarding the issue and to see the political manipulation firsthand. It also gave him a chance to object to the forced taking of Indian children from their homes to "Westernize" and "Christianize" them in foster homes. RT often talked about the "buckskin curtain" that kept people on the outside from realizing what was really going on with the Indians.

RT told many people, "I have been shot at, and they have tried to poison me many times. We even had FBI and CIA agents at Meta Tantay. We didn't care, because we had nothing to hide. We knew who they were all the time." Stanley remembers seeing a bullet hole in the wall of RT's home; RT told him that the person who tried to shoot him was a poor shot. I am glad that whoever it was couldn't shoot straight!

12

Shamanic Healing

For American Indians healing is Nature's way of restoring equilibrium to a system, human or nonhuman, that has lost its balance. Native American tribes were in agreement that the particular gifts of the universe can be transferred to medicine people when they heal. Medicine men and medicine women form alliances with spirits, animal allies, healing plants, and other agencies that are repositories of curative powers. These practitioners also use power objects such as amulets, charms, and crystals. The Cherokee medicine people use crystals in preparing their medicines where sunlight is guided through the crystal and onto an herbal preparation to potentiate its power. Sometimes they access the world of Spirit by burning sage, tobacco, sweetgrass, or other sacred plants. Another technology is the use of special songs, chants, and stories. The shaman's repository of power differs from tribe to tribe, but all use sacred technology in the service of their patients and their communities.

For example, the Plains Indians direct their sacred pipes to Six Directions: North, South, East, West, Up, and Down. Navaho sand paintings create a tiny universe that represents the cosmos as a whole, and patients who sit in the center of a painting are the recipients of what the universe bestows on them. The Pawnees use sacred songs to hasten the growing of their crops, both those plants that feed their tribe and those that heal its sick tribal members. Christina Pratt observes that shamanic healing takes place in a broad context: "As we address the healing needed outside of ourselves, we are shown the need for healing within. And as we address and transform the need for healing within, the need to reflect healing back to our suffering world is revealed."

It is customary to dismiss these technologies as triggers of the placebo effect. However, placebo effects produce actual physiological changes. They are not caused by a physical intervention but arise from the patient's making of meaning during his or her interaction with the shaman and his or her environment. Furthermore, the placebo effect provides patients the opportunity to become active agents in their own recovery. Spiritual experiences and practices involve a number of neurological reactions that resemble placebo effects. So it should come as no surprise that Native American healing has strong spiritual components. In fact, the ancient Greek philosopher Socrates realized this when he observed that a remedy is far more useful when accompanied by the proper words than if used without them.

All healing practitioners operate from a model. Shamanic models generally differ from the Western allopathic model in that they involve facilitating a devotion to the well-being of Nature, of one's body, and of one's spiritual growth. Moreover, they encourage people to make life decisions in a way that reflects the ideals of harmony and knowledge. Shamanic models represent a structured and thoughtful approach to healing that attempts to mend the torn fabric of a person's (or a community's) connection with the Earth as well as the splits that frequently occur between the individual and the social group, between the spiritual and the secular. But in the last analysis, medicine people take the position that there is no division between the sacred and the secular, because every plant and animal, every stone and tree is sacred. At the same time, understanding the cosmos through conceptual models involves simplification, abstraction, fragmentation, objectivity, and distancing; it allows the power of reason and logic to bear on particular phenomena. Models reflect reality, but Native American inquiry permits direct connections with the energies, spirits, and powers of Nature. This is the principle way in which Native American medical concepts differ from other frameworks that describe healing.

One of the most sophisticated Native American healing models is that of the Pima Indians in the southwestern United States. They classified sicknesses into two groups, the "wandering sicknesses," which can be treated by herbs and purification ceremonies, and the "staying sicknesses," which cannot be treated. Mental retardation is a staying sickness. People who are crippled for life have a staying sickness. Some sorcerers have the power to bring about a staying sickness.

The flexibility of the Pima healing system was apparent during the tribe's first confrontations with Europeans. When it was observed that the newcomers violated sacred objects without dire consequences, the Pima Indians concluded that the Europeans had their own deities and restrictions and hence were not affected by the Pima ordinances. Later, when Pima shamans were told about germs and communicable diseases, they subsumed this knowledge under their category of wandering sicknesses in which invisible forces "wander" through the body, leaving afflictions in their wake.

E. Fuller Torrey, a psychiatrist, holds that the nature of any effective treatment, whether conducted by shamans or other practitioners, inevitably reflects one or more of four fundamental principles: (1) a shared worldview that provides meaning to the diagnosis or naming process, (2) those personal qualities of the practitioner that facilitate the patient's recovery, (3) positive expectations (for example, hope, faith, placebo effects) that assist healing, and (4) a sense of self-mastery on the part of the patient that engenders empowerment. Torrey surveyed indigenous psychotherapists, concluding, "Many of them are effective psychotherapists and produce therapeutic change in their patients."

The Practitioner's Personal Qualities

Much of a shaman's effectiveness as a healer rests on the fact that his or her concepts of Nature are the same as those of the patient. Maria

Sabina, the Mazatec shaman, explained to Stanley how she and her patient would jointly ingest mind-altering mushrooms in a sacred ritual, attempting to identify the patient's physical, psychological, or spiritual problem. It was doña Maria's belief that Jesus Christ assisted them in the diagnostic process.

The shaman may often be a unique individual in relation to the people of his or her community. Some shamans may have been quite neurotic but stuck close enough to reality to use the shamanic technologies required for success in healing. The shaman's imaginative resources have been emphasized by Jeanne Achterberg, a psychologist who pioneered the use of mental imagery in Western medicine. She considers dreams and visions a source of vital information on human health and sickness, in part because of the symbolic images and metaphorical stories they contain. Among a shamanic society's symbols and metaphors is that of the "wounded healer." If a potential shaman has overcome a personal tragedy, sickness, or debilitating condition, his or her community often will bestow respect and deference for this impressive feat.

Positive Expectations and a Sense of Mastery

There is abundant evidence that demonstrates the importance of expectancy. What a person expects to happen in healing often will happen if the expectations are strong enough. Remedies such as lizard blood and swine teeth have no known medicinal properties, but if they have worked over the centuries it is because patients expected them to work. Jerome Frank and Julia Frank, in their classic book *Persuasion and Healing,* conclude that the state of mind conducive to healing depends on a practitioner's ability to arouse the patient's hope, bolster his or her self-esteem, stir him or her emotionally, and strengthen his or her ties with a supportive group. Hence, efforts to heighten the patient's positive expectations may be as genuinely therapeutic as specific therapeutic techniques.

Frank and Frank claim that the heightening of the patient's sense of mastery is a direct or indirect effect of all successful psychotherapies.

Shamans have used a variety of methods to empower their patients, such as pronouncing incantations, singing sacred songs, carrying out symbolic ritual acts, appearing to remove disease, removing objects from the body, placating appeasing spirits, interpreting dreams, and administering herbal remedies. The patient's emerging sense of mastery equips him or her with knowledge that can be used to cope with life's adversities. The patient may learn self-regulation, dietary and exercise regimens, and other disease prevention techniques to prevent a recurrence of the ailment. The patient also may learn the proper prayers or amulets that counteract malevolent spirits, the healthy attitudes that counteract depression and anxiety, and the dream interpretation techniques that provide personal empowerment.

For many centuries Western investigators had little respect or regard for shamanic healing, for Native rituals, or for altered states of consciousness. In recent years, however, such prominent psychotherapists as Achterberg, the Franks, and Torrey have found many Native practices to contain elements instructive for Western practitioners, for instance, the use of imagination and altered states of consciousness for health maintenance and personal growth. However, in the United States, shamanism is often misinterpreted as Satanism, and ritual is misrepresented as ritual cult abuse.

Practitioners of Western medicine do not have a flawless record. A study published in 2011 reported that between forty thousand and eighty thousand Americans die in hospitals each year due to misdiagnosis. Based on autopsy studies, researchers have found that American physicians have misdiagnosed illnesses between 20 percent and 40 percent of the time. According to the system fostered by the International Classification of Diseases, there are more than 13,600 possible diagnoses, so mistakes are inevitable. Wiser U.S. physicians realize this and are modest when discussing their own practice and tend to be more open-minded regarding non-Western medicine.

David Feinstein—a psychologist and the husband of Donna Eden, who was mentioned previously—and Stanley Krippner have adapted some of the principles described by Achterberg, Torrey, and the Franks for Western audiences, integrating them into their systematic program of personal growth. These procedures have been designed to help people find a "personal mythology" that will help them wend their way through life. This system involves finding one's "inner shaman" and is described in a self-help book, *Personal Mythology,* devoted to helping their readers discover and transform their outdated and/or dysfunctional personal myths. Like Native American healing stories, the search for one's personal mythology involves a narrative. The value of this narrative resides in its aesthetic factors, in its beauty, and in its meaningfulness.

Perhaps Western psychotherapy has been overly focused on cognitive content. Western psychotherapists can learn a great deal by exploring the stylistic principles of literature, of poetry, and of American Indian healing myths. Human experience is inherently messy and difficult to describe. But developing a mythological framework for one's life experiences can provide integration and wholeness that bestows purpose on his or her past, present, and future endeavors.

An Overview of American Indian Medicine

An elder who admired Kenneth Cohen's knowledge of Native American medicine gave him the name Bear Hawk. Cohen rightfully points out that this system is as worthy of respect as Chinese medicine, ayurvedic medicine, and other traditional healing systems. He echoes Rolling Thunder's belief that in Indian healing, the time, place, healer, and patient need to be in harmony. He also notes that there are many American Indian medical systems, not simply one. However, they all are guided by an emphasis on balance, prevention, and spirituality. They all believe that spirits can help or harm the healing process. And they all hold that Nature is an important source of health and wisdom. People deepen the connection to their Creator by finding their life purpose, and a medicine person can assist this quest.

It was quite appropriate that Cohen was given the name Bear Hawk. Some Native American traditions tell how Bear brought medicine to humans and taught them how to use it. Some Bear clans devote themselves to the practice of healing, both for themselves and others. In general, Native American healing involved the whole of Nature in a web of exchange, relationship, obligation, and renewal.

In Native American medicine there is no clear-cut difference between treatments that are used to help others and those that are used to help oneself. For example, either the healer or the patient can go on a vision quest to obtain information used in treatment. To practice massage, or "hand doctoring," a Native American healer learns how to perceive and project energy through the hands and also learns about the inner workings of his or her own body.

Native American healing is multisensory. In the winter spirit dances practiced among the Salish tribes in the Pacific Northwest, tribal members gather in huge smokehouses to honor the spirits with dance and song. Participants are stimulated visually by the imagery of the dance masks, auditorily because of the intense drumming and singing, kinesthetically by dancing and foot stomping, and mentally by hearing the words and rhythms of songs and prayers. The sense of smell is stimulated by "smudging," using the smoke and scent of a sweet-smelling plant to purify a person or space. Taste is involved in the plethora of healing herbs used in treating sick people.

Cohen discovered that traditional masks and dolls are seen as living beings, and this is why many Native people are distressed to see them in gift shops and museums. People think nothing of putting kachina dolls in display cabinets or hanging masks on their walls. However, the spirits in these dolls and masks may get restless and exert negative effects on people living in that house.

Plant medicine, according to Cohen, is probably the most widespread tradition on the planet. Native Americans taught the French explorer Jacques Cartier how his sailors could avoid scurvy by brewing a tea from pine needles, a substance containing vitamin C. Native Americans knew how to rid themselves of parasites by eating a type of parsley, how to treat wounds with yarrow plants, how to calm anxiety with bergamot flower tea, and how to cure headaches by drinking a tea made from willow bark, which contains the same chemical now synthe-sized to produce aspirin.

Cohen had a dream about Rolling Thunder before he met him. After several visits and observations, Cohen concluded that RT "was the most traditional of all the medicine people I have known. Not con-tent to speak about Native American tradition or only to practice it, he lived it." RT told Cohen about his calling and that once someone is called to the Red Road of Native spirituality, lessons and training are not a matter of choice. One needs to find a teacher, or teachers, and start working.

Cohen was impressed by RT's penetrating eyes and knew that light-ning was his ally. RT seemed to project lightning from his hands or feathers when he healed someone. On the one hand, Cohen observed that RT "flirted too much," and no one wanted to be around him when he was angry. On the other hand, he admitted his faults and made no attempt to pass himself off as a guru. Cohen was impressed by life at Meta Tantay. He observed that a generator provided electricity but was rarely used, because one could not see the stars when they were dulled by the use of electric lights or hear the coyotes due to television noise.

One of the most concise descriptions of RT's approach to heal-ing can be found in his appearance on the television show *Thinking Allowed,* where he was interviewed by psychotherapist Jeffrey Mishlove. Here are some excerpts from the interview.

Jeffrey Mishlove: Our topic today is the unity of humanity and Nature. And with me is Rolling Thunder, a traditional Native American medicine man.

Rolling Thunder: I'm very glad to be here as your guest.

Jeffrey Mishlove: It is only recently that American Indian medicine people, such as yourself, have been able to share your teachings with the larger community.

Rolling Thunder: We do what we think is ready and right. My dreams tell me what I am supposed to do, and at this time we can share some things that we couldn't before. Now it is necessary because sometimes people are foolish and aggressive, and they might destroy the Earth. Smog originates in the mind. But there are ways of cleaning up smog and other results of pollution, but it must originate in the power of mind. Mind brought about these problems, and mind can correct them. I do my best to show people why greed and aggressive thinking are wrong, and why they must be stopped.

Jeffrey Mishlove: You are wearing a very unique turban.

Rolling Thunder: This is my own tribal headdress. And the seven-pointed star with turquoise represents where we came from. We came from Atlantis and from the seven stars before that, the Pleiades I think you call them.

Jeffrey Mishlove: And you ended up in North America.

Rolling Thunder: That's right. And then the white men came from Europe, and they stole almost everything they could get their hands on. They even stole our women and children. They took the natural wealth and left us a very poor people, homeless in our own country. But at least they left us our way of life, because that had no value to them.

Jeffrey Mishlove: And you are trying to tell people how to live as part of Nature?

Rolling Thunder: That's right. We are the caretakers of this land. We are one with Nature. We don't hold ourselves up to be better than the animals or even a grain of sand or dirt. I've read the Bible and books from other religions, and then I put them away because they don't have a lot in them about the oneness of people with Nature, with the storms, with the trees and the plants and with the Earth. Now it will take hundreds of years to clean up the mess we have made here.

Jeffrey Mishlove: Is this something everyone can do together?

Rolling Thunder: The white people need us, and we need the white people. We need all the help we can get. The Earth is a living body, just like we are. All people at one time had a Tree of Life, even in Europe. It was an oak tree, and people could eat acorns from it and from other gifts from Nature. And then the Europeans got greedy and started building ships to sail and raid other people and to discover other worlds. They used up their own natural resources, and they started to steal them from others. And then they would carry their diseases from one place to another. Before that, they followed their natural regional ways. They went with the circle, and you can see this in Ireland, in Scandinavia, and in other countries. We should think more about our children and our grandchildren and what is being destroyed. People ask me how we stop this destruction. I tell them that we don't believe in violence. We are not going to take up guns or blow anything up. That's not our way. I ask them, "Do you know how to pray?" You'd be surprised how many people admit they don't know how to pray. If they pray, they might ask for a Cadillac or a gold mine, but that is not the Indian way.

Jeffrey Mishlove: Do you pray when you gather your healing herbs?

Rolling Thunder: Yes, I do. When I gather my plants, I go between sunrise and sunset only. At nighttime I let them sleep and rest. They have a tribe. They have a family. And they have a chief just like we do. They communicate on a much higher level. They don't have to make a lot of noise when they communicate, but they know what's happening. They can read our thoughts. I've seen some plants fold their leaves in fear when some people approach them. They know those people will start yanking them up or maybe poison them. But I like to see the plants happy. And I explain in my prayers how they're going to be used in a good way, and they should be happy for what they're going to be doing. I don't take too much, never more than half. And if I only see one or two, I let them be so that they can reproduce. After I have made my prayers and my offering to the chief and the ladies around him, I still take only so much. I don't believe in killing those plants or destroying them. And if I take some from below the ground for their roots, then I smooth the

Earth back just like it was. And maybe I will plant a seed or a piece of the root so the plants can grow again.

Jeffrey Mishlove: Where do you see your patients?

Rolling Thunder: Well, I don't like to do "doctoring" in my home. It's better to do it in a natural setting. And if people come here with mental and emotional problems, those issues can keep hanging around the house and can be pretty destructive. My home is where I live and rest and raise my family. And I like to keep it that way.

Jeffrey Mishlove: You must have many female patients. Do you give them health advice?

Rolling Thunder: Yes, I do. And I give them practical advice. For example, I tell them that using douches is good, and don't let anyone say that it isn't. Pregnant women should not douche until after the eighth week from conception or until after the cervix opens. A sage douche is good for yeast infections, and a vinegar douche is good for cleanliness.

Jeffrey Mishlove: How do you prepare for a healing?

Rolling Thunder: In the first place, I take a good bath. I ask the other person to take a bath too, one without soaps, perfumes, and shampoos. Some of that stuff can knock me down! My sense of smell is very intense, and I can smell the sickness. Then I become an animal, or I let the animal spirit move into me, snakes especially. I use them in my way of healing, whatever animal is meant to be. And I make a lot of noise. Sometimes I sing a song; they come to me, and some of them are very ancient. Then I put my animal spirits together with the power of the moon, the sun, and the stars that guide our way. I put all of these things together in my mind, and I don't have room for any other kind of thought, drinking, sex, or anything else. And I put in my mind what is happening after I look into the person, for example, broken bones coming together and healing.

Jeffery Mishlove: Do you have assistants?

Rolling Thunder: I have all kinds of helpers. Some of them stay with me a long time, and some stay just a little while because the work is so intense. And somebody has to stay with the people I "doctor" until they are well, no matter how long it takes. And the helpers tell me what happened, because I don't always remember what I've done after I've done it. Sometimes the mind of a medicine man goes blank except for focusing on the job that has to be done. I have different ways of doing things. I suck things out of a person with my mouth. But I don't swallow anything, because it might be infection or poison. And sometimes I use my finger. I don't need a knife. I can use my finger or an eagle feather if I have to cut into the body. And I use a lot of herbs when I "doctor" someone. I also pray a lot.

Jeffery Mishlove: What kind of people have you worked with?

Rolling Thunder: All kinds of people. I've worked on doctors, even a world-famous brain surgeon. Sometimes a person comes along who is sick, and I feel a sort of sympathy for them. I might even pick up their aches and pains in my own body. If they want to give some money, I usually give it to my helpers. I accept nothing for myself. If they want to give me an offering, I use that for transportation. After all, I don't travel on a broomstick.

A first-person account of RT's healing abilities was shared on Canadian radio by Karie Garnier, a well-known photographer. He told a compelling story.

Just before I met Rolling Thunder I was bedridden, bone thin, and dying. I suffered from severe hypoglycemia, depression, adrenal exhaustion, and supraventricular tachycardia. My heart raced uncontrollably at two hundred beats a minute, my hair was falling out, and I could barely walk. I had been terribly sick for two years. My doctor warned me, "Your heart will not last much longer."

At the lowest point of my illness, as I faced death's door, I had a crazy dream: Some madman with a high-powered rifle was trying to shoot an eagle out of the sky. As he fired off numerous rounds, the great invincible eagle, with its pair of powerful wings, dodged and dipped and flapped its wings and transformed into a pair of galloping horses! With horrendous energy the pair of charging horses roared down from the sky. They flew in like a pair of jets, thundered across the plane of the Earth, and disappeared into the horizon. When I woke up I was dazed and confused.

My landlord at the time was also a Jungian psychologist, and he told me, "Karie, that's not a crazy dream! That's a powerful, archetypal dream. This was a near-death vision that came into your mind, sent directly from God, and it's trying to show you the way to survive."

A series of coincidences then brought me into contact with Steven, a local resident who told me about a Native American healer. Steven urged me, "Take your dream to Rolling Thunder. I met this man, and I can assure you, he's no lightweight!"

In August 1982, at a gathering on the outskirts of Falls City, Washington, I had the privilege of sitting in front of Rolling Thunder during his two-day healing circle. That weekend Rolling Thunder healed me spiritually and physically. Simply listening to his voice and being in his presence began to produce changes in my body. By the end of those two days, I had never felt better. He also gave me advice on herbal medicines I could take to maintain the healing process. The experience changed my life forever.

Due to the far-reaching impact of Rolling Thunder's work, I was not only completely healed, I was also inspired to create a photographic show, "Our Elders Speak," which was featured at Expo '86, the University of British Columbia's Museum of Anthropology, and at the United Nations as well as other venues around the world.

Stanley's Comments

In 1976 I participated in a smudging ceremony with RT. Rock Scully, a road manager for the Grateful Dead, was about to begin a jail term for a minor offense and asked RT for help. RT gathered a dozen of us together and smudged our foreheads with a collection of twigs and herbs that had been burned to produce the ashes needed for smudging. We prayed that Scully would endure the incarceration and could find some way to learn from it. Suddenly RT interrupted the ceremony by saying that he had a short vision of Scully in jail, obtaining important information from another prisoner.

A few weeks later it was discovered that Scully's neighbor in his cell block at a federal prison in Lompoc, California, was H. R. Haldeman, Richard Nixon's chief of staff, imprisoned for conspiracy and obstruction of justice during the 1972 Watergate scandal. The scandal resulted when Nixon's aides were caught breaking into a political opponent's office at the Watergate Hotel in Washington, D.C. It was in this prison setting that Haldeman, who was sequestered in an adjoining cell, spent hours giving Scully a detailed account of the questionable Nixon White House activities and also admitting to Scully his own devious acts. Haldeman later confessed his misdeeds in a memoir, contrary to other Watergate conspirators, most of who insisted that they had done nothing wrong. Haldeman also told Scully that his children were impressed that he had become friends with the road manager of the legendary Grateful Dead rock band.

An understanding of ceremony and ritual is essential to appreciate the complexity of shamanic experiences, and I have proposed a model that separates them from the pathological terminology often imposed by Western social scientists and psychotherapists. I have combined the parapsychologist Rhea White's description of "exceptional human experiences" and the anthropologist Ruth-Inge Heinze's identification of a practitioner's degree of volition and concomitant degree of dissociation. The term dissociation is used when one is disconnected from his or her usual flow of memory, identity, and/or behavior. A patient suffering from loss of identity in a mental hospital may experience uncontrolled *dissociation,* whereas a tribal shaman, whose identity supposedly has been transformed or replaced by discarnate entities, may be engaging in controlled dissociation. A seasoned camper might awaken to a morning sunrise, reporting a spontaneous onrush of uncontrolled awareness, that is, an intense appreciation of Nature that appears to have occurred with no apparent volitional control. A mathematician may spend hours in a condition of highly controlled awareness, concentrating on a perplexing problem.

This model recognizes that the degree of control and awareness may fluctuate during the same event and that seemingly opposite descriptors may even complement each other, such as the wild but disciplined frenzy of some shamanic dance rituals and the "effort of no effort" in Vajrayana Buddhist practices. Western dualities, such as control versus lack of control, make little sense in the spiritual practices of many collectively oriented cultures.

Borrowing terms from White, I also ask if a shamanic ritual or other experience is personal (reinforcing one's identity) or transpersonal (transcending one's identity). A transcendent glimpse of the oneness with all things (in other words, the All) can occur in any of Heinze's four varieties of experience.

1. One practitioner may become aware of this oneness in ritual prayer in which his or her self-identity gradually merges with the transcendent All (in controlled awareness).
2. Another practitioner may contact the transcendent All while dissociating from self-identity, as when channeling messages from a source of universal knowledge (in controlled dissociation).
3. A third practitioner may suddenly feel a oneness with nature, with an infant, or with one's lover (uncontrolled awareness).
4. A practitioner may ingest an unfamiliar but powerful drug, entering a void in which self-identity is lost (uncontrolled dissociation), yielding to terror, bliss, or something in between.

This model also acknowledges the Indian stance that a ceremony can be done anywhere and with any number of people. A person alone can have a ceremony while making a prayer to the Creator.

Hypnosis at Meta Tantay

In 1979 I made one of several visits to Meta Tantay. Each visit was marked by surprises, and this one was no exception. Upon my arrival RT asked me to hypnotize William Grant, a young man he had been "doctoring." William was a Native American who had come to Meta

Tantay because he was an alcoholic. He was desperate for help, and RT had put him on a "purifying diet" for three months, accompanied by the ingestion of herbal medicines. The day of my arrival RT had told William that a psychologist would hypnotize him that evening at a special ceremony attended by the entire Meta Tantay community.

I assumed that I would meet William before the ceremony so that I could fathom his expectations and adapt my intervention accordingly. However, William held a job in a nearby town, and so I did not see him until the ceremony began. When I arrived at the campfire William was already there, seated in a comfortable chair and flanked by some four dozen community members. Drumming, chanting, and singing proceeded for about ninety minutes in preparation not only for my hypnotic procedure but also for a healing ritual by RT himself.

When the drumming stopped, RT introduced me to the group and I walked to the center of the circle. I observed that William seemed somewhat apprehensive, probably in anticipation of being hypnotized. He also showed the effects of listening to the rhythmic sounds for an hour and a half; when I told him he might be more comfortable if he closed his eyes, William's eyelids dropped shut immediately. I suggested that he imagine what it felt like when he craved an alcoholic drink. He easily re-created the feeling and briefly discussed it with me. Then I asked William to transform those sensations into an image of some sort. He quickly told me that he had visualized a dreadful monster that was intent on destroying him.

I reminded William that there were some fifty people around the campfire who cared for him and were concerned for his well-being. I suggested that he imagine that they were giving him a gift that would help him to destroy the monster. Instantly William reported a mental image of an arrow. Remarking that the gift reflected his Native American heritage, I told William that he could use the arrow to kill his enemy. He imagined drawing a bow and shooting the arrow into the monster's heart. The beast collapsed, and William breathed a sigh of relief.

I led William through a brief relaxation exercise before I initiated the next step of the hypnosis session. Then I asked him what healthy beverages he enjoyed. He responded with a list of fruit juices and herbal teas, so I asked him to imagine drinking and enjoying one of them. After William reported imagining drinking a cup of herbal tea, I led him through an exercise that was a rehearsal for his future behavior. Whenever he desired alcohol he would change the craving into an image of the monster, shoot it with his bow and arrow, and (either in his imagination or in reality) drink some herbal tea or fruit juice. I told him that the more often he repeated this procedure, the more successful he would be in combating his yearning for alcohol.

I stepped back and joined the circle around the campfire, allowing RT to step forward. Resplendent in a white buckskin suit and a feather headdress, the medicine man asked the group if they had heard the hooting of an owl during my hypnosis session. Various members of the group nodded their heads in agreement, and RT commented that the owl was a symbol of death. Therefore, William was engaged in a life-or-death struggle with his nemesis, alcohol. Then RT asked if the group members had heard the owl hoot seven times. Again, several people nodded affirmatively. He commented that seven indicates good luck, especially for Native Americans. The owl, he said, is not only a symbol of death, it also can symbolize transformation, so William's chances of winning his struggle were quite favorable.

RT proceeded to poke William's skin with an eagle feather until he winced in discomfort. RT then cupped that particular area with his hands, sucked the skin to extract negative material from William's body, and then spit a mouthful of dark fluid into a pail. He explained that this was part of the three-week purification process and that the fluid would be taken away and buried.

Frankly, I did not recall an owl hooting, much less hearing seven hoots. However, I was concentrating on William's reactions to my suggestions, so I might have been oblivious to external sounds. Nevertheless, William appeared at the airport when I left Nevada. He had left work for a few minutes to say good-bye and to thank me for my help. He expressed his gratitude intensely, his eyes filled with tears. He left Meta Tantay the following year but kept in touch with the group. Two years later he had retained his sobriety.

I suspect that my hypnotic intervention had played a relatively minor role in William's apparent recovery. However, it might have catalyzed the purification work he and RT had done before my arrival, work that came to a climax with RT's dramatic campfire performance. And my suggestions might have provided William with a means to take an active role in attaining and maintaining his sobriety. I have observed more than one hundred shamans working with their patients, and most of them use techniques and procedures that enable the patients to become dynamic participants in what is going on, often giving them "homework assignments" so that they can continue to get well when the shaman is no longer present.

Sidian's Comments

I interviewed Larry Dossey, a well-known physician and author, after I had made a presentation in Dallas, Texas, in 2008 at the Society for Shamanic Practitioners. Dossey recalled:

During the early 1980s at the height of his popularity, Rolling Thunder was invited to give a talk at Unity of Dallas Church, which was just down the street from my office in the Medical City Dallas hospital. Although I was unable to go to his lecture that evening, I was told it was well attended and warmly received. Not everyone agreed. A reporter from the Dallas Morning News *published a critical account of his talk the next day. Although I did not read the write-up, I was told it was skeptical and cynical and implied that Rolling Thunder was a fraud.*

According to Rolling Thunder's volunteer escort, who was a friend of mine, the medicine man felt deeply embarrassed and hurt by the article. Rolling Thunder, he told me, called the reporter and told him he regretted that he harbored such negative impressions of him. In order to prove his genuineness, he told the reporter he would give him a sign later that day, one that would make clear why he was called Rolling Thunder and, he hoped, would change the reporter's mind.

A friend of mine, who worked in air traffic control at Love Field in Dallas, reported an extraordinary event that occurred that same afternoon while he was on duty. His comments were relayed to his wife, who worked in my medical office, and she related them to me. On this perfectly lovely, clear day, a violent storm suddenly materialized and hovered over the city. In all his years of watching weather patterns over this part of Texas, the traffic control officer said he had never seen anything quite like it—its sudden appearance out of nowhere, its violence, its dramatic thunder, lightning, and rain, and its static localization. And suddenly it was gone. He knew he had not witnessed a typical North Texas thunderstorm.

The fact that this report came from this particular person was in itself noteworthy, because he is one of the most precise, understated, reserved, and trustworthy individuals I know. I have never known him to exaggerate anything. The fact that he chose even to relate this event is evidence of its singular significance. In any case, I witnessed the storm myself and was stunned by its ferocity and sudden appearance and disappearance. I knew at the time that I had experienced something highly unusual.

After his conversation with the reporter earlier that day, Rolling Thunder told my friend, his escort, that he would "make the thunder roll" to indicate his authenticity. Perhaps he had done just that. Did it change the reporter's mind? I cannot say. Was it all a mere coincidence? You decide. But if I were a skeptic, I'd think twice before tangling with a genuine shaman.

An Interview with Everlight

One of my interviews that taught me a great deal about RT's approach to healing was with Everlight, a spiritual counselor.

Sidian Morning Star Jones: What did you learn from RT?

Everlight: I don't remember everything that I learned from him, because so much of it was informal. I learned a lot from him by observing, going with him on errands, and doing things with him like driving down the road. One time we were heading toward San Francisco. And all of a sudden he yelled, "Stop!" He had spotted some things he needed for medicines, and he wanted to collect them. He didn't miss a thing. In this particular case, there was a little bit of swamp in one area, and there were pussy willows and other green, growing things that other people would call weeds or wildflowers. So we pulled over to the side of the road, and we approached the special things that he wanted to gather in a very meditative way, with prayer and respect. And, in a very quiet way, he sprinkled the tobacco near the plants and told me, "We're letting them know, our brothers and sisters, that we need some of their medicines." He asked permission. He looked around like he was in mental communication with all the plants and everything around us. I was just picking up from him what was going on.

Sidian Morning Star Jones: It sounds as if you were taking in the experience.

Everlight: It was like osmosis. I would be able to get into his head and understand what he was doing, at least to a degree. Again and again he would be communicating in a silent way and with love. He would communicate from his heart. The Native American way is love. It's the heart energy. And he would talk about love a lot. So we would spread the tobacco, and then we would pick up some greens, and he would say, "You never take more than you can use. And remember that one medicine is always growing next to the opposite of that medicine. If you doctor someone with one medicine and you use too much of it, you can counterbalance it with another medicine." And he knew how to gather the different plants that would provide for the balancing of the other plant.

Sidian Morning Star Jones: It looks like you could have a big rainbow pie wheel. Each of the plants has its own segment. There are some that are opposite and some that are very similar.

Everlight: All plants are medicine from his viewpoint. But for certain sicknesses I saw him go back and forth, using trial and error. He learned how to deal with medicines by poisoning himself and finding the antidotes. RT told me that he almost killed himself a number of times doing that. And usually this was when he was looking for medicines for other people. So something that he may react to might be the right thing for someone else. But he had to find out himself what was too much and how to counterbalance it. And he learned by talking with the plants. He would ingest these medicines and then have to take the other medicines to bring himself back into balance. He was walking the razor's edge, literally. But that's how he made medicines. And he learned from the plants which ones would work in a certain way on each other. There was a balance. It wasn't so cut and dried as a wheel, with absolute opposites. It wasn't that way at all. It was getting to know the plants themselves. And also you had to take certain times of the year into account. Certain medicines would work during one season, and during other times they wouldn't work. This is how he would make his medicines and do "doctoring."

Sidian Morning Star Jones: It may be more like each kind of plant has its own personality.

Everlight: He saw these plants as his brothers and sisters. One day we gathered cattails, which are very poisonous. But if you use them in a certain way, as a poultice, they can be very powerful.

Sidian Morning Star Jones: What's a poultice?

Everlight: It's when you make a mushy kind of substance by smashing the plants and their juices and you place it on something. Not all of his medicines were ingested. When he did healings at the Association for Research and Enlightenment in Virginia Beach, I saw him chew stuff, and then he would put the mush on the wound. And he would often make the poultice with his own teeth. But some of it was too powerful, and he couldn't do it that way. So he had to do it the way the old alchemists used to do it. They used to pound it out without chewing it.

Sidian Morning Star Jones: Is there anything else you learned about the plants?

Everlight: So basically you don't take more than you need. You only take a certain amount, at most never more than half of what might be growing there. And you don't take it all from one spot. You walk around and take it from the whole group of plants that are in the area. And then you thank the plants after you have taken what you need. And one of the things RT used to do was to tell them, "One day my body will come back and nourish you. I'm your sister, I'm your brother. We're all one." It would be part of his prayer.

Sidian Morning Star Jones: How long did you know RT?

Everlight: I would say ten years.

Sidian Morning Star Jones: You were close to RT. Did you observe him at a time when his powers seemed to be declined?

Everlight: I could see those in moments, not just over a time period. I could see him decline when he was drinking.

Sidian Morning Star Jones: But I thought he outlawed alcohol at Meta Tantay.

Everlight: He was dead set in the camp about anybody bringing any alcohol into the camp, and nobody was allowed to bring drugs either. And when visitors came, the young men checked their cars for drugs or alcohol. But he said his own drinking was for medicinal purposes.

Sidian Morning Star Jones: Did you believe him?

Everlight: He had bottles of vodka at his house, and I challenged him on it. I was feisty. I used to challenge him on things and get away with it, because he always knew I spoke the truth. That's also why I was sometimes called the Owl Woman. Now, the Owl Woman is someone most people are afraid of, because they tell the truth. But I was given an owl feather by RT's family. They tried to give me an eagle feather, but I said, "No, that's not my feather." I was also given a medicine necklace that had been handmade by Buffalo Horse. He took the shells from one of his own medicine practices and put them into the necklace.

Sidian Morning Star Jones: Is there any special significance to the owl?

Everlight: The Owl Woman typically takes on the role of an owl for someone who is dying. And that's why most traditions are afraid of owls, because they think their presence means someone is dying. This is only partly true. The point is that the owl can see through the darkness, and people cannot hide secrets from the owl. The owl can see into your darkest corners. And if the owl speaks to you, you have to listen because it may be a life-or-death message. And you can't lie to the owl, because the owl can see through lies and can see through darkness. An Owl Woman can perceive the truth, and this is why RT would listen to me. This is the only reason he would listen to me, because he knew that when I spoke from that place, I was speaking the truth. But I was not always called the Owl Woman. I was sometimes called the Seer. But that was also scary for some of the people at the camp. And some of them called me the Witch. I'm not a witch, but witches can do a lot of good, so I didn't mind the name. Aside from being called the Owl Woman and being given the owl feather, which I still have, I hold the secrets of the family. I could look at all of them and know exactly what was going on. And that's why I was trusted. It's also why I was sometimes feared. A number of the times when I would go up there, it was because I was getting a message from Spotted Fawn that help was needed. RT never himself called on me; it was always through Spotted Fawn knowing that RT was unbalanced and they needed some help. And when I go someplace like that and they say, "She's coming, she's coming," everything in someone's heart that they don't especially feel proud of comes up, and they think, "Oh, she's going to see it." And a number of times I would arrive at the camp and everyone was apprehensive, because they knew I was there to sort out who was behind some of the problems. And the person who was really causing the problems had everybody riled up so that they all looked like they were guilty. They were all feeling guilty about something.

Sidian Morning Star Jones: Probably, they all played a tiny part, and some played a much bigger part, but they all were thinking, "Oh, shit. It's me!"

Everlight: That's exactly what went on. A number of times I would go up there and run into this wall of denial because everyone was doing their drama. And so I would have to take a couple of days until everyone settled down. And one by one, people would come to me and confess. And by process of elimination, everyone would settle back down again. Once your grandmother Spotted Fawn had been screwing around with a young guy who had come into camp. Yeah, she was feeling guilty about it because she hadn't gotten permission from RT to screw around with this young man. But this particular young man was actually the one who was causing the problems and was using her for his own purposes.

Sidian Morning Star Jones: You needed to get rid of him?

Everlight: We did. Let me start at the beginning of that story. I was in Redwood City, California, visiting my mother. I was sleeping on her roll-out couch, and all of a sudden I woke up from a sound sleep, and I heard screaming and yelling. And I could see flames, and I knew it was the camp. I thought, "Oh my God, the camp's on fire! Oh my Lord, they need help!" I heard screaming and yelling and saw fire. And so I called the gas station in Carlin, Nevada, and asked them to get the message to the post office, and I knew the post office would get the message to Spotted Fawn. Then she would know that I had gotten her message. And she called me back within a couple of hours. And she said, "How did you know?" I said, "You sent me a message." And when I described what I saw she said, "Yes, there have been fires breaking out, and everybody's fighting. RT is walking around with a shotgun. He's ready to shoot everybody. He is so unstable. He doesn't trust anybody. He knows something is terribly wrong, but he is so messed up himself at that moment, he can't see that he is contributing to the problem." And so when I got there it was the heaviest psychic attack on me that I had ever experienced. I had to work hard to keep balanced. And that night I had a dream about the psychic attack on me.

Sidian Morning Star Jones: And that was when Spotted Fawn was messing around with that one other guy?

Everlight: I didn't find that out until later when she came and confessed it. As I said, everyone came and confessed different things to me. This man had come into the camp to "learn medicine from RT," as he put it. But instead he had the intention of disrupting the camp and killing RT. And RT was picking it up, knowing that someone wanted to do him in. So he was walking around with a shotgun. And everybody was fighting. And when they weren't fighting, everybody was having sex with everybody. Everyone was just going nuts. It was just a mess when I got there. And on the night I arrived I dreamed about the forthcoming attack. But it was symbolic, an animal was biting my heel. RT and Spotted Fawn listened to me, because they knew that my dream was the key to finding out what was going on. My dream contained the symbol of an animal biting my heel, the universal Achilles heel. If the heel was wounded, the entire person would die. And that's how RT saw it as well. When an animal bites your heel, they are trying to find your weakness and knock you off. I was the one being targeted. The Seer was there. The young man was thinking, "I've gotta knock out the Seer." Again, the dream warned me to stay within the circle of the family and not try to fight the young man directly. That would have been fighting back from a place of my ego. But I knew not to get outraged that someone had the audacity to try to attack me.

Sidian Morning Star Jones: If you had fought back, he would have tried to overpower you even more.

Everlight: The young man tried all kinds of ego stuff on me. He said, "I hear you're powerful, I hear you're sexy. Oh yeah, do you want to have sex?" He was like doing the whole number. He seemed like a sweet, nice young man. But I could tell he was evil. And again, I knew most of the people there but not everybody there, so he was definitely on my list of suspects. I knew it wasn't a member of the family. And I could see that someone else was stirring everyone else up. That's the way it usually goes. There's a troublemaker. And by the process of elimination, it finally got down to the point where he was just plain annoying me. I pretty well narrowed it down to him. And I finally had a heavy confrontation with him. This is a process when you name a person with full intention and focus, and RT was good at this too. Basically you look right into them and tell them that you know who they are and you know what they're doing. You do this with such power and such intention that they crumble before you. It's an intention of confrontation, basically making a mirror and making them look at themselves. But it has to be done correctly.

Sidian Morning Star Jones: This can be difficult. You have to make sure that you are correct.

Everlight: But if it's right on, you make it simple. You don't say, "You did this, you did that." You just tell them that you know who they are and that you know what they're doing. This confrontation with me hit him as a physical force, because it was his garbage that went right back to him. And this turnaround is one of the other tools that RT used. You have them return to the source of their negativity, without emotion and without ego. You send the negative energy that someone is sending to you back to them. Again, it is like a breeze that passes through you, and then you send it back to them. Do you understand that principle?

Sidian Morning Star Jones: I do.

Everlight: I know you do. So I just told him, "I know who you are, and I know what you are doing." And he fell back. He was very angry. And he ran out of the camp, got in his car, and took off. That night he came back, started a fire again, and tried to burn down the house. But everyone was alert to him. And then he disappeared again, and we thought, "All right, he's gone." And everyone celebrated. There was great joy. The whole energy of the camp rose up. It was a marvelous feeling. Of course RT was happy. He didn't thank me; he just put his rifle away.

Sidian Morning Star Jones: It was kind of like, "Well, it's over."

Everlight: I didn't explain anything. I didn't have to. It worked out perfectly. And I rested for a day because I was exhausted. That visit was very intense. Very intense. And I was happy, and I was feeling good. It was just a good feeling of love and nourishment all around the camp. RT didn't have to say, "Thank you." I didn't need a thank you. I didn't need anything, because I did it for love, loving the whole family. And it was wonderful. And I'm driving along, and as I am driving back to the Bay Area, all of a sudden my back starts to burn.

Sidian Morning Star Jones: What was happening?

Everlight: I was smoking cigarettes at the time. Somehow the cigarette flew up and landed on my back. And it was itching and burning. I just kept on squirming in my seat. Finally I stopped and undid my bra. I reached back under my shirt and felt a welt. And I thought, "Oh shit! That son of a gun is going after me." I thought, "I can't take this energy back into my mom's house." So I stopped at a friend's house and told her I needed to meditate. I needed to be quiet. I needed to focus on what's attached to my back. And I showed her my back, and she said, "Oh my God! You have this huge welt on your back." I said, "What does it look like?" She said, "It looks like a paw." And I knew the paw would be right in back of my heart. And it was raised and red. I said, "I need to trace it back to where it is coming from." This is something I learned from RT. When someone is attacking you, you can trace it back to them. And you can turn it against them. And there can be changes in their body that occur so you know it was not just your wishes or your imagination.

Sidian Morning Star Jones: Otherwise you wouldn't be able to see it.

Everlight: Exactly. So you can trace back when something is attached to you and find out where it is coming from. Literally, you can go back to the source, especially when there is such a physical manifestation. And so I got into a quiet state and focused on what was going on. Basically it led back to this young man's cave. He went back to his cave after he left camp. And he was conjuring up a brew of stuff that was evil. It was some really nasty, evil stuff. And part of it was Wolf Medicine that he was using in a very negative way. RT and I would talk about using the Earth energies and the animal energies in a positive or negative way. They could be used both ways. And people working with the dark forces knew how to use it in a dark way. So I knew that this young man had some powers and was really pissed off at me. And so I basically took that energy and returned it to its source, because it was almost solid mass and it was manifesting in a solid way because there was so much energy in it. And the only thing I can describe that I saw happen to him in his cave was that he imploded, he blew apart from the inside. And all I know for sure is that he was never seen again by anyone.

Sidian Morning Star Jones: It reminds me of a martial arts technique in which someone would throw a punch at you and you use their own momentum to throw them into the ground.

Everlight: Right. RT was interested in Eastern spirituality. He believed in karma too. We talked about karma, cause and effect, and he understood that principle very well. He actually liked the Dalai Lama. He read things about the Dalai Lama, heard about the Dalai Lama, and later he actually met the Dalai Lama. And RT had a great affinity with the Dalai Lama and thought that he would have loved to have changed some of the old religious rituals but didn't have time because he had to leave Tibet. But the whole principle of detachment is the Buddhist way. And RT and I would talk about that as well. When you free yourself from attachments, you can use that energy for walking the Red Road, the path of service.

Opinions of Family Members

I also interviewed family members about RT's healing abilities, and I got some surprising responses. I have attached no names, because I encouraged them to speak frankly and anonymously.

First female voice: Wasn't RT away from home a lot?

First male voice: Once RT became famous he spent less time at home.

Second male voice: But he needed that time at home. He had to have that time when he was just human.

First male voice: You see, with RT, he liked that.

Second male voice: I went on some of those talks and tours with him. He definitely has talent.

First male voice: He could make people feel good, because they believed in his power. They thought they were healed, and they probably were healed. But if you don't believe in that person's ability to heal, then it doesn't work for you.

Sidian Morning Star Jones: It's kind of like a placebo.

Second male voice: But do you think that it was because he actually healed them, or was it because they believed it?

Sidian Morning Star Jones: I think they are both the same.

First male voice: What is a placebo, a type of medicine man?

Sidian Morning Star Jones: It's a treatment that doesn't work unless a person believes it will work.

First male voice: That sounds gross. I've never seen a placebo call down the rain.

Indian medicine can combine energy, power, spirit, relationships, balance, and walking the Good Red Road. Doug Boyd, in his book *Rolling Thunder,* recalls the day that Spotted Fawn gave Boyd a dozen herbal capsules when he had an attack of hay fever. Her instructions were to take three capsules each day. He followed the directions, and the hay fever never returned.

On the other hand, there is the well-known account of one of RT's spiritual warriors whose young son developed an ear infection. The spiritual warrior's friends in San Francisco urged him to see a physician, but he and his child's mother refused, placing their faith in RT's remedies. Unfortunately, their son became deaf, first in one ear and then in the other. The family left Meta Tantay in order to find work in a city on the East Coast, where their son could attend a school for the profoundly deaf. In this instance, RT's antipathy to Western medicine had unfortunate results.

Gary Sandman's Observations

During my interviews with Gary Sandman, he provided a firsthand report of RT's preparations of herbal remedies. Gary recalled:

I remember I helped him make an herbal concoction. RT had some great stuff for earaches and other health problems. He would say, "Put a handful in." And I would reply, "What's a handful?" And he would say, "Everyone knows what a handful is." His measuring was pretty subjective, and it was based on how he knew it had to be. But I hoped I didn't put in too much or too little. And RT said, "Don't worry so much. Just put it in there, I'll tell you if it's enough or not."

He was always laughing and joking with us, but sometimes he scared us because we didn't want to do the wrong thing. We really respected him and wanted to have him tell us what to do. We felt pretty honored to help out. And whenever we went out to pick herbs, he said, "You have to ask permission from the plants if it is okay to pick them." And we would walk over to a group of flowers, and he would say, "Now see the biggest flower? That's the king. That's the medicine man of the flowers. You never pick the biggest flower or the second biggest, because that is his wife. You speak to them, and you give them an offering." And I said, "But I don't have anything to give." And RT replied, "Do you have any money on you?" And I said, "Yes." And he directed, "Put fifty cents out there. This is a part of you that is of value. If you have tobacco, use tobacco, if you have coins, use coins. But always give an offering first."

In fact, there was one time when we were rushing because we were late, and we started picking before we said a prayer. But we couldn't break the branch, and nothing was going right. And RT said, "Whoa, wait a minute. You know what we need to do." Everybody stopped, and we said a prayer and made an offering, and then we would just go back and "click," the branch would break off in our hand. It was as if the tree was willing if we were willing to be respectful. Now, that happened in so many instances that I am not just making it up.

Another instance I remember was when RT was pointing out "horse tail" that looks like asparagus. He said, "Now, here is a very interesting herb, because the time you pick it determines how it acts. Depending on whether you pick it in the spring or the fall, it will either put calcium in your body or take calcium away. And you need to know when it was picked so that you're taking it at the right time of the year; otherwise you could be hurting yourself." RT knew that healing plants had to be picked in the right way, at the right time, and for the right purpose.

RT was fond of saying that there wasn't that much difference between medicine people and medical doctors, because the medicine of both comes from the same place, from the Creator. He would say, "Look at the medical doctor's symbol, a cross with two snakes wrapped around it. The snakes meant healing and wisdom." For RT, the snake is the most powerful of all creatures; for example, a certain amount of snake venom constricts the blood vessels and deadens pain.

And he knew the background story of the herbs he used. I remember him telling us, "Jerusalem artichokes didn't come from Jerusalem but from the country where the Cherokees originated." And he often reminded his audiences that willow bark contains molecules directly related to aspirin, or acetylsalicylic acid.

RT used all of his senses in making a diagnosis. He often said, "I see different colors in and around people and smell odors that come from them. I can see these things and know what's happening inside a person." He was often asked his opinion of meditation and healing. He responded, "We believe in meditation, but it must have a purpose. I like to see the bones coming together. I might see a big tumor inside a person just vanishing and going away. That is meditation in its highest form."

RT purified water by boiling it and placing a few fresh bay leaves in it. He added sassafras, which smells good and, in his opinion, thins the blood and is good for the heart. Instead of spraying insects, he would take a spoonful of apple cider vinegar two or three times a day and avoid sugar through the mosquito season. Mosquitoes would bother people who ate sugar but would leave him alone.

RT did not apologize for eating meat. "One mistake I see vegetarians make is they fail to recognize that, like the Mother Earth, plants have living bodies and are also living beings. A vegetarian diet might be all right for some people if they get enough protein." He continued, "Organic food might be a little more expensive, but it might be cheaper in the long run. You might want to organize your own cooperatives."

At the same time he had no patience with people who claimed to have Indian genes, assuming that this entitled them to claim that they were Native Americans. RT objected. "Many people are wannabe Indians. If you aren't Indian, don't go around claiming you are, because it will catch up with you someday."

Leslie Gray's Observations

Leslie Gray added her comments from the perspective of both a shaman and psychotherapist.

Sidian Morning Star Jones: What sort of interaction did you have with Rolling Thunder?

Leslie Gray: The first time I met him was at the Humanistic Psychology Institute, now known as Saybrook University. It was back in the early 1980s.

Sidian Morning Star Jones: And you were both giving a talk, is that right?

Leslie Gray: Well, I was invited to do a presentation with him and Ketowa, a Cherokee medicine man who worked almost exclusively with crystals.

Sidian Morning Star Jones: It's interesting you mentioned crystals, because this is the first time I've heard of a Native American using crystals for healing.

Leslie Gray: I gave a talk on the Native American use of crystals a number of years ago, and a magazine printed the first half of the talk, and then it went out of business. But crystals are very much a part of some Native American healing traditions. They might not have inert medical properties, but their beauty makes them a powerful placebo. The Cherokees use crystals frequently, but so do other tribes, especially in California. There are burial sites that have been found here in northern California of medicine people buried with hundreds of crystals around their bodies. I've seen crystals from ten thousand years ago that were excavated in California burial sites. Native Americans used more technology than most people suspect. In preparing medicine, sunlight may be guided through a crystal and onto the preparation to potentiate its power. Medicine Wheels are built at powerful sites that favor concentration and focusing.

Sidian Morning Star Jones: So the three of you were giving a presentation?

Leslie Gray: Yeah, the three of us were presenting papers. And one of the things I remember about RT is that there were still a lot of dreamy-eyed, long-haired, countercultural people around. I remember this tall, young, blond guy with a sweet face who stood up and said, "We've been having a real problem with ants over here."

Sidian Morning Star Jones: Ants?

Leslie Gray: This guy said, "What I'd really like to know is if any of you has an idea of how to get rid of them in a good way." And RT spoke right up, and he said, "Yes, I do. The first thing you do is you go to where the ants are, and you pray over them. And then if the ants don't go away you get a pot of honey, and you make a trail from the ants out all the way to where the anthill is and leave the honey pot there. If they still don't go away then you kill them, because they have become pests." That's so typical of RT to me!

Sidian Morning Star Jones: That is RT—to the T. He had a really good sense of humor.

Leslie Gray: Well, you know, he was a very flirtatious guy, to put it mildly, but he flirted with a sense of humor, which is why I think it wasn't offensive. He even flirted with me when he was in his seventies. We would talk over the phone because he was in Santa Cruz, and he'd flirt over the phone. I mean—he just was unstoppable! During one of our conversations, he told me that he was sitting in a bar with Spotted Fawn, and another Indian offered him twenty-five horses for his wife. RT paused, furrowed his brow, and said, "Let me think about it." He turned down the guy's offer, and after he had left, both RT and Spotted Fawn had a good laugh about it.

Sidian Morning Star Jones: When was the last time you saw my grandmother?

Leslie Gray: I went to Letterman Hospital when Spotted Fawn was there, as did a number of medicine people. They streamed in, you know, to do work with Spotted Fawn when she was dying. So I arrived with my rattle, and I was very somber when I entered the hospital, which was a military hospital. Right off the elevators were these guys, these big Indian guys with red T-shirts on, standing on either side of the elevator door. And there were others in the hall on the way to her room wearing these T-shirts that said "We Know How." I knew they must have been RT's spiritual warriors.

Sidian Morning Star Jones: A bit intimidating.

Leslie Gray: You could see that the hospital staff was not sure what this was about, not to mention, you know, the drumming and singing and rattling that was coming out of the room, but they just kind of walked a wide berth around the room. So I saw RT on the way there, but when I got there RT wasn't around. So I just started doing some singing and rattling with Spotted Fawn. I gave her some Nevada sage, which she said reminded her of her girlhood, and it was an incredibly sweet-smelling sage. In fact, I haven't had any sage like that since. So then I finished, and I was standing there when RT came in, and he looked at me, and he said, "Boy, have I got a buck for you!" I had no idea if he was serious, but I think he did that sort of semiseriously. I mean, if you took him up on it he might actually do it.

Sidian Morning Star Jones: What about his ecological views? Were you familiar with his work on the environment, saving the pinyon nut trees and that sort of thing?

Leslie Gray: I attended a number of talks where that was a central part of the presentation. There was one in particular where he kind of rambled around a bit, but he got deeper and deeper as he spoke, and the more he spoke the more he was saying, "Wake up, the Earth is in peril, we're not taking care of her." He conveyed a sense of urgency about caring for the Earth and about life having gotten out of balance. And he became absolutely eloquent.

Sidian Morning Star Jones: Was this sort of a new topic at the time?

Leslie Gray: Well, it's a perennial topic, but to try to reach the prevailing dominant culture with those ideas was rather new. Chief Joseph tried to sound the alert, but he never reached the number of people that RT did.

Sidian Morning Star Jones: Yeah, RT usually had the sense of humor that did not turn people off. I only ever got to meet him half a dozen times or so, and that was when I was young, but I remember him.

Leslie Gray: How do you remember him? I mean, what kind of feelings do you have when you remember him?

Sidian Morning Star Jones: I remember feeling a kind of natural reverence.

Leslie Gray: Oh?

Sidian Morning Star Jones: Yeah, he kind of scared me though too.

Leslie Gray: Oh, yeah. He was tall and very handsome.

Sidian Morning Star Jones: He had all this regalia, and it was a whole different scenario than any of the life that I'd ever lived. He carried around a medicine bag that probably contained roots, herbs, fungi, feathers, pieces of bone and fur, and who knows what else.

Leslie Gray: I think he provided hope to a number of people who might have well been lost souls.

13

Retrieving Lost Souls

As we noted in the previous chapter, in their book *Persuasion and Healing,* the psychiatrists Jerome Frank and Julia Frank observe that all effective healing practitioners resemble shamans in that they bolster their patients' sense of mastery and self-efficacy by providing them with a myth or conceptual scheme that explains symptoms and supplies a ritual or procedure for overcoming them. This myth bolsters faith in the healer and in the treatment, triggering the well-known placebo effect. Any number of potions, lotions, salves, and concoctions have helped people feel better because the power of suggestion is so strong.

Suggestibility in other animals indicates that it is an ancient primary adaptation for reducing social stress and promoting relaxation. Some farmers take delight in "hypnotizing" chickens, having them fixate their gaze on a bright object. Dogs can be conditioned to salivate when they hear a bell, if that bell had been rung previously when food was offered. Suggestibility and conditioning often work together to promote healing.

In humans, suggestibility became a biological capacity for the recovery from disease. Human rituals produced an intergroup cohesion through suggestibility that was experienced as a oneness or union, a classic aspect of spiritual, religious, and mystical experiences. Suggestibility also increased access to unconscious processes. The interplay between unconscious and conscious processes was aided not only by suggestibility and conditioning but also by dissociation, fantasy proneness, and thin cognitive boundaries. These capacities had evolutionary advantages, because they encouraged healing through the stimulation of the patient's inner resources. We have had to use technical psychological terms in laying the groundwork for this chapter, but they provide a basis for explaining why what RT called "doctoring" so often had positive results.

For suggestibility to work, a relationship with the medicine person or other healer needs to be established through an exchange of some sort. With RT it was the gift of Three Brothers tobacco. The result may be a healing ritual that sucks or blows the sickness away or treats it with herbs or other substances. But according to RT it is not simply the medicine person who does the healing; it is the Spirit within the medicine or the relationship with Nature that moves in a circle of balance between the sick person, the medicine person, the plants, and the powers of Nature. This is why RT would ask people to pray over their medicine before they took it.

Shamanic practices of recovering lost souls, calling on animal allies, and communing with spirits reflect an interaction of the spiritual and social worlds that can produce personal power. Claude Lévi-Strauss, the noted ethnologist, observed that animal species provide a universal system for creating meaning, particularly representations of various aspects of themselves placed into social settings. Animal allies assisted the shaman's self-development as their characteristics were incorporated into the shaman's self-identity. An animal's "essence" also was observed and integrated into a tribal member's behavioral repertoire, especially if one was a member of the Bear Clan, the Badger Clan, or another group of people known to emulate that particular animal.

Shamans engage spirits to provide means for personal transformation and positive change among their patients. Spirits provide protection against stress and anxiety through models for the management of emotions and the handling of stress and anxiety. Dramatic interactions provide vehicles for self-transformation as well as interaction with the shaman's social world. Both spirits and animal allies are natural symbols that shamans and medicine people can put to good use.

The word *totemism* refers to establishing a relationship between the natural domains of animals and social groups. Totemism is played out in the establishment of animal clans. The establishment of animal clans is a way of expressing and creating meaning through the use of animal categorization.

We might say that shamans, medicine men, and medicine women create a theater of the mind that aids their self-development. From an external perspective, this is a social theater that links an individual to the community in a way that promotes healing. It is important to remember, however, that what the Western world considers a symbol or metaphor might be considered actual reality by a Native person, a reality that we have called the "imaginal world."

Human evolution produced a fragmentation of consciousness due to the modular structure of the brain. But shamanic activities, such as drumming, dancing, and the use of psychoactive substances, served to integrate the modules of the brain, combining all of the shamans' inner capacities to solve the problems they were requested to solve. Without this integration, shamans would be at risk for developing many kinds of health problems such as obsessions, compulsions, anxieties, dissociations, repressions, and excessive desires, including sexual desire. With this integration the shaman is capable of problem solving, of empathy, and of providing security for individuals and for the community. The integration of nonverbal information into the language-mediated activities of the brain is one way in which this feeling of union and unity takes place.

Procedures used by shamanic healers vary but may include diet, exercise, herbs, relaxation, mental imagery, surgery, prayers, purifications, and various rituals. Specific treatment procedures depend on the diagnosis and the cultural traditions. In some communities serious illnesses are felt to be due to the loss of one's soul. Diagnosis will determine whether it has been stolen, has been "spooked" away from the body, or simply "strayed" during some other activity. Treatment will aim to recover the soul through "soul catching" or similar procedures.

Other common causes of soul loss in shamanic societies are the breach of a taboo, karma for past actions (even actions from a former lifetime), the intrusion of a toxic object into the body, or a jealous neighbor "casting the evil eye." In recent years many shamans have added the germ theory of disease to their etiological schema and may refer some patients to allopathic physicians if they exist in the community. Shamanism is basically an open-ended system that can be modified, altered, revised, or changed due to the demands of historical circumstances and community requirements.

Symbolic manipulation plays a major role in shamanic healing. The drum is the most frequent vehicle with which the shaman "rides" into the spirit world, but others include rattles and stringed instruments. The blowing of smoke toward the directions may represent an appeal to the guardians of the universe's various dimensions. For the shamans and their communities, any product of the imagination represents a form of reality. As a result, mental imagery and imagination play an important role in shamanic healing. But as noted earlier, something that starts out as a part of the shaman's "imagination" may turn in to something that is "imaginal," in other words, a part of a different reality, a space and time that coexists with ordinary reality.

Shamanic healing usually involves the patient's family and community. Rituals of transformation are often the essential link in introducing synergy to a healing community. By providing experiences of bonding, these rituals enable individuals to realize their communal responsibilities and sense their deep interconnectedness. Even when a patient must be isolated as part of the healing process, this drastic procedure impresses the community with the gravity of the ailment.

There are shamanic methods of healing that closely parallel contemporary behavior therapy, clinical hypnosis, family therapy, psychodrama, and dream interpretation. E. Fuller Torrey concluded that shamans and psychotherapists demonstrate more similarities than differences in regard to their healing practices. In both practices patients respond to reducing symptoms of distress, but the shamanic worldview is more expansive than that of the Western psychiatrist. Lévi-Strauss called "mind-body healing" the ultimate enigma of medicine; shamans made no such division between mind and body: they would not have been puzzled when they saw someone recover from sickness in response to a ritual, a chanting session, or a dream.

Stanley's Comments

In April 1973 I was still commuting from New York City to complete my teaching assignments at Sonoma State College in California. Jim Hickman was now working on his master's degree in the psychology department, and along with a mutual friend (and Sonoma State student), Floyd Fox, a naval veteran who had seen duty in the Vietnam War, we drove to Mickey Hart's ranch to speak with RT. He had come to the area for a well-needed vacation. He was still working as a brakeman for the railroads as well as doing "doctoring" on his days off. When RT arrived at the Novato ranch, he expected to enjoy Mickey and Jerilyn's hospitality and relax. But no sooner had he settled in, he received a phone call from a member of the Dead's road crew. A friend of his was in the hospital; Midge and her female companion, Jan, had been driving on one of San Francisco's curvy, narrow roads when the brakes failed as they were making a turn. Their car went off a cliff and landed far below, killing Jan instantly. Midge survived but was in a hospital, comatose. The phone call was from a friend of Midge's seeking RT's assistance, and so he requested a ride to the hospital, and within an hour he was at the bedside of Midge, the young woman who was in a coma.

As RT told the story, his diagnosis was one of soul loss. When someone suffers a physical or emotional trauma, a part of his or her soul (and sometimes the entire soul) becomes disconnected from the body. RT simply sat down near Midge's bed, closed his eyes, and projected himself to the site of the accident. In the shamanic literature this purported feat is often referred to as a soul flight. Metaphysical books frequently call it an astral journey. In the parapsychological literature it is referred to as an OBE, an out-of-body experience. RT had spoken of these experiences before, especially in connection with his reputed ability to transform himself into an eagle and fly in the sky, where he could commune with other eagles about what they had seen on their travels. In this instance he found the place where the car had landed and where Jan had been killed. Nearby was a large rock, and the soul of Midge appeared to be sitting on the rock.

RT spoke to Midge's soul, urging her to rejoin her body. But the "soul of Midge" was stubborn, and she replied, "I am waiting right here for Jan." RT retorted, "Your friend is with the Great Spirit. But your time to join her has not yet come. Let me bring you back to your body." Midge was adamant. And so RT called on his ally, the North Wind. The wind blew Midge's soul from the rock right into the hospital room. And within a few minutes, Midge opened her eyes. The nurses were very excited and called for a physician. The first act the physician took was to order RT out of the room. He muttered, "That old Indian simply went to sleep; he wasn't performing a ritual or doing anything useful." It is just as well that RT was sent from the room as this gave Midge an opportunity to tell her own story without RT being nearby to influence it.

When Midge had adjusted to her strange surroundings she told the physician and the nurses this story.

When I crawled out of the car, I saw Jan's soul beginning to float up into the sky. Jan said, "I will not be seeing you on this Earth again." But I wasn't going to give up so easily. I replied, "I am going to sit on this rock and wait for you to come back and rejoin your body." So I sat on that rock for the longest time, waiting for Jan to return. Then suddenly I felt a strong wind against my back. I tried to grasp the rock desperately, but the wind was too forceful for me. Finally I let go and felt myself zooming through the air. Then I realized that I was in a hospital bed.

If these two accounts are accurate renditions of what took place, there was an independent verification of RT's narrative. I had read similar accounts in the shamanic literature, but it was noteworthy to have a comparable experience related to me by an actual participant.

I also took advantage of this meeting to check out a story told to me by Dr. Irving Oyle, the osteopathic physician who had met RT in 1970. Oyle was so impressed with the meeting that he later asked RT if he would serve with me on the advisory board of a free clinic Oyle and some colleagues were creating in Bolinas, California. RT agreed, and Oyle contacted him by telephone for advice from time to time. However, sometimes more than advice was required. The free clinic attracted a number of young hippies and street people who had found their way to the California coast, only to fall ill with no way of paying a medical bill. The Bolinas clinic was run by donations and saved many lives of patients who were suffering from an infection or a disease that might have been fatal.

One memorable day an attractive young woman walked through the door of the clinic. The physician on duty, Jerry, started to do a routine examination only to have his patient curse at him using very inappropriate language. Ignoring the foul words as best he could, Jerry continued his examination, at which point his patient fainted and fell to the floor. Jerry immediately initiated artificial respiration, breathing into her mouth until she recovered. Finally, Jerry concluded that she had a low-grade infection, gave her a small bottle of antibiotic medication, and asked her to return the following day.

Jerry never saw this woman again, but a few local people remarked that they had seen her catch a ride to San Francisco, apparently recovered from her malady. At around the same time, Jerry's colleagues at the clinic noticed a strange change in Jerry's behavior. The easygoing, laid-back physician became very temperamental, swearing and cursing at anyone who irritated him in any way. His wife reported that he had become abusive at home; she took their children to her parents' home for a quick "vacation" and told Jerry she would not return until he settled down. Jerry ignored her threat and kept working at the clinic, even though his behavior was alienating patients and colleagues alike. One day, following an extremely long harangue of expletives from Jerry, Oyle jokingly remarked, "Where is Rolling Thunder now that we need him?" A few seconds later, RT walked through the door. He had needed some time off and had decided that the calm and beautiful ambience of Bolinas would be the perfect place to get some rest and relaxation.

No sooner had RT walked through the door, but Jerry lunged at him. RT, with one stroke of his fist, knocked Jerry out, even though the young physician was half his age. As Oyle and his colleagues watched, transfixed, RT then engaged in a strenuous fight with an unseen adversary. Sometimes RT was on top, sometimes his adversary was on top, and sometimes punches were exchanged. One of the nurses claimed to smell "fire and brimstone," even though she probably didn't know the actual smell of those alleged demonic signals. Finally RT stood up, brushed his hands together, and said, "Well, it was a tough fight, but I don't think you'll have any more trouble around here." Jerry regained awareness, albeit with a sore jaw, and asked what had happened. He said, "The last thing I remember was administering artificial respiration to a young hippie girl who had passed out." I was told this story by Oyle and, separately, by one of Jerry's other colleagues. When RT told me his version of the story it was basically the same, except that he said he had encountered an intruding spirit that he described as an adversary that was a "low spirit who needed to return to the spirit world to get some more education before he mingled with humans again."

In both of these instances RT showed up at just the right time to be of help. How did this happen? Perhaps RT gave the wisest answer when he was asked why Mad Bear Anderson seemed to come out of nowhere when there was a crisis demanding his services: "Sometimes we'll know where Mad Bear is, and sometimes we won't. Yet he can be reached. Medicine people reach each other in spiritual ways, in ways where there are no days or miles." RT commented on his fortuitous appearance at these critical junctures by saying, "I guess this was a case of me being where I was needed."

I have discovered during my contact with shamans and medicine people from many other Native American spiritual traditions that a malevolent spirit is often described as immature or stupid. The remedy is not to consign that entity to hell or Hades but to "send it into the light" or to another place where some recycling and consciousness raising can take place. For RT, "Evil spirits are those who have passed on and didn't have a good life on this Earth. They are caught between this world and the world where they belong."

Sidian's Comments

Many traditionally oriented Christians have posted messages on my OpenSouceReligion website (www.OpenSourceReligion.net) saying that people who behave badly are often possessed by the devil or by evil spirits, and in these cases, a priest or minister needs to come to their rescue and send the devils back to Hell. This is done with an exorcism. With RT's technique he "exorcises" the harmful entity but sends it back to the spirit world for recycling. The intention is for these entities to get educated and grow up. This emphasis on rehabilitation seems to be a more positive attitude than sending an entity, real or imagined, to a place where it will be tormented for eternity. It is like sending juvenile offenders to jail with hardened criminals. They will not get rehabilitated; they will just get worse. They will learn more about crime than they ever knew and be much more dangerous when they are back on the streets.

Leslie Gray once treated a patient who insisted that RT had stolen his soul. In another interview that I did with Gray she recollected the following story.

Leslie Gray: In about 1982, I had a patient referred to me by a psychiatrist. The psychiatrist had been working with this man for about a year and not getting anywhere, and so he called me up and asked me if he could refer this guy to me. And the psychiatrist said, "The reason I can't get anywhere with this guy is that every time I tried to work with him on some problem that he had, he insisted that Rolling Thunder had put a curse on him and had stolen his soul.

Sidian Morning Star Jones: I don't think I've ever heard anything like this story.

Leslie Gray: This psychiatrist sent him to me, and the purpose of the referral was for me to remove the curse so that this guy could then go back and work with the psychiatrist.

Sidian Morning Star Jones: Right.

Leslie Gray: The first thing I said to the psychiatrist was, "Rolling Thunder doesn't put curses on people!" He replied, "Well, this is what this guy thinks. He was up in Carlin, Nevada, and he claimed Rolling Thunder put a curse on him, and ever since then he's been in a downward tailspin psychologically." And I said, "Well, you know, maybe Rolling Thunder said something to him that he interpreted as a curse because he's hypersensitive, but there's no way Rolling Thunder goes around cursing people and stealing their souls." The psychiatrist said, "Yeah, what you say is probably true. I don't know Rolling Thunder, but do you think you could remove the curse?" I said, "Okay, send him over." So I'm sitting there, warming up my curse removal, and in comes this guy. I'm listening, and he's going on and on about Rolling Thunder as if he were this evil person, and so I said to him, "I'm going to ask you to make a choice. What do you think is more important, removing this curse, or making you so strong that you're not vulnerable to curses? I could remove this curse, but you could go out and someone else could put another one on you just like that!" Nobody had ever asked him that question.

Sidian Morning Star Jones: I'll bet it took him by surprise.

Leslie Gray: It kind of short-circuited him.

Sidian Morning Star Jones: So then he didn't know what to do?

Leslie Gray: Right. He had to admit that what I had described was an even worse possibility than the one he was experiencing.

Sidian Morning Star Jones: He probably imagined that he would be vulnerable to losing his soul for the rest of his life.

Leslie Gray: So I forced him to choose. And he said, "I guess if you make me invulnerable to curses then I won't be suffering like this, and Rolling Thunder won't have this impact on me anymore."

And I said, "Yeah, you should be careful because you only had one curse from Rolling Thunder. Suppose he had put two or three on you." So what I did was to conduct a ritual that put this guy into an altered state of consciousness that made him powerful. I suggested actions he could take that would build up his power so that he would not be vulnerable to curses. And then I sent him back to the psychiatrist.

Sidian Morning Star Jones: Did you ever hear anything about him since then?

Leslie Gray: I did hear that he came back with energy and willingness to work on his issues. You have to work in therapy, you know. You can't just sit there playing a victim role. He was saying, "I can't do anything because Rolling Thunder put a curse on me."

Sidian Morning Star Jones: If you think that you can't do anything, then you won't do anything.

Leslie Gray: Exactly. If you think that you can't change, then you won't change. But when this guy went back to his psychiatrist he was in better spirits with a willingness to work. And before too long he got better, and the psychiatrist was able to discharge him.

14

Rolling Thunder in Germany and Austria

In *An Encyclopedia of Shamanism,* Christina Pratt notes that shamanism is not an institutionalized religion. We agree, because shamanism predated organized religion. We define shamans as socially sanctioned, spiritual practitioners who claim to deliberately and voluntarily alter their awareness so as to access knowledge and power from nonordinary reality. This nonordinary reality is what we have previously called the imaginal world, sort of a parallel universe that shamans (and some medicine people) know how to enter. They use this knowledge and power to help and to heal members of their community as well as the community as a whole.

From a psychological perspective, these practitioners constrict, expand, and/or alter their awareness in order to access information not ordinarily available to members of the social group who sanction their practice. This is the community whose physiological, psychological, and spiritual conditions shamans attempt to reinforce or ameliorate.

From our perspective, shamans appear to have been humankind's first psychotherapists, first physicians, first magicians, first performing artists, first storytellers, and first weather forecasters. They were originally active in hunter-gatherer and fishing tribes, and they still exist there in their most unadulterated form; however, shamanic and shamanistic practitioners also exist in nomadic-pastoral, horticultural, agricultural, and even urban societies today.

223

As we noted earlier, the word *shaman* is a social construct that originated in Siberia and was later applied to a diverse range of practitioners in many parts of the world. Some scholars doubt that the term should be used cross-culturally, because it is a European concept. The anthropologist Michael Winkelman has rejected this assertion, emphasizing the cross-cultural studies and evolutionary models that demonstrate the ubiquity of shamanism.

Historical Perspectives

Winkelman's seminal cross-cultural study of forty-seven societies focused on various types of magical-religious practitioners. These individuals occupy a socially recognized role that has as its basis an interaction with the nonordinary, nonconsensual dimensions of existence. This interaction involves special knowledge of purported spiritual entities and how to relate to them, as well as special powers that allow the practitioners to influence the course of Nature or human affairs in ways not ordinarily possible. Winkelman classified each type of practitioner separately on such characteristics as the type of magical or religious activities performed, the techniques employed, the procedures used to alter the practitioner's awareness, and the practitioner's mythological worldview, psychological characteristics, perceived power, socioeconomic status, and political role. Statistical analysis provided a division of four groups.

1. The shaman complex (shamans, shaman-healers, and healers)
2. Priests and priestesses
3. Diviners, seers, and mediums
4. Malevolent practitioners (witches and sorcerers)

The shaman appears most often in hunter-gatherer and fishing societies. The introduction of horticulture and agriculture was accompanied by the emergence of the priest or priestess. However, the roles of shamans and priests are quite different. Shamanic oral traditions differ from the sacred scriptures usually maintained by an organized religion and its priesthood. Religious doctrines tend to be rigid and dogmatic, but shamanic traditions remain flexible and adaptive, with each situation seen as unique. Political differentiation of a society led to a further division of labor into that of healers, mediums, and malevolent practitioners. Any given society may have one or more magical-religious practitioners. Among the African !Kung, for example, the majority of the men as well as a sizable minority of the women are magical-religious practitioners.

Using Winkelman's terminology, the shaman-healer specializes in healing practices, while the healer typically works without the dramatic alterations of awareness that characterize the shaman and, to a lesser extent, the shaman-healer. Diviners, seers, and mediums claim to incorporate spirits, after which they act on a patient's request to heal or to prophesy. These practitioners typically report that they are conduits for the spirits' power and claim not to exercise personal volition once they incorporate or are possessed by the spirits. Shamans, on the other hand, frequently interact with the spirits and sometimes incorporate them but remain in control of the process, only suspending volition temporarily.

For example, volition is surrendered during some Native American ritual dances when there is an intense stimulation. Nevertheless, the shamans purportedly know how to enter and exit this type of intense experience. Malevolent practitioners are thought to have control over some of the lower spirits as well as access to power through rituals. Typically these sorcerers do not see their mission as empowering society as a whole (as do shamans). Rather, they are employed by members of their community to bring harm to enemies (inside or outside the community) or to seek favor from the spirits for specific individuals through sorcery, witchcraft, hexes, and spells.

The more complex a society, the more likely it is to have representatives of each type of practitioner, except for the prototypical shaman. It should be kept in mind, of course, that categories are never absolute; some practitioners are difficult to classify, and others switch roles according to the occasion. Furthermore, in some societies, for example, the Diné, Lakota, and Yanomami, the boundary between sorcerers and shamans is quite thin. Many writers use the word *shamanic* to refer to practitioners and practices that clearly fall within the domain of the shaman or the shaman-healer. They use the word *shamanistic* to refer to practitioners and practices that are related to the shamanic realm but which are basically adaptations of it because one or more of the critical criteria is absent (for example, community sanction, voluntary control of shifts in attentional states). RT would probably be classified as a shamanic healer under this system.

Stanley's Comments

The growing interest in shamanism prompted a group of German entrepreneurs to organize a conference on the topic at a beautiful retreat center near Alpbach, Austria, in 1980. Participants flew into Munich and were driven to the site of the conference. Several of my friends were featured speakers. They included Albert Hofmann, who discovered LSD; Michael Harner, an anthropologist who had done considerable field research with the Jivaro tribe of South America; and his wife, Sandra Harner, who, with him, had created a training program in shamanic counseling.

Another friend, don Jose Rios, was a Huichol shaman based in eastern Mexico. To obtain a visa for travel to Austria, he needed a passport, and to obtain a passport, he needed a birth certificate. However, he had been born in the late 1800s, when birth certificates were not required for Native people. One of his students, a young American named Brant Secunda, came from a family who had legal connections, and within a few weeks, with Secunda's assistance, they had obtained a visa for don Jose from the Austrian government, and the elderly shaman took his first trans-Atlantic trip. When we picked him up in Munich, don Jose was surprisingly spry and vivacious. We queried, "Don Jose, you have just crossed the Atlantic Ocean after a grueling trip from Mexico. How did you come through that ordeal in such good shape?" Don Jose smiled and confided, "I ate a few buds of peyote before I boarded the airplane, and I've been flying ever since."

We introduced don Jose to Rolling Thunder at dinner that night. In the meantime, the program committee had decided that RT would design the opening ceremony, as he was the best known of all the shamans assembled from Asia, Europe, and the Americas. But RT would not hear of it. He responded, "Don Jose is my elder; he must open the program." The two of them had only met a few hours earlier, but RT's comment demonstrated the respect for seniority that crossed cultural lines. The next morning don Jose and Secunda spread a large blanket, or *mesa,* on the stage of the conference center. The purpose of the ceremony was to "raise" the mesa (symbolically) to create a community of participants. Each of us was asked to place a personal item on the blanket, one of some special significance.

After this was done, Secunda began beating his drum, and don Jose began to chant. I could hear don Jose telling Secunda, "Something is wrong; the mesa is not moving." I was sitting near RT, who asked me what was going on, and I told him that the blanket was not rising as expected. RT casually replied, "Of course it is not moving; many people have placed weapons or money on it." In the meantime, Secunda kept drumming and don Jose kept chanting until sweat covered their faces and arms. Finally, don Jose noticed a bit of movement and announced that the mesa had risen and that community had been established.

A week later RT and I were giving a joint workshop in Cologne, West Germany, sponsored by Jürgen Kremer, a German psychologist and psychotherapist. RT began the workshop by laying a blanket on the floor and asked people to put a personal possession on it—but not to use money, knives, or other weapons. RT's spiritual warriors, who had accompanied him to Europe, beat furiously on their drums while RT chanted. Within minutes he claimed that the blanket was "elevated" to a sufficient degree to ensure that the community had congealed. The workshop lasted more than a weekend and was well attended. I used several exercises demonstrating how people wittingly or unwittingly construct their own personal myths, the narratives that shape their lives. The exercises employed an "inner shaman" who helped them find a power animal and, after a search of the immediate vicinity, a temporary power object.

RT used his time to great advantage, outlining the principles of Native American medicine, at least a version that reflected his own heritage. Later, he told me that everything I said was in accord with his teachings and that the exercises were capable of "helping a lot of people." It was one of the most important compliments I had ever received following one of my workshops.

The workshop had been preceded by a press conference in Cologne. As RT walked into the press conference, a woman brought her baby to him. His hand had been caught in a door, and the infant was in extreme pain. Kremer recalls RT simply placing his own hand on the baby's hand. The baby immediately stopped crying and remained silent during the remainder of the conference. RT had undergone many of these inquiries before and handled the journalists with aplomb, again emphasizing the importance of honoring Mother Earth. As usual, he recalled the old prophecies foretelling dire consequences if human beings continued their rampage of destruction, deforestation, and pollution.

Once again RT was accompanied by several spiritual warriors who were on constant guard to protect RT. Sometimes they gave the journalists a difficult time if the questions were too complicated. RT, however, was very gracious and treated the journalists with dignity and respect. But RT wanted to be sure that he would not be taken advantage of, and his crew of young spiritual warriors worked diligently on his behalf. They also supplied him with his daily ration of garlic, which he insisted was the healthiest of all herbs, and they cooked his favorite foods. Not being professional chefs, they left a messy kitchen behind them, filled with blackened pots and pans that were burned beyond repair. However, RT congratulated them on their good work, and they returned to Nevada with unforgettable memories of the trip.

One memory was the good-bye dinner party that Kremer organized for the group. RT frequently insisted that he could never get enough garlic and that most restaurants were very stingy when they used that life-sustaining herb in their dishes. Kremer made reservations at one of

Cologne's best hotels and told the chef to put garlic on every piece of meat, every slice of tomato, and every serving of salad. The chef complied. RT and his group were in tears, and they were not tears of joy. They were tears induced by the overdose of garlic, and for once RT could not finish the dinner because his taste buds were inundated.

The last event in this European adventure was a lecture RT was scheduled to give at a town hall in Cologne. More than one thousand people were in the audience; some of them had traveled hundreds of kilometers to listen to the teachings of the famous Native American medicine man. In introducing RT, I noted that another well-known American, President Ronald Reagan, had spoken in West Germany just a few days earlier. I asked the crowd to compare the two worldviews and judge for themselves which was likely to bring about international cooperation and world peace. RT, of course, won hands down. The crowd was enthusiastic, and the lecture hall was filled to overflowing. It was one of RT's most successful trips.

RT could not resist making a comment about the current U.S. government. James Watt was Ronald Reagan's secretary of the interior. According to RT, "He insulted the Indian people. He dwelt on the fact that there is much more alcoholism, drug abuse, and other bad things among our Indian people. You find the same thing among a conquered people anywhere when they have nothing else to do and no hope for the future, where everything, including most of their land, was stolen from them."

RT also could not resist interjecting a piece of German history into his lecture.

The people who broke other people on racks during the Inquisition and burned people at the stake said they were Christians. Anyone could be a witch, women especially. Once they were denounced, they'd usually confess, especially once they'd pull out their fingernails or started to burn them. In one place in Germany there were only two women left in town when they got through burning the witches. The first Pilgrims were real bad; they burned witches on Sundays, whipped people for kissing on Sunday, put people in stocks, and bad things started to happen over here.

For RT, renunciation was not a necessity for spiritual development. He believed that renunciants are being false to themselves and to Mother Nature. His focus was expanding the senses, not withdrawing from the senses. He ended his comments on religion by stating, "I'm not a Christian, but I have more respect for their own great teacher than they have."

Sidian's Comments

One of the people I interviewed was Peter Meech, an author and screenwriter who was at the Alpbach, Austria, conference. He told me:

A group photo of the guest speakers was being organized in one of the large conference rooms. I was in the room at the time and noticed a scowl on RT's face. I could tell that he didn't like the way the photographer was ordering him around. After the group photo was over, I asked RT if I could take his photo with my camera, and he didn't answer. I asked him a second time, and he still didn't answer. He was still in a bad mood. So I took a few shots and forgot about the incident. A week later when I had the film processed, I discovered that none of the pictures had come out. That's when I reflected on what RT had said in his opening remarks to the conference participants. He said it was always important to get permission from a medicine man before you took his picture or recorded his voice. He spoke about the time he was at a news station and someone had turned a camera on him without first asking his permission. Moments later, he said, all the electrical equipment in the station ceased to work. His image and his voice were never recorded.

During mealtime RT would always sit with his braves at a long table. There were no women in his entourage. To ameliorate this situation, one night he had one of his braves ask a gorgeous Filipino healer if she would like to join them for dinner. She turned down the invitation, citing her poor English as an excuse. Later she told me that the reason for her refusal was that she could tell by the way RT looked at her that he wanted to have some romance. The fact that they were both married did not seem to be an issue for him.

Peter's story is one of several I was told about RT's romantic predilections. When my grandfather was not preoccupied with flirting, I think he would have agreed with what Albert Einstein once wrote: "The most beautiful thing we can experience is the mysterious. It is the source of all true art and all science. He to whom this emotion is a stranger, who can no longer pause to wonder and stand rapt in awe, is as good as dead: his eyes are closed." Einstein's comments certainly apply to shamanism, a composite of spiritual practices and rituals found worldwide. In their book *Shamans through Time,* the anthropologists Jeremy Narby and Francis Huxley concluded, "Even after five hundred years of reports on shamanism, its core remains a mystery. One thing that has changed, however, is the gaze of the observers. It has opened up. And understanding is starting to flower." In my opinion, RT was one of those people who planted the seeds that facilitated this growth.

Much of the mystery surrounding shamanism is perhaps attributable to the fact that it emerged during a time of preliteracy, and, therefore, little is known about its origins. Although the term *shaman* is of uncertain derivation, it is often traced to the language of the Tungus reindeer herders of Siberia, where the word *šaman* translates into "one who is excited, moved, or raised." An alternative translation for the Tungus word is "inner heat," and an alternative etymologic derivation is the Sanskrit word *saman,* or "song singer." Each of these terms applies to the activities of shamans, past and present, because they enter what is often described as an ecstatic state in order to engage in spiritual rituals and psychological practices for the benefit of their community. RT once said that his traditional name had two meanings. One was "speaking the truth," and the other was "singing to the gods." Both of these meanings fit into one or more of the derivations of the term *shaman.*

As we know, my grandfather never called himself a shaman. He would sometimes say, "Some people call me a shaman, but I don't know about that." This modesty contrasts with charlatans who advertise their "shamanic services" in popular magazines and offer weekend courses on shamanism to people who hope to become part of this select group. Some naive people do not realize that shamanism involves challenges from dangerous entities. There are frequent confrontations with malevolent entities that refuse to leave the mind and body of a person who has become possessed. There are also temptations that seduce anyone who achieves fame or notoriety. RT had great success in banishing negative entities from a sick person's energy field. However, he had a mixed record when it came to refraining from the sensual enticements that tempted him.

The adaptive character of shamanism is confirmed by its appearance around the world, even though the cultural diversity is obvious to anyone who makes a serious study of the topic. Shamans are labeled differently in different cultures, and their roles have evolved in tandem with the needs of those cultures. The ethnologist and philosopher Mircea Eliade provided a list of what he considered universal functions of shamans, but the anthropologist Ruth-Inge Heinze found many exceptions. For example, she worked with shamans who did not claim to control animals, who did not have immunity to fire, and who did not claim to have had experienced "dismemberment" or to have had a near-fatal illness that constituted a shamanic call. Eliade placed all of these traits and experiences on his list of "shamanic universals."

Heinze did find a universal response to community needs among the shamans she interviewed, and this need often required mediation between the living and the dead, between the sacred and the profane, between the Upper World and the Lower World, and even between a shaman's own masculine and feminine attributes. Wearing clothes of the opposite gender is a common practice in many shamanic traditions, a custom that alarmed European visitors to Siberia and the Americas because it violated their habitual gender boundaries.

As noted in chapter 5, shamans often play the role of tricksters who violate societal conventions in order to challenge a person, a family, or a community for a variety of reasons, providing a way for the participants to conceptualize problems in novel ways. It is noteworthy that shamanism is currently attracting increasing interest as an adjunctive therapeutic technique in the disciplines of psychotherapy and medicine.

Furthermore, many contemporary investigators propose that shamanism has emerged worldwide and has survived because it involves adaptive potentials derived from the structure of the brain and consciousness. This is a departure from the earlier dismissal of shamanism as a condition characterized by psychopathology, charlatanism, or both. In contrast, the Society for the Anthropology of Consciousness is a group of professors who are convinced that attention must be paid to shamanism because it is worthy of academic study.

For professors and students to grasp the nature of shamanic phenomena, there are useful research strategies, many of them pioneered by anthropologists and ethnologists, but some developed more recently by psychologists and neuroscientists. Phenomena such as shamanic imagery, shamanic journeying, shamanic incorporation, shamanic healing, and so on can be described in ways more understandable from an academic perspective. However, these attempts must not reduce the power and utility of these phenomena; they are merely recasting them. The anthropologist Barbara Tedlock, in the seminar I attended with her, kept emphasizing that shamanism needs to be studied from an inside perspective, not from the outside. Shamans need to tell their own stories or find writers who are acute listeners and will help them do so.

Although so-called neoshamanism or new shamanism is becoming increasingly popular in the West, indigenous shamans are endangered. It is crucial to learn what shamanism has to offer the social and behavioral sciences before archival research in libraries replaces field research as the best available method for investigating these remarkable men and women. Neoshamans are usually well-meaning people who have picked up some shamanic techniques and often have taken courses with practicing shamans. However, they can be utterly clueless when faced with a terrifying spirit who threatens the life of their patient and that of the neoshaman as well. A well-trained shaman has undergone ordeals and tests that prepare him or her to cope with unexpected emergencies and intrusive spirits. If a neoshaman is able to rise to those tasks, the patient is in good hands. If not, the results might be catastrophic.

Shamanic epistemology, or ways of knowing, depended on the

shamans' ability to deliberately alter their awareness or heighten their perception to contact spiritual entities in the Upper World and the Lower World, as well as in Middle Earth. For the shaman the totality of inner and outer reality is fundamentally an immense signal system, and the shaman's entry into what have been called shamanic states of consciousness was the first step toward deciphering this signal system. Members of the species known as *Homo sapiens* were probably unique among early humans in the ability to symbolize, to mythologize, and, eventually, to shamanize. This species' eventual domination may have been due to its members' ability to enter the imaginal world and use what they found as a bridge to produce narratives that facilitated human survival. Shamanic technologies, essential for the dramatic production and ritual performance of myths and other narratives, interacted with shamanic epistemology, reinforcing its basic assumptions about reality.

The stories and images that shamans bring back from the imaginal world are not mere hallucinations. They describe a world that is just as real for the shamans as the ordinary world is for the community they serve. Sometimes a community member will glimpse the imaginal world in a dream, in a vision, or in a state of awareness induced by peyote, dancing, chanting, or drumming. However, the shaman is able to enter the imaginal world at will, whenever the occasion demands it.

Carl Jung was the first major psychotherapist to take the imaginal world seriously. He wrote about archetypes, symbolic images that occurred in his patients' dreams. These images differed from ordinary dream images because they had a numinous, universal quality about them. Understanding and appreciating them could be life transforming, and Jung often sent his patients to libraries to study such archetypal images as the Great Earth Mother, the Wise Old Man, and the Magical Child. Jung also asked them to discover their Shadow archetype, that element of their psyche that they had avoided, shunned, or disparaged, even though there was something of value that could be learned from it. Jung wrote that everyone has "something of the criminal, the genius, and the saint." He found that his patients' psyches contained "pretty well everything that moves upon the checkerboard of the world, the good and the bad, the fair and the foul." Making contact with these archetypes often unlocked the blocked energy that was needed to solve a personal problem and move them on to a deeper level of integration.

Rolling Thunder often described the tests and challenges that faced people who, in his words, were "training for the medicine." In one of them the person being tested goes alone to a sacred place without a weapon of any kind, only with an eagle feather. The person being tested must spend the night in that place, facing his or her fears. And everything most feared will come and will try to frighten the person so badly that he or she will give up the training. But to pass the test one only needs to sit quietly, holding the eagle feather, no matter what is seen or heard or felt or touched. To Jungian psychotherapists this description would characterize patients who are discovering their Shadow, facing it, and understanding what it has to teach them. This is not a simple task; one can come near to death during the night, and a few may not survive.

I've always had an affinity with dark imagery, movies, and art. These days I understand that I was confronting my psychological shadow. Although I've had no interest in becoming a shaman, it's taken a great deal of practice throughout my life to "ride the beast," as I called it, who these days is little more than a tamed wolf.

15

Meta Tantay

A central aspect of shamanism is community service. Ritual serves a biological need for human communication that evolved to provide attachment bonds between infants and those who nurture and protect them. Humanity's evolutionary ancestry produced a neuropsychological desire for a social world, a need for a shared emotional life that is wired into the human nervous system. Shamanic ritual provided a group identity and a social support system, both of which could be called on when healing was required.

Native Americans had the experience of being a part of the universe, an integral part of the cosmos in which the lines between past, present, and future were dissolved. The modern individual's urge to restore this lost unity is an essential factor in such human activities as meditation, prayer, nature walks, and—for some people—sexual union.

There are Native American medicine women as well as Native American medicine men. Jasmine Hisha is a Cherokee medicine woman who counseled a non-Native woman by the name of Mare Cromwell in 1996. Cromwell found the interaction very helpful and wrote about it in some detail in her book *If I Gave You God's Phone Number,* published in 2002.

Mare Cromwell: If I gave you God's phone number, what would you do with it?

Jasmine Hisha: I would tell you that I already have it. And I use it every day. I talk to God about whatever is on my mind. And he talks back to me. That is what makes it fun, because he mostly laughs. He finds me humorous because sometimes I think I am important. But anybody can talk with God.

Mare Cromwell: Have you always talked to God?

Jasmine Hisha: My grandmother taught me how to do this. I call it "connecting." I connect when I wake up and before I go to bed. In the morning I go out and call, "Hey ho. Thank you that I am breathing air another day." Earth Mother speaks with me also. Her voice is very different from God's. It is very melodious. She gives me good wisdom whenever I ask for it.

Mare Cromwell: So you can talk with God and Earth Mother any time of the day?

Jasmine Hisha: Yes, my conversations really don't end. The Creator and the Earth Mother's messages are very clear to me because I've developed a relationship with them. People in mainstream society are not taught that they can have a relationship with God. They think they have to go to someone to intercede for them. That is not the truth. That has never been the truth. We can all communicate directly. I don't just talk with the Creator and the Earth Mother. I talk to all the trees. I talk to the brook. I talk with the swan family in the spring. I like talking with the Canada geese because they see so much from year to year because of the amount of land they fly over. We have really great conversations.

Mare Cromwell: How do you start talking with God?

Jasmine Hisha: It is always best that when you talk with God you call it by whatever name you are comfortable with. It could be God, Universal Creator, Allah, Brahman, whatever. Then claim a relationship. You are a daughter or a son. And then give the one thing in the Universe that does not automatically belong to the Creative

Force. That is your love. And people can learn to do this directly. They do not need to be in an organized religion to do it.

Mare Cromwell: It sounds as if you are rather judgmental of organized religion.

Jasmine Hisha: I have promised my true parents, the Creative Force of the universe and Earth Mother, that I would not become aligned with a religion, that I would stay free of the dogma. Take some of the Christian dogma. They would have us believe that homosexuality is wrong. But that's their personal opinion. The universe doesn't care who we sleep with. The universe loves it when people love. What are you sending into the universe? If it is love, that is great! Native people have no problem with homosexuality. When two people love each other, that is just fine. And when the Christians pulled fidelity on us, we didn't understand. We believe that if a woman loved a man and he loved her, they could bond and have children. But it was not necessarily a lifelong commitment. Why should it be? People change and love other people. The Creative Force loves us. And the Creative Force is actually thrilled when we turn to it and give it our love so it is able to move its way into our lives.

Walter Williams, an anthropologist, devoted an entire book, *The Spirit and the Flesh: Sexual Diversity in American Indian Culture,* to the topic of sexual diversity. Williams notes how this acceptance of diversity was condemned by the Europeans, with their rigid notions of uniformity of sexual behavior that applied to all people, regardless of their natural inclinations. Most American Indian cultures took what the Europeans considered negative and made it positive; many shamans engaged in homosexual or bisexual behavior, while others wore clothing favored by the opposite gender in special ceremonies when a different perspective was needed for divination or healing. Two of RT's associates, Running Wolf and OhShinna Fastwolf, have been outspoken advocates for sexual diversity. In speaking about the Great Spirit, OhShinna commented, "I don't relate to the Great Spirit as male or female. It's both masculine and feminine, and how we're working that balance out within ourselves is a matter of free will." Running Wolf added, "We don't distinguish between a man and a woman when it comes to spiritual practices, nor do we distinguish between a person's sexual orientation. We are all children of our creator, and we are supposed to treat each other with dignity and respect."

In his perceptive book, *Blackfoot Physics*, physicist David Peat observes that the Europeans brought to Turtle Island a set of assumptions about the way that the world works, and those assumptions ignored the Native Americans' understanding that not everyone sees the same world. Peat observes that the quantum world is basically ambiguous and that American Indians understood this principle better than did the European invaders. A Crow elder remarked, "We don't waste people the way white society does; all people have their gifts." The Cree language has a special word, *ayekkwew,* which can be translated as "neither man nor woman." The Lakota Sioux term *winkte* can be translated as "wants to be like a woman." Still other labels refer to "two-spirited people." RT frequently spoke out for all types of diversity. In a 1982 lecture he told his audience, "People are not the same. We were made differently and come in all types, just like the many colors of flowers."

Stanley's Comments

Upon retiring from the railroad, Rolling Thunder organized a small spiritual community called Meta Tantay, a Chumash word meaning "go in peace." RT created Meta Tantay with the earnings he had made from international lectures and workshops. Visitors, primarily from Western Europe and North America, spent various amounts of time at Meta Tantay studying Native American medicine and traditional lifestyles. *Shaman's Drum* magazine observed that the camp was created as an experiment in cooperative living and as a place to teach traditional Native American lifestyle and culture. Meta Tantay survived for a decade, planting the seeds of indigenous spirituality in the hearts of many people who visited the site or who lived there, including celebrities such as the famous American athlete Muhammad Ali and the architect Buckminster Fuller. RT envisioned the community as a living example of "the brotherhood of peace," adding, "The others have had their chance, and now the Indian will show them the right way." In fact, the motto of Meta Tantay was "We Know How," a statement emblazoned on the T-shirts of those who lived there.

On January 29, 1976, I gave a seminar in Virginia Beach, Virginia, home of the Association for Research and Enlightenment, a group promulgating the teachings of the American seer Edgar Cayce. While there I met Tom Helsabeck, a young man who had recently returned from Meta Tantay. Helsabeck reported that when he was there, Meta Tantay housed nearly one hundred men, women, and children. It boasted a kitchen, a school, and a healing center and was run according to a code of ethics: "No drugs, no alcohol allowed on land."

Later I found out that the Grateful Dead had provided a generous subsidy to help RT obtain the equipment he needed for this ambitious undertaking. This was not the first time that the Grateful Dead had come to RT's assistance. In 1972 a group spearheaded by Doug Boyd and several Indians began to meet to establish a foundation to preserve Native American customs. Semu Huaute, RT, and other Native American leaders attended this meeting, and the Grateful Dead put on a benefit concert to raise the original funds needed for the undertaking. This undertaking might be seen as the precursor to Meta Tantay. Sidian interviewed Helsabeck more than three decades later, obtaining the following additional details about the community.

The first time I went to Carlin was in 1974. I remember being invited into the family house and sat down in the living room. Nobody else was there. So after a while I got up and went into the kitchen and the bedroom. Everyone had left to do errands. I was pleased that they trusted me. Later I found out that when RT worked on the railroad he would bring hobos to the house. They had no other place to stay. And later he would bring hippies to the house. At first he would give them haircuts.

But then he began to like the long hair because he remembered an old prophecy about how times would get better for Indians when young men started to wear their hair long. Also, RT had good intuition about who he could trust and who he wouldn't let stay at his house.

So they found me a place to sleep. And the next morning I was invited to the sunrise ceremony. After the ceremony they told me I had passed the test. They left me alone to see if I would steal anything or touch things that were none of my business. I passed the test. So from then on they trusted me. They were very paranoid. But they had to be. Narcotic agents suspected RT of having drugs on his property because of all the hippies they saw hanging out there. Well, I came back for visits many times, and I learned something new from RT during each one of my visits.

In Doug Boyd's book *Rolling Thunder,* RT observed that he had never planned to build a camp in the desert. But his sons really wanted the barren land, and he thought that buying the land would help them learn more about Nature. "When I went out to look at the land," he recalled, "a golden eagle flew overhead, circled around, and flew off to the East, so I knew it was a good place and meant to be." RT continued, "Our camp was located in a position where they built earth mounds and pyramids, that is, in the middle of four sacred mountains." He knew it was a place of power where sick people could get well and healthy people could get better.

According to RT, "We lived in wickiups that we built ourselves with willows and without government help and bank loans." RT described covering them with canvas, old rugs, nylon material, and recycled fence materials. When some local authorities started harassing RT for violating building codes, he told them that his tepees and wickiups would be standing when their own buildings had fallen to the ground. RT continued, "We found water in a well at seven feet and another at twelve feet. I believe in scientific methods and technology, so I used a willow stick. When that stick broke, that's where I drew the stake in the ground." Meta Tantay used wind power, solar power, and recycled older machinery. According to RT, "Nothing was wasted." Other forms of Indian dwellings were the longhouses of the Iroquois, the hogans or kivas of the Navahos, the wigwams of the Plains people, and the cliff dwellings of ancient Southwest tribes. So the structures at Meta Tantay added to this venerable tradition.

During one of my visits, RT told me that he was able to buy the land at a low price because there was no source of potable water. Nonetheless, he told me the story about his dowsing willow stick and how when it snapped, signifying a water source, he had his crew dig until they found a spring. He did this not once, but twice; as a result, there was drinking water at each end of the property. Using American Indian farming techniques, the community grew two-foot cabbages, huge Jerusalem artichokes, burdock plants, and other crops on soil that its neighbors had predicted could not grow anything.

Meta Tantay's kitchen was always a busy place. A friend of mine named Mushroom (whom we have mentioned before) left San Francisco to live in the community for about one year and brought her expertise as a member of a catering and cooking team to Meta Tantay. Newcomers to the community often started out with kitchen duty. Such was the case with Fred Swinney and his wife, Jeannie Eagle. Fred came to me after experiencing a number of dreams and visions that I recognized, from my reading of the literature as well as my conversations with neophyte shamans, as being a call to shamanize. Fred and Jeannie spent more than two years at Meta Tantay, eagerly learning anything RT had to offer. Fred left Nevada for Oregon with a new name, Graywolf, the funding to set up his own healing center near Grants Pass, and a determination to forge a type of psychotherapy that integrated what he had learned from RT.

Another friend, Kenneth Cohen, whom we also discussed earlier, was also a frequent visitor to Meta Tantay; his classes in tai chi and Taoism were the only non–Native American spiritual disciplines encouraged by RT, who observed the similarities between traditional Chinese Taoism and his Cherokee and Shoshone worldviews. Tai chi, which seems to have originated among Taoists, uses bird and animal names for many of its movements and emphasizes the ambience between humans and the rest of Nature. As Alan Watts might have phrased it, "A berry bush berries. The living Earth peoples."

I did not witness RT's dowsing firsthand, so I cannot vouch for its accuracy. However, I did see the wells, and I did drink the fresh spring water. I did have a firsthand experience that demonstrated RT's closeness to Nature. One night RT asked me to walk around the property with him. As we approached the outer limits of the property, he began to howl. If I had not known RT's "medicine ways," I would have thought that he was going over the edge. Rather, I took his behavior in stride, and soon I heard a similar howl. A few minutes later, half a dozen coyotes appeared.

One of them approached RT, and they howled back and forth. After they ended this conversation, the coyotes slinked back to their own homes. I asked RT what was decided. He replied, "Every so often, I renew the bargain. The coyotes will not raid our chicken coops if we ensure their safely when we see them on our land. So far they have kept their end of the bargain, and so have we."

In one of his lectures RT observed, "Sometimes the coyotes ask us to pray for them. Coyotes are our neighbors at Meta Tantay. They don't bother our livestock, and we don't bother them. They keep the rat and the mouse population down. They also help keep down the rabbit population so that the rabbits don't eat our vegetable gardens. In Idaho the farmers have killed most of the coyotes, so the rabbits multiplied and overran the farmers' fields. The farmers retaliated by killing thousands of rabbits, and this destroyed the natural food for the remaining coyotes. The result was that the coyotes turned to eating sheep and cattle to survive. It seems as if those farmers in Idaho are at odds with Mother Earth. We hope that they will wake up, and in the meantime our prayers go out to the coyotes. In fact, some people use the wrong language when they pray. They say 'I want.' The Great Spirit doesn't give a damn about what you or any of us want. The Great Spirit is interested in what's good for you and what you could benefit from."

RT's Pharmacopeia

During another visit to Meta Tantay, RT took me to see his latest acquisition, a secondhand trailer (please see plate 13 of the color insert). It was no longer roadworthy, but RT had accepted the gift with gratitude, knowing exactly how he would put it to use. When I entered I saw rows and rows of medicines, most of them herbs ensconced in paper bags with an identification written on the outside of each bag. RT explained where some of the herbs came from, and the roster of states was impressive. He also showed me some medicinal samples that physicians had given him, along with instructions on their application. RT smiled, "I'll use anything I'm given if I think it will help one of the people I am 'doctoring,' even if it comes from a physician's office." I also noted a great variety of Chinese herbs; RT said those had come from traditional Chinese physicians who had dropped by for a visit.

Some months later I took a trip to Guatemala; while there, I visited a local market and bought half a dozen bags of herbs, along with instructions on how to use them. RT was delighted, and he eagerly tried them out with some of his patients. By promoting them as "the latest medicine from the markets of Guatemala City," it is no wonder that his patients got better. RT, as well as other medicine people I have observed, knows how to make maximum use of the placebo effect, as well as expectation, to maximize the positive effect of the treatment. But to ascribe all of RT's success to placebo effects and suggestion is doing him an injustice. Several visitors to Meta Tantay who knew a great deal about healing plants told me that they were impressed by RT's herbal knowledge and by the cures they observed once RT had skillfully used herbal teas and poultices. But RT also used food as a type of medicine. The third issue of the *Meta Tantay Newsletter* observes, "Healthy, good tasting food is the result of right thinking, right attitude, right respect. One should not be so concerned with seeking 'health foods,' but healthy foods that nourish us in body, soul, and spirit. Healthy foods, in essence, are the start of understanding what is considered 'good medicine.' One's thoughts, one's attitudes, one's respect for food determine whether the food cooked will be beneficial and nourishing."

Sidian's Comments

Alpha Lo, a physicist and community planner, spent time at Meta Tantay and introduced RT to a large audience in northern California in 1976. Fortunately, Alpha Lo tape recorded RT's lecture as well as his introduction.

Alpha Lo: I spent some time with Rolling Thunder at Meta Tantay, a community near Carlin, Nevada, about 250 miles east of Reno on Route 80. I was there a few times and noticed how RT would be guiding the people to live in a natural, harmonious way. Each time I came away rejuvenated and amazed with how the Great Spirit had guided me to be with those people. I always left his presence with a new awareness of how to watch my thoughts and to be calm within myself.

Rolling Thunder: Alpha Lo described our camp pretty well. Most of us live in wickiups that we built out of willows. We weave them like a basket upside down, and we made them big. We dug down in the ground a little, threw the dirt around the outside, and put old rugs over them. Remember Christo's fence in Marin County? It was a fine example of environmental art. We recycled some of that fence and covered the wickiups with that heavy nylon material. And that worked out pretty well. Those wickiups were warm in the winter and cool in the summer. It's five thousand feet high where we are. We've got a huge garage where we can work on our cars. We've got animal sheds and lots of animals. And we're going to make our own gasoline out of methane.

There are different kinds of nationalities living there, and they all look the same to us as they follow our Indian tribal rules. We don't make many rules, but the ones we have are very strictly enforced. No alcohol. No drugs. No foreign religions either. We've nothing against the religions, but I must admit there are some parts of them I don't like. They brought that devil into this country. I don't like that guy. We've got no use for him, and so he's fired. And we won't let the missionaries in. There is no way they can fit in. So we've fired your missionaries, we've fired your devil, we've fired your booze, and we've fired your drugs. And we've got a lot of young Indians back from the streets and the bars of the big cities. We've been doing very well at it.

I used to hang out with a Japanese friend of mine. He couldn't speak much English when he first came over from Japan. He wore a long samurai robe. And a young student from Norway joined us, and he spoke the ancient Viking language. And the three of us traveled around together healing people. We were quite a sensation. We just went around doing our thing and having fun together. And one lady gave birth to a little boy, and her hip went out of place for some reason. She went to different doctors and chiropractors and osteopaths, and the hip would go back, but it wouldn't stay. The three of us worked on that lady, and when her hip went back in, it stayed. That's why we say the Indian way really helps. I told my Viking friend that Columbus did not discover America. We were already here. And the Vikings came long before Columbus did, and there were Asian people who came from the other way. The ocean was not a one-way street.

This van I am driving in today came from the husband of a young lady who had a horse that stepped on her back. The hospital was already making the braces when I came along. But they took her right out of the hospital so that I could "doctor" her. She got well, and her husband bought me the van. I never have money to buy anything for myself, and I do not charge for healing. But sometimes I accept donations. And that van was a great donation.

But when it comes to medicine, nobody has a limit on knowledge. Any of these methods are good as long as they help. Acupuncture, chiropractic, white medicine can all be good for some people and at the right time. But we don't want to guarantee or advertise anything. They could throw us in jail in a minute if they said we were practicing medicine without a license.

I hadn't been back to Oklahoma, my country, for many years. I found some of the Cherokees there still living in the woods, still holding out, their morale high, no drinking, no fighting. And they are still doing the stomp dances and all the Cherokee ceremonies.

We talked about rich people, especially people in the oil business. Their greed seems to be getting the better of them. Did you ever think that greed is a sickness? It is like a cancer. And what can we do about it? It doesn't do any good to turn to violence. I tell all our young people to put their guns away. I think there are better ways to fight. I know it's a temptation, especially when you get beaten up in jail. One woman told me that there was more power in my eagle feathers than there is in my fists. I never forgot that. So we don't underestimate the power of women, not among our people. Women have a great power, and it's greatly respected among our people. So let's get the women to get after those guys who are greedy.

And we talked about the prophecies and about the earthquakes that are coming. Some rich people in California wanted to pay me to tell them when California would be under water. But I didn't say a word. We talked about the prophecies about money. There was a prophecy that when your money goes down, your way of life goes down, your culture, as you call it, the culture that you brought over here. We wish that everyone could live like we do. No federal regulation. No bank payments. Nothing that you set up over here. Now the food famine will be the next thing coming. There will be shortages of this and shortages of that. So out in the desert we are growing new plants, and they are not delicate like the tame plants; the first frost didn't knock them down. And they thrive, and they are hearty, and many of them are more nutritious than the weak salads you get that have been sprayed. We found seven different things each plant does and does well, and we found seven side effects that you have to compensate for when you change your diet, like when you become a vegetarian.

We are not allowed to take money for our prophecies. But prophecies are not written in stone. All prophecies are subject to change, especially if people have a change of heart. And just a few people can make that change. They could change some of the bad things that are happening now if they had it in their heart and mind to do so.

Anyway, I am glad to be here. I am a tough old Indian, I'll tell you. Ho. What was that? I said, "Ho," and someone behind my back said, "Ho," like he agreed with me. But I'm not perfect. I have many bad habits. I have never met a medicine man who was perfect or who claimed to be perfect. If I get wound up I might talk all night long, and that's one of my bad habits. So I'll stop now, because that's the message I have for you at this time. Ho.

My interview with Franklin Fried provided me with additional insights as to what life was like at Meta Tantay.

Sidian Morning Star Jones: You told me earlier that you had arrived at Meta Tantay in time for a birthday celebration.

Franklin Fried: So, the birthday party was quite exciting, and all sorts of gifts were given, and of course there was no drinking or drug use. You didn't need it. We had a good time anyway. And I was just in culture shock. I'd never been to that part of Nevada; I was in Las Vegas when I was younger. Meta Tantay was a lot different from any other place. I felt like I was on Mars. There was a lot of sage and sagebrush.

Sidian Morning Star Jones: You grew up in New York right?

Franklin Fried: Yes, I am a native New Yorker. So that whole time to me was as if I had landed on another planet. I would go back and forth to Meta Tantay over the years, but the experience of the first day was the high point. And over time I became close to RT, and I'd stay at the house where RT had his gardens. He was very proud of his rhubarb and his turnips that could fit in a five-gallon bucket. He used to brag to people about it: "We grow turnips here that could fit in a five-gallon bucket."

Sidian Morning Star Jones: I don't understand. They don't normally fit in a five-gallon bucket?

Franklin Fried: One big, huge turnip.

Sidian Morning Star Jones: Oh, just one huge one?

Franklin Fried: A really big turnip for some reason.

Sidian Morning Star Jones: It would like fill up the bucket?

Franklin Fried: Yeah. Huge turnips. And sometimes I would tend to his garden, but he always had his friends, the rattlesnakes, around. So, one day I am walking over a plank, and I'm hearing, "Shhhhh." It was a snake pit. I had to take a bath, and the bath was in a separate building. I wanted to make a medicine bath to soak in, but to do that I had to walk over the snake pit, just like I tended his garden. There would always be all of these snakes coming out, but I never got bitten.

Sidian Morning Star Jones: Were they all rattlesnakes?

Franklin Fried: Rattlesnakes or copperheads, I don't remember what they were, but they were highly venomous. So they would slither by my feet, and I had to stomp the ground when I walked. RT had always told me, "When you're walking, make sure the animals know that you're coming. Especially the snakes, so they feel your vibrations."

Sidian Morning Star Jones: Then they'll get away from you before you get there?

Franklin Fried: Yes.

Sidian Morning Star Jones: Walk hard when you are in dangerous territory.

Franklin Fried: Yeah. I like that. So at first I was in shock because I had really never seen rattlesnakes before, growing up in New York, but soon I just kind of got used to it. One time, I came in from the outside area and said, "There's another snake." And a woman named Owl Feather gave me the nickname Little Reptile.

Sidian Morning Star Jones: Little Reptile?

Franklin Fried: Yes, because I would always see those snakes. That's what Owl Feather used to call me. That was okay. I didn't mind being called a little snake. That was RT's medicine.

Sidian Morning Star Jones: That's true. They had RT bitten by a rattlesnake in the Billy Jack movie.

Franklin Fried: One day I was at RT's house in town, and Grandfather Semu Huaute was there too. Stanley knew Grandfather Semu and stayed in touch with his widow. So Grandfather Semu comes inside, and RT said to him, "Did you meet Franklin?" RT said, "He's from New York." So Semu turns to me and said, "You know, I like those bagels, but if I eat too many of them I get constipated." And RT replied, "Yeah, white flour is not good for you." That was another thing he didn't like, white flour. He was against white flour and sugar but was a big fan of using cayenne pepper.

Sidian Morning Star Jones: Really?

Franklin Fried: Yes. He was ahead of his time.

Sidian Morning Star Jones: I eat cayenne pepper every day. I put it on everything.

Franklin Fried: That's good. And that's what he would tell you to do. Sometimes it was so cold in the wintertime at Meta Tantay that we used to put cayenne pepper in our boots and in our socks so our feet would get warmed when we put them on in the morning. That's a trick RT taught me.

Sidian Morning Star Jones: Didn't it stink?

Franklin Fried: Well, look, we lived on a ranch. You smell strange when you live on a ranch. RT also really liked garlic.

Sidian Morning Star Jones: Did he eat a lot of it?

Franklin Fried: He sure did. He was way ahead of his time; he ate a lot of garlic and cayenne pepper. Another fond memory was when I was at his house and RT cooked fry bread for me, and he would get so excited. "Frank, we're going to make fry bread!" Then he told me a secret: "It has buttermilk in it." So now everyone will know his secret.

It was also at Meta Tantay where I first met your relative Patty. That was the first day that I arrived there. Oh, she was so beautiful, and my heartbeat was rapid whenever she was around me. And one time when I was at RT's house I met his wife, Spotted Fawn, and she really started to like me. That's when she told me how we date people at Meta Tantay. She was the clan mother, that's what Spotted Fawn was. And she explained to me what to do if I wanted to date a particular woman or whatever.

Sidian Morning Star Jones: Say you wanted to date Mushroom.

Franklin Fried: Mushroom, exactly. The first time I wanted to date Mushroom, I said, "Spotted Fawn, I really like Mushroom, and I would like to go on a date." And our dates were pretty nice.

Sidian Morning Star Jones: So you would go out places?

Franklin Fried: No, we just hung out. Yeah, the town was far away. We would just hang out in someone's wickiup or whatever, and we had dates like that.

Sidian Morning Star Jones: So you would have to ask the clan mother?

Franklin Fried: Sure. Maybe she had a boyfriend I didn't know about; maybe she liked someone else.

Sidian Morning Star Jones: So, Spotted Fawn would sort of take care of and look out for the females.

Franklin Fried: Yeah. So also you wouldn't get hurt. You wouldn't get rejected like if she was already with someone or something like that. She helped protect you too.

Sidian Morning Star Jones: And that makes for less drama.

Franklin Fried: Yeah, and let's say I liked someone who was married or had a boyfriend. Spotted Fawn would ask both of them if it was okay. So it was quite interesting on my first date at Meta Tantay. I was about eighteen, and I didn't understand that when you went on a date instead of hanging out, it meant you would probably have intercourse.

Sidian Morning Star Jones: Okay, so you got down to business pretty quickly around there.

Franklin Fried: Oh, yeah. I guess I did. Everybody else's business is their business, but I had fun. But you see the thing was that I was the youngest adult. That was kind of weird for me because everyone was older than me, and there were no girls my age.

Sidian Morning Star Jones: How old was Mushroom?

Franklin Fried: I was eighteen then; how old would Mushroom be? She had to be in her middle twenties. So there weren't any women my age. So it was quite interesting, because I was with someone that was older than me.

16

Spotted Fawn Says Good-Bye

Visitors to Carlin told us that Spotted Fawn made sure there was coffee on the stove and lemonade in the refrigerator so that they would be assured of her hospitality from the moment they stepped into her home. Sometimes visitors were treated to chicken soup or beef stew as well. Richard Clemmer-Smith, an anthropologist, recalls, "Despite his posturing and perhaps fakery, my interactions with RT were positive. I learned a great deal from him and met many great Shoshone people. But actually I learned just as much from Spotted Fawn and met wonderful people through her too." Clemmer-Smith did more than observe; he was one of the spiritual warriors who helped RT photograph the tractors that were ravaging the pinyon nut trees in the late 1960s.

Visitors were also welcomed by a number of dogs, which RT said were needed not only for companionship but also for protection. RT claims to have been the object of various curses and hexes, not only by sorcerers and so-called black magicians but also by people with no special powers except their weapons. RT took pride in showing visitors a bullet hole in his wall, from a bullet that would have killed him if he had not left his customary chair to visit the bathroom moments before the shot was fired. When asked about protection, RT replied, "There are different ways to protect yourself. We medicine men wouldn't be here today if we didn't know something about how to do that. Everyone in this life needs help all the time—standing alone is very hard. One of the best is to surround yourself with true friends and brothers and sisters."

Indians often speak of people walking a road through life. Certain steps along that "Earth walk" are marked by ceremonies, visions, dreams, fasts, or initiations. Spotted Fawn played an important role in all of these activities. In his book Doug Boyd describes her as "a large woman with a very beautiful face. She wore long black beads and a necklace. I believed that she was enchanted."

It was at Meta Tantay that Spotted Fawn finally came into full bloom. Regarded as the heart of Meta Tantay, she had taken on a maternal role with runaways and outcasts, a supervisory role with the kitchen staff who prepared three savory meals each day, and a spiritual role when she told campfire stories, led songfests, and counseled troubled group members. She also played an instructional role with women entering the "moon lodge" during their menstrual cycle. Menstruation is not looked on negatively, as it is in some social groups in Western society. Instead it is seen as a time for prayer, introspection, and rejuvenation. If a woman was being "visited by Grandmother Moon," she was not allowed to sit near RT during his lectures, not because of discrimination but because her power at that time of month would create an imbalance with the energy of RT and the message he was attempting to convey. It was believed that a woman who is menstruating has such power during that time of the month that she would disturb the balance of energy and spirits within the medicine, the ceremony, or the tribal council.

Some of Spotted Fawn's most memorable contributions were her spontaneous discourses on relationships between the genders, illuminated with graphic examples, practical guidelines, and dramatic case histories that were as candid as they were comical. The young women at Meta Tantay could not have had a more knowledgeable—or a more outrageous—director for these sex education classes! Jean Millay, an artist who spent a considerable amount of time with Spotted Fawn during her San Francisco visits, observed, "This lady was the prototypical clan mother—sweet, loving, gentle, healing, and yet imbued with a special power."

Spotted Fawn was also a ritualist, reminding her husband when a sunrise ceremony was needed and actively participating in many of the sacred ceremonies held at Meta Tantay. She felt that rituals were one way to "spot the phonies," because the rituals they performed lacked the proper context, organization, and respect for tradition that characterized authentic performances. Kenneth Cohen, the Taoist master, marveled at how "Spotted Fawn was the great organizer; without her work, neither Rolling Thunder nor Meta Tantay would have been half so effective."

The third issue of the *Meta Tantay Newsletter* provides a succinct description of Spotted Fawn's role. "The Clan Mother has the final authority over all matters regarding women. Further, a veto power over all community decisions is part of the Clan Mother's authority. But Spotted Fawn, in her own wisdom, prefers instead to exercise a mediating role. Her opinion is sought and is respected on all levels."

Stanley's Comments

It seems as if all good things must come to an end. Once he retired from the railroad, RT spent considerable time away from Meta Tantay, earning the money needed to keep the place running. In his absence his wife, Spotted Fawn, played an important role in organizing and supervising the daily routine: the meals, the school, the labor force, the clean-up crews, and—perhaps most important—the classes where Native American traditions were being passed down and preserved. RT did not limit participation in these classes to Native Americans. As he once told me, "Those long-haired hippies were probably Indians in a previous life. So why should I turn them away when they want a refresher course on what they used to know?"

When it came to the preparation of food, Spotted Fawn told the kitchen crew that they were not only providing nourishment for the body but also for the spirit. In regard to "moon customs," Spotted

Fawn reminded young women that this was a sacred time. It was one in which they could purify themselves and rejuvenate their strength. "When Grandmother Moon comes to visit," Spotted Fawn remarked, "it is the time for prayer and renewal." Menstruation was a time when the power of women was self-evident; to maintain the balance needed both by Rolling Thunder and Meta Tantay, during their menses women sat in the rear of the audience and maintained a low profile. They avoided sunrise ceremonies and often stayed in the moon lodge. Spotted Fawn explained to me that this was in no way discrimination against women but recognition of their power and special needs during moon time.

During the years of Meta Tantay, Rolling Thunder was in constant demand as a speaker. I introduced him to student groups at Sonoma State University and Saybrook Institute (now called Saybrook University) in San Francisco, California. In the meantime, Spotted Fawn, often aided by other family members and by Meta Tantay veterans, provided the cohesion so badly needed to hold the community together during the turbulent 1970s and early 1980s. On one occasion she traveled to San Francisco without Rolling Thunder to visit family members. I arranged an impromptu party for her; she was genuinely touched, because, in her words, "No one has ever held a party in my honor before." I replied, "Well, it's about time!"

In 1955 I was working in Richmond, Virginia, and I remember watching a film, *The Conqueror,* a highly fictionalized version of Genghis Khan's empire-building exploits. Several months earlier a minor event in cinema history had taken place—with dire consequences for the film company and indirectly for Spotted Fawn as well. On July 6, 1954, in St. George, Utah, a local men's club played a charity softball game against *The Conqueror*'s film crew, which was on location for the movie filming. The actress Susan Hayward kicked off her shoes, ran the bases barefoot, and scored a run. John Wayne (improbably cast as Genghis Khan, the Mongol emperor) and Dick Powell (who directed the opus) scored several runs each. Agnes Moorehead, another of the film's stars, cheered from the grandstand. Three decades later all four were dead from cancer, and half of the two-hundred-member cast and crew had been diagnosed with cancer as well.

St. George was later called "the world's most active test site" by *Shaman's Drum* magazine in its summer 1992 issue. The article noted that the cumulative fallout of the many nuclear tests of 1951, 1952, and 1953 had covered the ground there in uneven blotches, most intensely in and around the area where most of the movie footage had been shot. During the filming there were dusty battle scenes, and during the battles actors and extras rolled in the sand. Electric blowers were brought in to simulate windstorms, and so much dirt collected in the costumes that actors had to be hosed down before they took them off. This land rightfully belongs to the Western Shoshone Nation, but neither the United States nor Great Britain asked the tribe's permission for the detonation of the nuclear weapons that both countries were testing there. This area became the most active test site in the United States, and more nuclear weapons were exploded there than anywhere else in the world.

Many fission products like strontium 90 and cesium 137 decay slowly; they are driven below the surface of the soil by rain and snow. When the soil is stirred up, the buried poisons emerge again. Not far from the Utah and Nevada proving grounds, during the time that the bombs were being tested, Spotted Fawn was living with members of her family. In 1984, three decades later, she was hospitalized for cancer. She was taken to Letterman Memorial Hospital in San Francisco's Presidio Military Base, where, as a Native American, she was able to obtain low-cost medical care at the massive military facility. Spotted Fawn was diagnosed with abdominal cancer, a malady that RT blamed on the atomic bomb testing that had occurred near Spotted Fawn's childhood home, and he might have been right.

Soon thereafter Rolling Thunder accepted another of Mickey Hart's offers of hospitality so that he and his associates could drive the short distance from Mickey's ranch to San Francisco every day to comfort Spotted Fawn in the hospital. Rolling Thunder spent his meager resources to secure outstanding practitioners from both mainstream allopathic medicine and from alternative and complementary medicine.

In addition, I brought friends of mine to the Presidio Hospital who taught Spotted Fawn various types of self-regulation in an attempt to reduce her discomfort. These psychologists, physicians, and neuroscientists had backgrounds in biofeedback, meditation, autogenic training, the relaxation response, and other self-regulation techniques. Welcoming all this attention, Spotted Fawn followed the instructions meticulously. Rolling Thunder complied with the suggestions as well, stating that he used them to mitigate the personal stress his wife's illness had induced.

I made a special trip several times a week to visit her, and at RT's request I hypnotized Spotted Fawn to help ease her pain. The most effective image seemed to be a calming, peaceful blue light. When she merged with this light, in her imagination, the discomfort eased and sometimes abated completely. RT closed his eyes to attempt to use the imagery I suggested as well, viewing it as a case of "preventive medicine." RT spent a considerable amount of money bringing renowned medicine people to the Presidio Hospital. On my last visit to see Spotted Fawn, RT confided, "You have done more for my wife than all of those expensive healers put together." It was one of the most gratifying compliments I have ever received.

RT had paid a great deal of money to "psychic healers," many of them nationally known. He had a great deal of trouble simply allowing his wife to join the Great Spirit. I had seen RT's stubborn streak on several occasions, but it was never more evident than at the Presidio Hospital. Jürgen Kremer was with me during one of these visits and knew that Spotted Fawn's condition was terminal. He also knew that RT was virtually unable to let go.

On one July afternoon, I spent an hour with Spotted Fawn, taking her through a series of progressive relaxation exercises, ending with the image of the blue light that had provided her so much relief in previous sessions. Spotted Fawn told me that this session had been especially compelling and that she had difficulty returning from the light. At that point I sensed that Spotted Fawn was close to death and had made her peace with her condition. Both Rolling Thunder and Spotted Fawn had told me about how spiritual healing begins with respect for the Great Spirit—the life and love that can be found in all of Nature's creations. Each element of creation has its own will, its own way, and its own purpose. These ways need to be respected, not exploited, by human beings.

In August 1984 I was attending a parapsychology conference in Mexico. On the night of August 15 I had a dream that I had arrived at Mickey Hart's ranch. As I drove in, Rolling Thunder and his group were driving out. He had a sober expression on his face, as did the other members of his entourage. I asked, "Where is Spotted Fawn?" He turned his head slightly toward the back of the truck, where I saw a wooden coffin strapped to the floor. I knew that it contained the earthly remains of my dear friend Spotted Fawn. That morning I experienced what is called a hypnopompic image. Although most such images are visual, this one was auditory. I heard Spotted Fawn's voice telling me, in a very unpretentious way, "You know, I won't be seeing you anymore." Upon arriving back in the United States, I learned that Spotted Fawn had passed away that same night. Mala Spotted Eagle and his wife, Sky, organized a memorial service for Spotted Fawn. Jürgen Kremer, the psychologist who had organized events for RT in Germany, attended the event and was impressed by the testimonials given by those whose lives Spotted Fawn had so profoundly touched. There were about one hundred people at the memorial service, and it was obvious that Rolling Thunder had suffered an irreplaceable loss.

Once Spotted Fawn died, RT went into deep depression, and people slowly began to leave Meta Tantay. Gert Reutter, a German physician who spent several months each year with RT, visited me in 1985 with the sad news about the demise of Meta Tantay. Without Spotted Fawn the heart of the community had stopped beating. Nonetheless, Gert felt that he had learned a considerable amount of useful information during his stays at Meta Tantay. His medical training evoked some skepticism on his part when RT would engage in metaphysical discussions such as the Cherokee's origins in the lost continent of Atlantis. He also was skeptical about RT's claim that "some people are meant to die because they have to pay for something from as far back as seven generations."

But when RT spoke about Indian healing principles, Gert learned insights about the healing process that had been overlooked in his medical school. For example, RT emphasized the importance of social support, the active participation of the patient in getting well, and the ritualistic aspects of the healing process that Gert was able to carry into his own work once he returned to Germany. Gert also observed RT's modesty, remembering him saying, "I never claim to have cured somebody. If I started making claims I might lose my powers. They come from a special relationship I have with Nature, and I do not want that relationship to get out of balance. I was taught to be humble before the Great Spirit. It is the Great Spirit who has the power, not me." And Gert felt that he had assimilated lessons from Spotted Fawn as well. She found something positive about everyone she met and knew how to help them develop their strengths and overlook their weaknesses.

Sidian's Comments

When I interviewed family members about RT, Spotted Fawn's name came up time and time again. Here is an example (I have attached no names because I encouraged them to speak openly).

Female voice: There was that balance of Mom and Dad. Mom would keep Dad in line.

Male voice: But she never said, "Shut the fuck up." She'd just say, "Shut up." She would never use the "F" word.

Sidian Morning Star Jones: She would be like the grounding?

Male voice: For sure. When she would say, "Shut up," he would shut up. We all did. Because I only saw her get mad like that once or twice in my life.

Female voice: Well, she saved it for when she really meant it.

Male voice: Yeah, the true power in a tribe is the clan mother. And she was the clan mother of Meta Tantay. But when Mom died, all control was gone. And then Dad was left with the realization, "Hey man, I suck. I'm not really special."

Sidian Morning Star Jones: I never thought about it until now. But when Spotted Fawn died, Meta Tantay kind of fell apart, didn't it?

Male voice: Well, that's the truth.

17

The Future of Earth

The creation stories of many Native American tribes are sophisticated from a philosophical point of view. For example, the Muskogee Indians believe that the world and all it contains are the products of mind. The Omaha tribe believes that life can be found in everything, both organic and inorganic. The Sioux believed that Spirit is the source of energy in all of Nature.

The Hopi creation story holds that at first there was only the Creator, Taiowa. All else was endless space. There was no beginning and no end, no shape, no time, no life. Then Taiowa, the infinite, created the finite, and the universe came into being. The Blackfoot believe that all living creatures gain their power from the Sun and that the Sun is a living being.

These creation stories demonstrate the interaction between humans and the rest of the universe. It is not that people are stewards of Nature. People are a part of Nature itself, and what harms any aspect of Nature ends up hurting human beings as well.

The pine trees spanning many of the mountains and hills of Idaho turn scarlet red at the beginning of August. This is a beautiful sight—beautiful until people realize that the trees are not supposed to turn color this early. These pine trees are dying, falling victim to beetles that used to be controlled by extremely cold winters. Global warming has reduced the severity of the cold, and the beetles are staying alive at the expense of the pine trees and other evergreens. Global warming has increased the incidence of forest fires and has dried up ponds and lakes that nourish forests. Huge stretches of Siberian forests have been destroyed by fires, and the Amazon valley's foliage has been decimated by uncommon dry spells.

Droughts, floods, heat waves, insect outbreaks, wildfires, tsunamis, and polluted air and oceans are examples of the changing climate people encounter every day. Nobel Laureate Al Gore's film *An Inconvenient Truth* won an Academy Award and alerted millions of people to the fragility of the Earth.

Chaos theory argues that epidemics arise out of interlocking systems. Predator and prey, disease and host are locked in a battle that goes beyond the simple cause-and-effect germ theory of disease. According to David Peat the West's desire for progress, growth, and wealth has brought about the very diseases that have become its scourge.

The famed Nez Perce leader Chief Joseph saw the U.S. government take back almost six million acres of the tribe's land once gold was discovered on the territory. He resisted all efforts to force his band onto the small reservation in Idaho, and in 1873 a federal order gave the tribe back some of its land. But this decision was reversed a few years later, and a cavalry attack seemed imminent. Chief Joseph reluctantly began to lead his people toward the reservation, but they never got there. A small group of Nez Perce warriors raided nearby settlements, killing several white settlers. Although he had always opposed war, Chief Joseph and his brother Olikut cast their lot with the warriors.

What followed was one of the most brilliant military retreats in U.S. history. General William Tecumseh Sherman was impressed with the 1,400-mile march, observing that a band of two hundred warriors and five hundred companions held off two thousand U.S. soldiers for several months. When Chief Joseph finally surrendered, he mourned the death of his brother and eloquently asked for time to treat the sick and bury the dead. He continued to be an indomitable voice of protest, pleading his case to President Rutherford Hayes in 1879. He died in

1904, according to his doctor, "of a broken heart." He often reminded people, "The Earth and I are of one mind."

RT frequently referred to Chief Joseph and echoed his sentiments, referring to the Earth as a living being, one that encompassed him, his family, his people, and "all our relations." RT would keep asking why psychotherapists could not see the relationship between mental illness and the pollution of the Earth. He recalled that Chief Joseph, even while fleeing U.S. troops, would get off his horse to inspect and smell a flower that was new to him. RT commented, "If that's what they call fierce or savage, we need more of them."

For Peter Tadd, a college professor, his encounter with RT demonstrated the medicine man's closeness to Nature. Tadd wrote us a letter.

I had read the book by Doug Boyd. It touched me deeply. One thing that stood out was his arrival by rolling thunder and his departure by a gentle rain. I have had my own experiences with Nature that left me with the knowledge that we are no less a part of Nature than the trees and the stars. Somehow we Westerners lost that understanding.

One day Rolling Thunder came to the college town of Amherst, Massachusetts. This was in the summer of 1994. My wife and I were planning to go to the lecture in the evening when out of nowhere, out of the blue on a sunny day, we literally heard rolling thunder. The sound on this cloudless day was both eerie and natural. There was no doubt in my mind that this was the calling card of this great medicine man.

That evening RT gave a lecture in a large auditorium at the university. There was a very large attendance. I recall him on stage as someone with a great presence that was mixed with a certain degree of resentment toward our dominant culture. What was of particular interest to me was that he was indeed an incarnation of one of those fierce, determined, and powerful Celts. In fact he mentioned Celts during his lecture.

The day he was to leave, a gentle rain blessed the land. It had not been forecast. I thought to myself that the legend was real.

Stanley's Comments

Rolling Thunder frequently pointed out that the sickness of the natural environment is a reflection of the sickness of human beings. Native Americans had designed a number of ceremonies to purify the Earth, but the Europeans exploited Nature rather than working with Nature. For RT, one's inner ecology was matched by the community's outer ecology. The two worked together, and when one was out of balance the other lost its equilibrium as well.

RT ascribed great knowledge to wildlife, especially their sense of oncoming disaster. He would not have been surprised to hear that animals and plants across the world are reacting to global warming much more quickly than ever before. The movements of these animals have been tracked, and what is clear is that about two thousand species are moving away from the equator at an average rate of some fifteen feet per day. Species also are moving up mountains to escape the heat, perhaps in an attempt to avoid extinction. Gases from the burning of fossil fuel, especially carbon dioxide, are trapping heat in the atmosphere, warming the Earth and changing the climate in several ways, according to the overwhelming majority of scientists and the world's leading scientific organizations.

For example, the city copper butterfly, the comma butterfly, and the purple emperor butterfly in Europe have moved more than 135 miles in the last decade of the twentieth century and the first decade of the twenty-first century. The British *Silometopus* spider has moved its home range 8 miles per year in the same time span. The American pica, which resembles a rabbit, did not go higher than 7,800 feet in 1900, but a century later it was seen at 9,500 feet in Yellowstone National Park. The farther north that the species live, the faster they moved their home base. This makes sense, because northern regions are warming more than those closer to the equator. A team of scientists at England's University of Exeter calculated that one in ten species could disappear by the end of the twenty-first century due to global warming.

Other factors that threaten life include the rising acidity of oceans due to pollution and the similar deterioration of the atmosphere, the rain forests, and the coral reefs. When the world's population reached five billion people in 1985, the amount of Nature's resources being used became more than the planet could sustain indefinitely. The loss of biological diversity is a major issue, because it is part of humanity's only life-support system, helping to deliver everything from food to clean water and air—all the things that sustain human civilization—and we even count on it for recreation and tourism. Peter Sale, a marine biologist working with United Nations University's Institute for Water, Environment, and Health, made these dire predictions.

There are some scientists who scoff at these notions, but their ideas and data are not strong enough to be published in major scientific journals. They claim that prejudice and censorship prevent their claims from being aired, but I know better from personal experience. My own work with telepathic effects in dreams is highly controversial, but my colleagues and I have had no trouble publishing our results in major international psychological and psychiatric journals.

RT was not the only Indian elder who was concerned with the Earth's future. In October 2010 the *New York Times* published an interview with Earl Tulley, an elder of the three hundred thousand member Navaho Nation. He called for replacing coal with solar farms and wind power. Similar statements have been made by leaders of the Navaho Green Economy Commission and the Diné Hataalii Association, a group of medicine men and women.

Native American women are playing an important role in ensuring the future of Mother Earth. Women are the world's leading gardeners. Many women in developing countries are taking leadership roles in recycling sugarcane leftovers and other foodstuffs discarded as trash and are finding substitutes for plastic bags, one of the leading polluters of the world's oceans. The motto of Meta Tantay was "We Know How," and that claim extends to female Indian environmentalists as well. In a worst-case scenario, Leslie Gray reminds her audiences, "We are not going to get rid of life. Mother Earth will take a few million years to shake off her skirts and start all over again."

We do not want to romanticize indigenous people and their care of the Earth. Raymond Williams, in his book *The Country and the City,* presents the opinion that the arrival of human beings on the face of the Earth altered its ecology for the worse. The natural environment was well cared for by many tribes, but others engaged in destructive practices that led to a slow erosion of the land. This wearing down of Nature took a turn for the worse when agriculture appeared on the scene and plummeted more rapidly as the result of urbanization and industrialization. This is a pessimistic assessment, but it rings true.

Sidian's Comments

RT constantly spoke about the future of Mother Earth. Leslie Gray, when I interviewed her, recalled these comments.

Leslie Gray: When he talked he kind of rambled around a bit, but he got deeper and deeper as he spoke, and the more he spoke the more he was saying, "Wake up, the Earth is in peril; we're not taking care of her." He conveyed a sense of urgency about caring for the Earth and about life having gotten out of balance that not a lot of people were talking about then.

Sidian Morning Star Jones: It was still a pretty new topic?

Leslie Gray: Well, it's not a new topic, you know, it's a perennial topic; but to try to reach the prevailing dominant culture with those ideas, that was rather new. You know, Chief Joseph tried it but, I mean, not on the scale, not going out to get that message across, not promulgating that idea. But the things Chief Joseph said, you know, showed clearly that he saw what was coming down the road. If you're going to treat the Earth this way, there will be a big problem coming.

Sidian Morning Star Jones: Yeah, and Rolling Thunder was really out there, getting people together and talking about it.

Leslie Gray: Yeah, he was like an organizer around this and even, I think, set up a way of living in Nevada that would be different from the way people were treating the Earth, one that would be based on common sense. The alkaline soil was not suitable for farming because it lacked nitrogen, iron, and other minerals. But RT added manure and compost to the soil and planted crops according to the appropriate phase of the moon. I think he wanted people to return to a good way of living, but I don't think he was sentimental about it. He knew there was a role for technology.

Sidian Morning Star Jones: It was just a practical way to look at things.

Leslie Gray: Yeah, I really think so. He even had windmills and solar showers at Meta Tantay. And he used solar power to heat the water for washing the clothes and washing the dishes. And he helped install all of this technology.

Sidian Morning Star Jones: That's really cool, because Rolling Thunder really seemed to be one of those kinds of people who worked alongside of the people he was teaching. There are too many instructors who say, "Well, you should do things like this," but they don't follow through, and half the time they do the job some other way.

Leslie Gray: You know, it is possible for the interaction between indigenous and technological worldviews to be mutually enhancing and generate solutions to many of our world's greatest dilemmas. Your grandfather didn't exclude technology from Meta Tantay. Many of the young people who came there went on to have splendid careers in the computer industry, in environmental technology, and in alternative energy production. Indigenous traditions have always understood that a caring relationship with the environment has to be taught; it does not come naturally. And RT was a master teacher because he had great teachers himself.

18

Rolling On

Many friends, family members, and associates told us that Rolling Thunder never completely recovered from Spotted Fawn's death. However, as the Grateful Dead song lyrics say, he felt he had to "keep truckin' on" because his mission was an essential one.

As a part of his mission, RT conducted the sacred rituals with which he was familiar and continued "doctoring" people, many of whom reported remarkable relief from symptoms.

Stanley's Comments

Fame has a way of entrapping people, and once the spotlight is turned on, it is hard to order it turned off. In 1986 I was on the planning committee of a banquet held at the California Institute of Integral Studies (in San Francisco) in honor of RT. The surprise attraction was buffalo meat, something that many of the dozens of guests had never tasted. But the cooks told me that the buffalo meat couldn't be rewarmed; once it is ready to serve, it must be eaten promptly or it will become dry and unpalatable.

RT was accompanied to the banquet by a troop of his spiritual warriors and the omnipresent lovely young lady. I told the young lady that as soon as the buffalo meat was ready, a university official would give a short prayer, and then she would take RT's plate to the buffet, where it would be filled with buffalo meat, potatoes, and garden vegetables. Everything was beautifully timed. Nothing could go wrong. But the trickster had other plans. Once the invocation ended, I signaled RT's guest to take a plate and serve him.

Suddenly one of the spiritual warriors proclaimed, "Just a darn minute. We can't start eating until we've done some singing!" The chef and I were exasperated. We knew that we could not countermand the young brave, who started to lead the group in song, but we also knew that the buffalo meat was more fragile than the diners realized. So we had a trick or two up our sleeves. The chef and his crew immediately turned the oven controls down to "low" for the potatoes and other vegetables. They turned the controls for the buffalo completely off. As the singing ran down, they turned the controls for the gravy up to "high heat." By the time RT was served, followed by the remainder of the famished participants, the hot gravy had been poured over the tepid buffalo meat. The vegetables were a bit overcooked, but nevertheless a good time was had by all.

Sidian's Comments

RT really enjoyed music. I am told that he took to the Grateful Dead right away. One of the tapes that Mickey Hart lent us is filled with songs. RT comments on some of them, and before one selection he remarked, "The next song is one of my favorites. It's a song about freedom. Isn't that shocking that we Indians have never forgotten freedom? Many people speak of freedom. And they don't know the first meaning of the word. We Indians understand about freedom. For one thing, we see it in Nature. We have songs about it like this one, 'Free as an Eagle.' I am proud that the name of one of my little grandsons means free as an eagle."

When RT lectured in Sonoma County, California, he occasionally stayed at the Westerbeke Ranch. He left an indelible impression on his hostess, Patricia Westerbeke.

Patricia Westerbeke: You graduated from a college up in Boise named what?

Sidian Morning Star Jones: I graduated from a college named Stevens-Henager, where I studied graphic design.

Patricia Westerbeke: Are those black things you are wearing the shin bones of a deer?

Sidian Morning Star Jones: They very well could be. I know that they are bones. What kind of experience did you have with Rolling Thunder?

Patricia Westerbeke: It's been a long time since I've seen your grandfather. He used to come to our ranch, you know. Our ranch is in Sonoma Valley, about an hour's drive from San Francisco. We have a couple of hundred acres, and when we were youngsters and the property was bought all we did was ride horseback. In the 1950s it began to be a full-time conference center, and I did most of the cooking.

Sidian Morning Star Jones: What is this conference center called?

Patricia Westerbeke: It's called the Westerbeke Ranch. And it's quite well-known and most of our advertising is just word of mouth and people have had marvelous meals there and it's in a very beautiful setting. It's in the beginning of the foothills on the west side of Sonoma Valley, the Valley of the Moon, and of course Sonoma had Indians years ago. It was a place where everything grew very easily, and there were a lot of deer, a lot of natural wild animals. There still are, and we still have mountain lions and quite a few deer on the property. Anyway we can accommodate about fifty people.

By the time Rolling Thunder came to the ranch we were in full swing as a conference center and there was a full kitchen staff and there was a full massage staff and there were swimming pools. And he would come with a small entourage. Basically Rolling Thunder came to give a speech or talk to an anthropology class or a sociology class over at Sonoma State University, which was about maybe thirty minutes away. I was a friend of Stanley Krippner's, and at the time he was teaching at Sonoma State College in northern California. He really is a very, very unique man, and he was going all over the world to research psychic phenomena and shamans, and he would also give lectures and workshops at the ranch.

At the same time, my husband, Don, had been diagnosed with a pituitary tumor in his head, and it was right behind the sella tur-cica, which is known as the Turk's saddle, which are little bones, and he was advised to have this very long operation under a very famous surgeon at the University of California. But before he did that Anna Kay, a woman who had seen psychic surgery in the Philippines, came to the ranch for a weekend. She was also a yoga teacher, and she had these amazing movies, and they showed this man doing all these things to people's bodies, you know, without anesthetic.

You'd see a slit in the stomach done with a hand, and conse-crated coconut oil was wiped on the belly, and then there is a slit made, and you could see, you know, a little blood coming out, and then the psychic surgeon would take his hands and go in and get something, and he'd say, "Look, these were all fibroid, you know, this shouldn't be here," and the assistant would hold the bowl out, and he'd dump this stuff in, and it was all very, very, very strange.

I mean, it was very hard for me to take seriously, except some of the people who would walk in with crutches would leave the crutches at the door and walk home. There were some strange healings. In fact, when my husband was first diagnosed with this tumor, it was the very weekend when Anna Kay came, this woman who had seen these operations and had some crazy movies, and so right after that he called the healer in Manila. It was Tony Agpaoa, and Tony said, "Well, there's a group coming to see me this coming month." And Don, the idea of going with a tour to a healer was just an anathema; he didn't think he could he do that. He had been a colonel in the Air Force and quite a well-educated man and had a master's degree in chemistry.

Sidian Morning Star Jones: This was like the furthest thing from what he ever expected to do.

Patricia Westerbeke: Yes, I always say it was kind of a cosmic angel who flew over and looked at this conservative couple and said, "Hmm, I'm going to stir them up a bit." To think we'd be involved with psychic phenomena and psychic surgery was really quite bizarre. But Don was curious about everything, and so he flew to the Philippines and had the surgery. I have a lot of super-eight movies of Americans who were over there. Don just kind of hung around there, and then Tony worked on him. And we have these pictures of what was going on, and all I can say is that most likely Don was healed. I mean, the tumor just stopped growing. It caused no more trouble, and Don died of something totally different some thirty years later.

As a result of our trip to the Philippines, I wasn't surprised at any unique or interesting person coming to the ranch. Larry LeShan would come and teach psychic healing. And Luis Gasparetto from Brazil would visit and would draw pictures that he said were directed by spirits of famous artists like Monet and Picasso. He would take colored chalk in his toes and draw pictures of whatever artist had taken him over. I mean, he could draw pictures like Toulouse-Lautrec did, and this guy was pretty amazing. Now let me go back to good old Rolling Thunder and his group of Indian braves.

Sidian Morning Star Jones: I think he called them his "spiritual warriors," those men who were undergoing special training with him and who spent time protecting him and making road trips easier for him to handle.

Patricia Westerbeke: Yes, spiritual warriors. So they'd come and we always had very good food at the ranch and there was no charge at all, they were just guests. I'd put them all together in one cabin. There were just a couple of times, you know, I would go up to the main house where my bedroom was, and there'd be Rolling Thunder in my bed. I'd say, "What in the world are you doing here? I gave you a very nice guest room." And he said, "Oh, I'd thought this would be nicer for both of us."

Sidian Morning Star Jones: That's RT all right.

Patricia Westerbeke: And I'd say, "I don't think so." I mean, it was funny, and so I'd sleep in the guest room, I'd just leave him there.

Sidian Morning Star Jones: Really?

Patricia Westerbeke: Each time I'd put him, you know, where I wanted him, and finally he gave up. Heavens! He was a perfectly charming fellow as long as he stayed out of my bed.

Sidian Morning Star Jones: He was known for loving beautiful women.

Patricia Westerbeke: Well, I guess I should have been flattered.

Gail Hayssen, now a parapsychological researcher, wrote me a letter recalling her reaction to RT's flirting.

In the early 1970s Rolling Thunder stopped in to shop at Moby Fruit, my fresh fruit stand in Guerneville, California. He was on his way to the Emerald Valley Ranch, where Nicki and Rock Scully and the Grateful Dead had a country retreat. Rock Scully was the road manager for the Grateful Dead then. The ranch was a communal hippie scene that was very typical at that time in that part of California.

My customers were crowding about the famous Indian medicine man and were planning to attend a talk he would be giving that evening. Everyone was so excited about this medicine man that their eyes lit up when they said his name, "Rolling Thunder." Nicki Scully, one of my best customers, invited me to meet him at the Emerald Valley Ranch. I was thrilled to meet a real medicine man, and so I showed up right on time.

At the door of Emerald Valley Ranch I was approached by a woman who asked, "Excuse me, are you on your period?" I replied, "What? Why do you want to know?" She answered, "Women who are on their period are never permitted to be in the room with a medicine man." I assured her, "No, I'm not on my period now." She was relieved and told me something about conflicting energies. However, I was 17 at the time and very sensual, and she might have picked that up from me.

There were all sorts of hippies in the house, milling about and sitting around Rolling Thunder. They were sitting on the floor and were literally at his feet. He looked up at me. My instant reaction was a feeling that I was being undressed with his eyes. I saw a dirty old man like the ones I had seen before ever since I had reached puberty. I was not impressed with the claims that he was a very spiritual man because I felt him looking at me with desire. I wondered if there was something wrong with me. Why did I not think he was so energetically amazing, when everyone was so glassy eyed? Instead, I found him rather lecherous. I had been pursued by enough "spiritual" dirty old men that year. My belief at that time was that you could not be a spiritual teacher and also be sexually attracted to young girls.

I am sure he was an amazing man who inspired others. But that was not my personal experience as a teenager who owned a fruit stand, hanging out among all the adults who were admiring him. I just could not put him on a pedestal. I had several uncomfortable moments when people would come up to me in awe of Rolling Thunder. I would think in my mind as they spoke, "I don't want to burst your bubble, but I think he is a dirty old man."

But now I have come to learn that with a tremendous amount of power, which he obviously had, comes a tremendous amount of sexual drive because sex is powerful energy. I was young and filled with the type of sexual energy that would naturally be attractive to men who had a lot of power. It took me years to understand this. So my encounter with RT taught me something after all.

19

A Crisis in Carlin and Beyond

We learned that later in his life Rolling Thunder devoted more time to discussing the spiritual aspects of his work, ranging from prophecy to reincarnation. During one of his lectures in southern California, he remarked:

I read the Bible once, that's it. I've read the Qur'an. I've read Jewish books, like the Kabbalah. I never went to school, but I've read a great deal, and I've traveled a great deal. These books from different religions differ in some ways, but in other ways they say the same thing. And it is here where their teachings are similar to what is practiced by the American Indians. So that's why we are not alienated from each other. If one of us gets hurt, all of us get hurt. But that's why we are concerned about the future. So-called civilized people have gone way too far with destruction, with war, all of which are unnecessary, absolutely unnecessary. Now you will have one more big war, and that's all you are going to have. I've seen it on the rock writings, I have read it in many places, and it tells you that you'll see a trail of light and you'll see circles that represent three worldwide wars. And you will see it in the Milky Way, if you can read the stars at nighttime.

To us Indians several hundred years is a short space of time, a very short space of time. And I tell you we're coming back, only this time some other people are coming back along with us. And so it looks good that way. But if we are able, we can prevent the destruction of this land and life right now. I think they should have started a long time ago. But it is still not impossible, because the prophecy among the Indian people is that four people can protect this land, if they are sincere enough. But what is meant by this prophecy is that a small group, if they are sincere enough, could change the course of world events.

I saw something years ago up in New York City that I didn't like. I don't have too much against New York, except that I wouldn't want to live there. But I saw old ladies living in the streets. I had seen nothing about it in newspapers or magazines out here in Nevada, not one word about it. But I saw it, old ladies walking the streets with a pack on their back. I asked some of my New York friends and told them it was the first time I'd ever seen old ladies hitchhike. They said they are not hitchhiking, they live here but they have no homes, and that's what they told me. And I asked my friends, Where do they sleep? And they told me they sleep on the streets. In my religion we are concerned; I don't know if you want to hear this or not. But in my religion when we see something like that we are concerned right then, and we wonder what we might do about it. In other words we take action. We are militant. We are militant with the spiritual life as far as that part is concerned. And I'll tell you it's been our code.

When we come through San Francisco we see many homeless people too. One time when your [California] governor Reagan had made a big welfare cut, under different guises and excuses, it left a lot of people homeless and hungry. I have met some really hungry people. I remember a young lady and her family that walked up to the van we traveled in, and they were hungry and filthy and starving. And one of her kids was in a wheelchair, pushing it along. We didn't have much money, only enough money to get to our friends, who would help us out. But we had to give what we had. We had just come out of the food store, and we had bought ourselves groceries, because we eat in the car a lot of the time when we travel. But we had to give that family all our groceries and what money we had, and then we called for help.

Another time over in San Francisco there was a white lady who had been kind to Indians, and so we had to help her out. Because when we went in there we saw she was out of food. She had been letting a lot of Indians stay there, Indians who were coming back from the ceremonies at Wounded Knee. And she had let them stay there. And she was crying because she had no food left in the house. And she had three daughters to put through college. And she had lost her job too, and was on welfare. And she asked me what are the poor white people going to do? I told her, lady, I don't know the answers that your politicians claim to know. But I talked to her and sympathized with her a little bit, because I think she was entitled to get help. Some of the young warriors went out, and they bought a kitchen full of groceries and moved them in there.

But somehow I got a bad reputation; I tell you, we Indians all got a bad reputation. But I wish it were a hell of a lot worse. It would bring attention to what we are trying to do. Anyway, we travel in peace without guns. We brought our feathers and our drums. And it's been real good here. The energy is real high. I admit I am very particular in deciding where I'll go, and I have to have the feeling that maybe we can do some good, maybe we can wake some people up wherever we go.

Without that feeling, we don't go there. I've been offered big places, a lot bigger crowd than this. But I prefer this size of crowd. They can fit closer, they can hear, and they can communicate better than can a huge crowd. Maybe members of the huge crowd are there for show, and maybe they don't want to hear the message. So the chief up in our country told me a long time ago it was all right to use my Indian name if it would carry the message. He said that the message would be carried in many different ways, and that it might be carried in moving pictures.

Then Tom Laughlin came along and wanted to use my life story for his Billy Jack movies. I did my part on the Billy Jack movies by directing the Indian parts as well as seeing to it that we had clear weather. It did stay clear during the entire filming. I gave them most of the story board, I wrote some of the script, but I acted very little in it because I have very little desire to be a movie actor. But I did approve of the message bringing out what was going on. I think those movies carried a message based on the reality of things happening on the reservations that the public was totally unaware of. So I helped make those Billy Jack pictures and a few others, but I still don't want to be a movie actor. But the message can be carried in many different ways. And it's being carried among the Indians nowadays, because Indians are moving in all directions.

A group of Blackfoot Indians from Montana recently traveled through our camp, and they were on the way back from Arizona. And a group of Eskimos came from Alaska recently, and we get together and in a council sometimes. It's not that we still don't know how to communicate. When we had that big spiritual meeting of all the different tribes in Oklahoma, no letter had been written. Yet there was a group that showed up from Samoa way out in the South Pacific, and they gave their ceremony. Ancient peoples always had communication around the world, and it was more accurate than yours is.

One night a group of us from different tribes sat out all night and talked. What are we doing? Well, I'll tell you what we were doing. We were comparing our different dreams, our different prophecies. We were doing what you should be doing. You'll find out that what comes out of dreams can be more accurate than anything you see in the newspapers. Now I understand there is somebody from the newspapers here today. Okay, that's all right too. I am not out to put anybody down. But I say what I understand, that nobody has a monopoly on anything.

Now I think that's where some of us got off on the wrong foot. I know that some people think they have a monopoly on religion or God, as you call it. Whatever made them think that? Do you think that the Great Creator or God or Allah or whatever they want to call him, do you think he would go for such a petty thing? Do you think he would really understand or deal in that kind of way? Of course not. We are all created by the same Creator, the Grandfather, the Great Spirit. But we are not all the same. We are told in our religion, be respectful for differences. In other words if a person has a different color skin, respect that difference. I want to tell you something. We were created like the flowers, in different colors. There were white flowers, red ones, black ones, there were yellow ones, and people were created the same way. But we were supposed to live that way too. We were created to live in beauty.

Spiritual Components of Healing

Rolling Thunder's remarks remind us that both the endogenous and exogenous dimensions of traditional healing include a spiritual component. Hundreds of articles have appeared in peer-reviewed journals on health and spirituality. They include such dimensions of spirituality as intrinsic values, life meaning and purpose, community relationships and faith-based support groups, and reported inspirational incidents that go beyond one's ordinary, everyday experiences.

These articles contain considerable amounts of data indicating that people with internalized spiritual values score higher on measures of both spiritual and mental health than those without such values. These spiritual values and attitudes can occur with or without adherence to a religious belief system or membership in a religious organization. Indeed, there are some data that link certain rigid and dogmatic religious myths and belief systems with poor mental health. The growing body of such data requires health care providers to be aware of both the spiritual and religious dimensions of personal, familial, and cultural belief systems concerning health that are brought to their hospitals, offices, or clinics by an immigrant, refugee, or displaced person.

Does the positive association of spirituality and health provide evidence for the existence of a spiritual aspect of the cosmos? From the perspective of evolutionary psychology one could make the case that human beings who experienced their uniqueness and their connection with spiritual forces probably took a greater interest in their own personal survival as well as the survival of their family and neighbors. One's sense of self-worth became important, that person held greater expectations for oneself and his or her children, and if someone was gifted with something so special perhaps it persisted even beyond death. These personal and social myths may not be open to refutation or confirmation, but they could well have been adaptive. Natural selection favored those who held these beliefs, while those who lacked them fell out of the gene pool.

Because shamans played a key role in creating the cultural mythologies that reinforced these spiritual attitudes, they were unwitting agents in the saga of human evolution. In commenting on Darwin's theory of evolution, biologist Richard Dawkins once remarked, "Never were so many facts explained by so few assumptions." The development of spiritual beliefs may be one of them.

Stanley's Comments

On May 29, 1989, I was planning to spend a relaxing Memorial Day (an American holiday) with my wife at our home in Fairfax, California.

However, the Tao was flowing in another direction. I received a frantic telephone call from Mickey Hart, who said, "Stanley, we have a problem." I asked what kind of problem, having experienced numerous rough times during my years in California. Mickey continued, "I just had a phone call from Morning Star, RT's daughter. She was crying her heart out, saying that her father was dying. He never would take insulin for his diabetes, and now his leg is infected, and she claims that she can see the infection spreading. You are the only one who can persuade RT to come to Marin County, where my private physician can look after him." Mickey and I agreed to meet at the Novato, California, airport the next morning and not to tell RT we were coming to see him. That would have given him time to elevate his defenses and give us numerous reasons to stay in Carlin, Nevada.

Mickey persuaded Bill Graham, the rock music impresario, to lend us his private airplane and pilot for the day. When I arrived at the airport, Mickey, his son, and a member of the Dead's road crew were preparing the airplane for takeoff. We were in Carlin an hour later, and Morning Star was there to meet us. Between sobs, she told us that RT knew that the condition was serious but refused to leave his beloved home. When Mickey and I walked into his bedroom, RT gave us the least pleasant welcome we'd received in the years we had known him. He bellowed, "I know why you're here, and I'm not going with you. So you might as well get out of here right now and save yourself some time. I'm getting the best of care from a local medicine man, and I drink my herbal tea every few hours." Mickey whispered to me, "I just can't cope with this, Stanley. You are going to have to get him on that airplane before the end of the day."

I took some time introducing myself to the couple who were caretaking RT, a pleasant Native American man and woman. They told me that RT, indeed, was seeing a local practitioner of Native American medicine. But on his last visit the medicine man told RT, "If you are not better in three weeks, I think you should go to the hospital." Armed with this information, I went back to RT's room and started to discuss his illness. The gangrene emitted a very foul smell, and it was difficult for me to sit by the bed and listen. However, I tried to ignore the stench while RT extolled the wisdom of the local practitioner.

When he took a break, I asked, "RT, you really think a lot of that medicine man, don't you?" RT replied, "You're absolutely right, and he is giving me the best of care." I asked, "Has he shown up lately?" RT replied, "Not for the last few days." So then I asked, "I understand that he told you that you should go to a hospital if you were not better in three weeks. And he has not been here for five days. Don't you think he might be trying to tell you something?" RT paused. Slowly, he responded, "Well, you might be right. But if I go to the hospital, I want to take my herbal medicine along with me." At this point, his daughter took a traveling bag and said, "Dad, I will put your medicine right at the bottom of this little suitcase so it doesn't get lost." Morning Star also started to pack some clothes and toiletries.

RT looked at both of us and proclaimed, "I'm not saying that I'm going, but if I go, I want a police escort to the hospital. And I want to be carried out the back of the house. It is not seemly for a medicine man to leave from the front of the house when he is sick." I rushed into the hall where Mickey and his friend from the road crew were waiting. I said, "Mickey, you are going to have to make a donation to whatever charity event that the police put on in Carlin." I explained my reasoning, and Mickey peeled off a few hundred-dollar bills from a stack in his billfold. We phoned the police, who were short-staffed because of the holiday. But when we mentioned the possibility of a monetary donation, they immediately found a reason to assist us. Ten minutes later two police patrol cars and their uniformed drivers were escorting us up the road.

Getting RT and his cot out the back of the house was a more difficult feat. The four of us holding the cot had to tilt it to go through the three narrow doors that were on our way to the backyard. It didn't help that RT was complaining about the bumpy ride and threatening to go back into the house and die there. Eventually we arrived at the car, where the airplane pilot had been waiting patiently for our return, and started to the airport, with the two patrol cars clearing the roads for our journey. On the way to the airport Mickey stopped to buy some balm to disguise the strong odor. He was not going to succumb to the gangrene stench, which was even more noticeable in the car. RT did not look good; we quipped that for once he was whiter than we were.

Once airborne, RT's feet were practically in my lap, Mickey only shared the fragrant balm with his son, and there was a storm coming up. Nevertheless, we reached the small Novato airport without serious incident, and there was an ambulance waiting to take RT to the hospital. Mickey's physician was waiting, and after a cursory examination, whispered to us, "That leg will have to go." But RT was more interested in the room next door, one that had a guard posted in front of it. A hospital staff member explained that the patient was a prominent Mafia gang member who had been released from jail for an operation. The guard was there to scare off rival factions that might have a score to settle with the ailing godfather. RT, naturally, wanted a guard of his own; I proceeded to telephone friends of mine, and the next day, David Sessions, a musician who had visited RT in Nevada several years earlier, reported for duty and took one of several twelve-hour shifts. Also, on May 31, RT had the first of two operations that severed his right leg up to the knee.

I visited RT frequently while he was in the Marin General Hospital. On June 1 my wife and I visited RT, noticing that a very sleepy David Sessions was again standing guard. On June 12 we returned and were soon joined by Jerilyn Brandelius. Although no longer the significant other of Mickey Hart, Jerilyn was still concerned with RT's welfare, as they had become close friends over the years. RT was in good spirits even though he had several complaints about his hospitalization. When commenting on his medical care, he remarked, "The nurses in this hospital know more than the doctors."

A few weeks later I was attending an annual conference on shamanism and alternative modes of healing taking place at the Santa Sabina Center of Dominican College (now Dominican University) in San Rafael, California. Mickey was a featured speaker. After speaking about "music and spirit" in a manner that was both entertaining and instructive, Mickey brought me up to date on RT's condition. He told me that RT had been moved to a rehabilitation clinic, where the staff was teaching him how to use his new artificial leg. Adjusting to a prosthetic device was not an easy task for him, but he was eager to leave the clinic and continue his rehabilitation among his friends in Santa Cruz, California.

Mickey Hart's Account of the Crisis

Several years after these events, Mickey and I had an opportunity to review the crisis in Carlin. Here is our conversation about that fateful day.

Stanley Krippner: I got your phone call on Memorial Day.

Mickey Hart: I said, "We have a situation here, Stanley."

Stanley Krippner: You added, "RT is dying. We have to bring him out to see my personal doctor and save his life."

Mickey Hart: That's right.

Stanley Krippner: And you had the use of Bill Graham's private plane.

Mickey Hart: I called Bill up and said, "Bill, I need your plane." He said, "What for?" I said, "Well, I got this medicine man, Rolling Thunder, and he's isolating himself in a room, and he won't see anybody, and he's sick, and we have to go to help him, to get him down here to see Alan Margolin, my doctor." And so Bill gave me the plane, and then I called you because I didn't think I could do this alone. You knew how stubborn RT could be.

Stanley Krippner: I sure did!

Mickey Hart: And he had just locked himself in that room, and we were going to have to convince him, and I took my road manager as well and Taro, my son, and you. And was that it?

Stanley Krippner: That was it. We had the plane filled up—and of course we had the pilot.

Mickey Hart: Yeah, and we had to get RT. Actually, it was six passengers including RT.

Stanley Krippner: Yeah, and when we got there he looked at us, and he was not happy to see us. He said, "I know why you are here, and I'm not going anywhere with you."

Mickey Hart: He said, "I'm not leaving." He said something like, "Go away."

Stanley Krippner: He did. He really did not want us around.

Mickey Hart: I said, "We are not going without you. We're not leaving." And then I realized that I didn't want to get into a big argument, so I just turned him over to you.

Stanley Krippner: And I could tell that he was sick, because his skin was whiter than yours or mine. He was diabetic, and the gangrene was creeping up his leg. You could smell it.

Mickey Hart: Oh, the smell! I'll never forget that.

Stanley Krippner: And his daughter Morning Star was there, thank heavens. Then RT said, "I'm being well taken care of by another medicine man, and he comes in and helps out." But I had done a little research with his caretakers, and I said, "RT, your caretakers said that the medicine man was only going to work with you for three weeks, and at the end of three weeks if you hadn't gotten any better, you should go elsewhere. And the three weeks ended two days ago." And then, as we've said earlier, RT replied, "Well, you might be right. But if I go with you, I'm going to take all my herbs with me." And then finally his daughter said, "Dad, I'm going to start putting your things in a suitcase right now." And that's what eased the way. RT said, "But I'm going to go out the back way, and I want a police escort." We phoned the local police, and you gave them a nice financial donation. And then all of a sudden we had a police escort, with two motorcycled officers leading the way to the airport.

Mickey Hart: What do you suppose that was all about? Why did he want that?

Stanley Krippner: I think he wanted to leave in dignity, with a flourish, even if that meant going out the back door so nobody would see him until he got this escort to the airport.

Mickey Hart: That wasn't really like him.

Stanley Krippner: It wasn't like him, but he had never been deathly sick before.

Mickey Hart: That's true. I never really put that together before. He always liked to be under the radar until he wanted to be above the radar, then he was in your face. I remember we wrapped him very carefully, with his leg in a plastic bag.

Stanley Krippner: Very carefully.

Mickey Hart: We put him in the plastic bag and taped him; we sealed him up inside. We didn't want the pilot passing out, the smell was so bad. And we put a little pleasant-smelling balm under our nose when we got in that little plane, but it didn't help cover the stench that much.

Stanley Krippner: That was an ordeal.

Mickey Hart: It was an ordeal. And then we got him to the hospital, and they informed me that his leg would have to be removed if we were going to save him. And that was not a happy moment, but he went along with it. I just told him, "RT, this is it. This is the way it is: give up your leg, you live; you stay with your leg, you die." He understood. He let it go.

Stanley Krippner: That decision gave him several more years of life.

Mickey Hart: It did. That was very dramatic. I remember it very well.

The Premonition

On September 19, 1989, my anthropologist friend James Swan and I drove to Santa Cruz, California, to help RT celebrate his sixty-third birthday. Spotted Fawn had been dead for five years, and RT was on the road a lot, spending time in Santa Cruz, among other places. The occasion of his birthday party was a festive one, with drumming, dancing, singing, and buffalo meat—served at the right temperature. RT's son Buffalo Horse was there as well as Kasob, a son-in-law, Corey Folsom, Carie Spotted Feather, Jerilyn Brandelius, and Norman and Carolina Cohen, who had run the Thunder Trading Post in Santa Cruz for many years. Someone had brought a video that charted the destruction of the rain forests, and I reminded RT that he made the same type of predictions some two decades earlier.

RT enjoyed his time in Santa Cruz, surrounded by family and friends. But about a month after the birthday party, RT announced that he was going to leave Santa Cruz. He said it had nothing to do with his hosts and the good care he had received from them. However, he mused, "Something terrible is going to happen, and I don't want to be here at the time." The Loma Prieta earthquake hit Santa Cruz and adjoining areas on October 17. I was walking down a San Francisco street when I felt the tremors and immediately ran to the side of a building for protection. It was a 7.1 magnitude earthquake, the worst in the area since 1906. Later, when I discovered where the epicenter was, I recalled RT's premonition.

By this point the ownership of Meta Tantay had become contentious. RT was on the road half of the time, with as many as six spiritual warriors accompanying him; he probably could have made more money from his lectures had he limited his entourage to one or two. In his absence there was a lack of effective leadership at Meta Tantay; there was no real sense of direction, and his spiritual warriors and other associates living there spawned several projects that were short-lived.

I recall receiving letters from the Association for the Worldwide Church of the Great Spirit, Thunder over the Earth, the Committee for Preservation of Indian Lands, the Committee for the Study of Ecology and the Traditional American Indian, and Amerline Enterprises. The last-named group had a catalog of goods for sale, ranging from knives to jewelry to T-shirts emblazoned with the motto "We Know How." They knew a lot, but could not take an ingenious idea and follow it through to completion. From my perspective it was well run when RT's son Mala Spotted Eagle and his wife, Sky, were at the helm. However, they left to create their own center for the preservation of Native American traditions, Nanish Shontie.

Several people had signed on as co-owners, even people who put no money into the project. Some of those people had disappeared, and others were no longer talking with each other. Eventually the land was sold for a fraction of its value.

In retrospect, however, and in a much larger sense, Meta Tantay had been a huge success, and it must be said that the Meta Tantay Corporation had gotten off to a good start, being legally registered under the state laws in both California and Nevada. Adventurous experiments in animal husbandry and soil enrichment had produced verdant crops that made the community virtually self-sufficient. Hundreds of people learned about Native American traditions and how sincere people could put those traditions into communal practice.

It changed the lives of many young people who spent time there, and it educated and informed countless others. Perhaps it is remarkable that it thrived for as long as a decade. In any event, the full story about Meta Tantay has yet to be written.

In 2011 social activism in the United States took many forms, one of which was the Occupy Wall Street movement. Hundreds of people camped out in a park near the bastions of wealth and privilege— and, some would say, greed—to protest the growing income disparity between America's rich and poor. Although the movement received a great deal of publicity, one aspect that was not widely reported was the Native American protest group that stated, "The United States is already being occupied. This is indigenous land." Jessica Yee, executive director for the Native Youth Sexual Health Network, observed, "New York City is Haudenosaunee territory and home for many other

First Nations." She and other members of the group told the protestors that they were guests on the very land on which they were protesting. I thought that if RT were still alive he would be raising hell along with the protestors.

Sidian's Comments

It is no exaggeration to say that Rolling Thunder's legacy is a major contribution to the field of ethnomedicine. The term *ethnomedicine* refers to the comparative study of indigenous, traditional medical systems. Typical ethnomedical topics include causes of sickness, medical practitioners and their roles, and the specific treatments used. The explosion of ethnomedical literature has been stimulated by an increased awareness of the consequences of the forced displacement and/or acculturation of indigenous peoples, the recognition of indigenous health concepts as a means of maintaining ethnic identities, and the search for new medical treatments and technologies. In addition, ethnographic studies are a way of representing pluralism, drawing on those aspects of treating pain and suffering to resist the reductionism of conventional Western allopathic medicine that bypasses social and spiritual components that would characterize an integral, holistic system of health care.

There are two basic conceptual frameworks within traditional medical belief systems, the endogenous and the exogenous concepts. As an example of the former, sickness is caused by the loss or capture of a patient's soul, or part of the soul, or one of the souls. The soul has left the patient's body, has entered another realm, and the patient suffers as a result. Treatment involves the practitioner's intervention to recapture the soul and restore the balance of the patient's spiritual forces. In the latter instance, sickness is caused by the intrusion of a real or symbolic object within the patient; these objects range from pebbles to small animals to chunks of plastic to toxic substances such as viruses. Treatment involves an intervention to remove, kill, or neutralize the intruding objects, restoring the patient to health.

If a traditional medical system yields treatment outcomes that its society deems effective, it is worthy of consideration by Western medical investigators. This consideration is highlighted by the fact that less than 20 percent of the world's population is serviced by Western allopathic medicine. However, what is considered to be effective varies from society to society. Western medicine places its emphasis on "curing," removing the symptoms of an ailment and restoring a person to health, while traditional medicine focuses on "healing," attaining wholeness of body, mind, emotions, and spirit. Traditional, indigenous medicine uses a variety of herbs and plant substances, but it also uses rituals and ceremonies that are directed toward activating the patient's inner healer, connecting it with whatever spiritual, social, biological, emotional, and mental resources are available.

Some patients might be incapable of being cured, because their sickness is terminal. Yet those same patients could be healed mentally, emotionally, and/or spiritually as a result of the practitioner's encouragement to review their life, find meaning in it, and become reconciled to death. Patients who have been cured, on the other hand, may be taught procedures that will prevent a relapse or recurrence of their symptoms. This emphasis on prevention is a standard aspect of traditional medicine and is slowly becoming an important part of Western medicine as well.

A differentiation can also be made between "disease" and "illness." From either the Western medical or the indigenous point of view, one can conceptualize disease as a mechanical difficulty of the body resulting from injury or infection or from an organism's imbalance with its environment. A disease exists whether or not a culture recognizes it and whether or not the patient is aware of its existence. An illness, however, is a broader, socially contextualized term implying dysfunctional behavior, mood disorders, or inappropriate thoughts and feelings, as well as physical sickness. These behaviors, moods, thoughts, and feelings can accompany an injury, infection, or imbalance—or can exist without them. These illnesses to a large degree are socially constructed, and the way that they are constructed varies from society to society. Some people claim that allopathic medicine treats disease but not illness. Western-trained physicians learn to practice a technological medicine in which disease is their sole concern and in which technology is their only weapon.

Western medical technology often determines what is thought of as authoritative knowledge and, in turn, establishes a particular domain of power. Western medicine typically extends this privileged position to economics, politics, and class relationships. The power of allopathic medicine is jealously guarded by legislation, medical schools, licensing, and medicinal terminology. It is no wonder that indigenous, traditional people frequently view Western allopathic medicine as serving powerful groups while, in the meantime, they are struggling for a vestige of power over their own lives.

The value of ethnomedical practitioners and their incorporation into Western medical systems have become widely heralded since their advocacy by the World Health Organization at a conference in Alma-Ata, Kazakhstan, in 1972. However, such incorporation has been hindered by the high cost of training folk healers, the reluctance of the medical bureaucracy to accept them, and the decline of ethnomedicine in many parts of the world. The World Health Organization's objective of available medical care for all people of the Earth depends on granting folk healers professional autonomy as well as educating them to abandon worthless—and sometimes harmful—practices and teaching them about effective public health measures. Many ethnomedical practitioners use adaptive strategies that are open-ended and dynamic systems, flexible to change in response to the community and the environment.

Allopathic medicine is far from perfect. A 2006 report observed that 1.5 million people in the United States are injured each year by medication errors, including the poor handwriting of some physicians that leads to incorrect prescriptions being given to patients by pharmacists. A related survey estimated that there are more than 2 million hospitalizations in the United States each year and more than 100,000 deaths from the side effects of pharmaceutical drugs. These numbers, combined with previously documented information that takes into account the mistakes and misuses of pharmaceutical drugs, brings the number to more than 5 million hospitalizations and more than 250,000 deaths annually, in other words, nearly 700 deaths per day. This makes mainstream biomedical treatment the third leading cause of death in the United States.

In the meantime, more than 40 percent of the U.S. population is estimated to be using generic drugs as well as complementary and alternative medical procedures. Americans spend more than $30 billion on these services yearly, even though the costs usually are not reimbursed. Visits to complementary and alternative practitioners exceed visits to allopathic medical physicians by more than 200 million visits per year. People who gravitate to these practitioners have been found to acknowledge the importance of treating illness within a larger context of spirituality and meaning, one that embraces a holistic orientation to life.

Many patients believe that their experiences have been marginalized because they challenge the dominant worldviews of Western medical professionals. The self-statements of these patients often appear to be mocking, angry, or despairing as they find their problems reduced by allopathic physicians and psychiatrists to "diseased brains" and biochemical reactions rather than acknowledged as the enigmatic but distressing problems they are experiencing.

Moreover, some widely prescribed drugs are ineffective for more than half the patients who take them, many surgical procedures are unnecessary, and some sicknesses are "constructed" by pharmaceutical companies, business corporations, and the medical system to ensure profits. Common life problems such as shyness, hyperactivity, and sensitivity to the weather are called disorders, and the recommended treatment includes medication.

PLoS Medicine, a respected medical journal published by the Public Library of Science, ran a special issue on this topic. Various observers accused pharmaceutical companies of "disease mongering," inflating the market for a drug by convincing people that they are sick and in need of medical treatment. The journal reported instances of campaigns to increase drug sales by "medicalizing" aspects of everyday life such as irritability in children, twitching legs, mood swings, and irregularities in sexual performance. These have become "corporate-constructed" illnesses, often labeled attention deficit hyperactivity disorder, restless leg syndrome, bipolar disorders, frigidity, and erectile dysfunction, all of them purportedly requiring immediate pharmaceutical treatment.

The Future of Western Medicine

Staunch advocates of allopathic medicine often view folk healing as a superstition-laden obstacle to the dissemination of Western medical care, while many traditional healers view allopathic medicine as detrimental to the holistic, community-centered health practices they have advocated for millennia. This conflict resembles a clash of worldviews or mythologies. When discussing a traditional medical system's confrontation with allopathic medicine, an "old myth" (in this case, traditional folk healing) is often challenged by a "countermyth" (in this case, allopathic medicine).

Several outcomes to this dialectic are possible. The countermyth can prevail, and the old myth can be relegated to ignominy (as occurred when "bleeding" of patients was replaced by more effective types of treatment, such as antibiotics). Or perhaps the old myth prevails, and the countermyth fades away (as occurred in parts of the Amazon rain forest, where Western medical practices are shunned in favor of ancient practices). Another possibility is that a compromise can be worked out in which both mythic worldviews continue to operate, sometimes together and sometimes apart (as is the case in Bolivia, where allopathic and traditional practitioners both serve their coteries of patients). Sometimes there is a synthesis, where the old myth and the countermyth merge into a "new myth" that preserves the best of both perspectives. This synthesis is exemplified by Leslie Gray, who has combined her training as a clinical psychologist with her training as a Native American shaman.

The future of ethnomedicine will hinge on how these mythic clashes are worked out in one part of the world or another. The World Health Organization is hopeful that a synthesis will occur, or at least a compromise will be reached. But for either to take place mutual respect is required, and courtesy needs to be given to each tradition by the other. The increased number of immigrants and displaced people in the world has brought these mythic clashes into the open. Sometimes the evidence dictates that old medical myths need to be replaced, notably in regard to the prevention and treatment of AIDS in sub-Saharan Africa. In some parts of this area, the myth that AIDS among men can be cured if the afflicted man has sex with a virgin has had disastrous consequences. In other parts of Africa the alleged cure is to have sex with a postmenopausal woman, and in still other places the rumored cure is to have sex with an infant. These myths are dysfunctional, representing extremely irrational ways of removing an entity or force, in this case the HIV virus.

Groups such as the Society for Shamanic Practitioners are making active efforts to provide a synthesis between shamanic procedures and those of Western medicine and psychotherapy. The 178-nation World International Property Organization is attempting to protect indigenous people from outside exploitation of their herbal remedies. The future of ethnomedicine will depend on projects of this nature, syntheses that nurture a careful examination of existing evidence regarding the effectiveness of traditional treatments, the resolution of quality control of the substances used, and the opportunity for research when no data are available.

The momentum of the past few centuries has led to the waning of shamanism and other traditional practices in developing countries. This may be an example of the "tomato effect" in medicine. This term refers to the rejection of worthwhile traditional procedures and treatments that clash with those accepted by mainstream practitioners. The tomato, brought to Europe from the Americas in the 1600s, was not seen as fit for human consumption by physicians because it was a member of the nightshade family. The fact that Native Americans had eaten tomatoes for centuries without ill effects was ignored by the members of the medical establishment. After two centuries of tomato eating by Europeans who rejected the medical establishment's prohibitions without falling ill, physicians stopped objecting in the 1820s. In this case ingestion of the tomato represented a countermyth that was rejected by the European physicians who championed the old myth that all nightshade plants were poisonous.

Objections to the tomato aside, power began to gravitate away from folk healers and neighborhood doctors to highly technical allopathic medicine practitioners with their pills, procedures, instruments, and immunizations. Authorities in white coats replaced the friendly folk healers and bedside physicians, multiplying like sorcerer's brooms into myriad specialists sweeping in and out of examination rooms. Costs went up, caring went down, and patients became seen as consumers as they struggled for survival and autonomy. Lives were prolonged, but satisfaction and practitioner gratification plummeted.

On the positive side, more than two hundred pharmaceutical companies are investigating plant derivatives, many of them in rain forests and jungles. More than six thousand alkaloids have been isolated from nearly four thousand varieties of plants. National groups such as the Fundação Brasileira and the Comisión Amazónica are monitoring the work of drug companies to be sure that indigenous people are compensated for any discoveries. An international database, the Traditional Knowledge Digital Library, contains some 140,000 treatments, establishing what is known in the patent world as prior knowledge, protecting them from exploitation. This is part of the legacy of Rolling Thunder and other practitioners of traditional, indigenous medicine around the world.

The *Vital Signs* Radio Interview

Even with the loss of a leg, RT remained active. In 1993 he was interviewed by Dr. Stuart Fischer, a physician in New York City, on Fischer's radio show, *Vital Signs*. Here are some excerpts from the conversation between RT and Stuart Fischer from their 1993 radio interview.

Stuart Fischer: Today we have the Native American medicine man Rolling Thunder on the line to talk about some of the incredible experiences that he's had. First of all, I can't express my gratitude enough at having the opportunity to talk to you. This is one of the highlights of my professional life. Good morning to you.

Rolling Thunder: Good morning to you.

Stuart Fischer: Tell me about diet. I work at a nutritionally oriented practice, and I am constantly telling people about the importance of diet and health. I'm sure that you would support that even more than I do.

Rolling Thunder: Yes, I would like to speak particularly about diabetes, which is seen in every Indian hospital in the country.

Stuart Fischer: As I recall, the Pima Indians are often studied because of the incredibly high incidence of diabetes. I believe it is the highest in the country, percentagewise, of any group.

Rolling Thunder: Yes, they have diabetes and tuberculosis, which we also have an abundance of. It all comes from the wrong kind of diet.

Stuart Fischer: Absolutely. In what we call type I diabetes, the body does not produce enough insulin. In type II diabetes, the body produces enough insulin but the cells have developed a resistance to it. In both cases, the cells are not getting the fuel that they need.

Rolling Thunder: We were defeated many years ago, and our land was taken by the settlers. We were shoved out into the desert and the high mountain areas where we couldn't get water for our gardens. Yes, we had gardens. During one of my lectures, a girl told me she didn't know that Indians had gardens, and I asked, "Where do you think your tomatoes and your melons and your corn all came from?" And yes, we had gardens, wonderful gardens. It's a fact that it was the Indians that taught the Pilgrims for three years in a row how to plant corn so they wouldn't starve to death and how to fertilize their fields using fish bones.

Stuart Fischer: Absolutely.

Rolling Thunder: I myself have suffered from diabetes, and I lost one leg because of it.

Stuart Fischer: I know about this.

Rolling Thunder: But even after I changed my eating habits, I've been eating too much "white man's food," you can call it, in other words, Caucasian food.

Stuart Fischer: Refined carbohydrates.

Rolling Thunder: And I have been eating too much sugar. Sugar in cake, sugar in coffee, and sugar in yucky stuff, and I had to pay for it. I shouldn't have done it. I don't blame the white man or anyone. I could have carried a bag of pinyon nuts, cornmeal, a piece of jerky, and a canteen of good water, and I would have been much better off. But instead of that, I was tempted, and I should not have been. Nowadays, I don't allow any sugar in my house.

Stuart Fischer: Carlton Fredericks, the famous naturopath, based so many of his teachings upon the fact that civilization, as you would say, "the white man's civilization," involves destroying the Earth's good grains and turning them into processed carbohydrates. That is the prime villain in developing diabetes.

Rolling Thunder: Yes, they are exactly right about that and also about sugar. I've known many medical people for many years and dentists too. The dentists have a big practice because of children coming in with cavities at a very young age. The consumption of sugar has increased twenty times in the past decade, and it is still going up. People think the way to be kind to little children is to give them candy and all that stuff instead of an apple or something that would be good for them. And you get plenty of sugar in oranges, apples, and some other fruits. You get plenty of sugar in orange juice, apple juice, and other fruit juices. Refined sugar is the worst, because it goes into the bloodstream real fast. If you have rheumatism or arthritis and if you want to know where it is located, all you have to do is eat a little bit of sugar in any form and you will feel the part of your body that gives you the most trouble. It can increase your misery, and your disposition gets worse. Whatever you do, don't give your wife sugar-coated candy or something like that, especially if she's got a cavity.

Stuart Fischer: What kind of food do you try to encourage people to eat on the reservation?

Rolling Thunder: Well, we're not all on the reservations, thank goodness. Not all of us yet. There are a lot of Indians who have surrendered and moved to the reservation. We have a confrontation about that going on out here right now. They are trying to take the cattle and horses away from the Indians who we call "off-reservation" Indians who never surrendered.

Stuart Fischer: Really?

Rolling Thunder: The ones who surrendered were marched to the prison camps called reservations.

Stuart Fischer: What I think of as a benign term is actually, as you just said, a prison camp.

Rolling Thunder: They were prison camps and guarded by soldiers.

Stuart Fischer: Also, one of the points that we certainly can agree on is that the type of food that was being fed them was, as you were saying before, food with high-carbohydrate content.

Rolling Thunder: The Indians were fed a ration when it wasn't stolen and stolen away from them. It was usually sow belly, the cheapest part of the belly of the hog. Also, they were given flour, white flour that was usually wormy. They were always given coffee, and it seems like there was always sugar to eat. That stuff would keep indefinitely because it was not fresh.

Stuart Fischer: What are the foods you encourage people to eat?

Rolling Thunder: Just the opposite of that. Well, I like rhubarb for one thing. It's good to guard against sugar diabetes. Good for the stomach. Also, I like a little of it every morning, and I like anything bitter.

My taste buds are active now, and food tastes so good because I don't eat sugar. I like natural fruit sometimes, and berries, and the more bitter they are the better I like them. I don't take insulin. I don't believe in chemicals of any kind. I don't need them in my body anymore.

Stuart Fischer: What about things like garlic and onions?

Rolling Thunder: I eat lots of garlic and lots of onions. Cherokees have always eaten onions and leeks. There are different kinds of foods growing up there in the Smoky Mountains. I tell you they are mighty good blood purifiers, all of them. I advise people to stay away from too many dairy products like cheese, butter, and milk. No-fat milk is fine, and so is yogurt. I suggest that they eat cooked greens and cabbage, raw carrots and watercress, soup, and poached eggs. They can't go wrong if they eat what Indians call the "three sisters"—beans, squash, and corn. If they eat meat, beef and chicken are better than ham and bacon. And I like a glass of hot prune juice in the morning.

Stuart Fischer: And this is one thing I think that modern medicine, actually modern alternative medicine, could agree with you on. Garlic has been demonstrated to be a blood thinner and can help protect people against heart disease.

Rolling Thunder: It's one of the best antibiotics ever invented, besides being a good preventive against high blood pressure.

Stuart Fischer: Cayenne pepper is useful too.

Rolling Thunder: Cayenne pepper is all right, especially as a treatment to prevent and treat tuberculosis. I got rid of my tuberculosis when I had it. That's how I became a medicine man. I had to go through every sickness I was going to treat, and I had to master them and get well from them. That was part of the test. I got rid of my tuberculosis. I had a craving for lots of hot chili, but I don't like it so hot anymore. I overcame it. I don't need it quite so hot anymore, but I still love it.

Stuart Fischer: Did it make you sweat a great deal?

Rolling Thunder: It made me sweat. Also, it broke loose the phlegm. I got it all out. It's a wonderful feeling to be rid of it. It's a good thing that I didn't smoke cigarettes and all the chemicals they contain.

Stuart Fischer: I was lucky enough when I was trekking in the Himalaya Mountains to watch my guide, a Sherpa, when he ate very hot chilies. He turned bright, tomato red, and there was profuse sweat coming out of him. I thought something dangerous would happen, but when the redness went away, he had a big, big smile on his face.

Rolling Thunder: Well, yes, that's the way it can happen. A good sweat can be used in the right way, the traditional way of doing things. Whoever runs the sweat lodge has to carefully select the people who will participate. When I am in charge, I can smell who is right for the ceremony.

Stuart Fischer: What type of meat do you eat?

Rolling Thunder: I do not eat pork. They rationed the Indians, and some Indians got addicted to this stuff. I don't eat ham or greasy bacon. I do eat other kinds of meat on occasion. I eat buffalo meat every chance I get. I can order it from a place where they raise buffalo in Kansas.

Stuart Fischer: It has phenomenally low fat.

Rolling Thunder: It's wonderful, and cooked right, it's tender and nonfat. I like it cooked well done where you can cut it with a spoon. I know how to do that, and I used to marinate it. I've taught other people how to cook it. I think that buffalo meat is coming back now that they've learned how to raise buffalo properly.

Stuart Fischer: It's making a comeback in the New York area because of the high-protein and low-fat aspects. It's an extremely high-protein food.

Rolling Thunder: The trouble with wild game meat like buffalo meat is that when you eat it, you don't want to eat beef anymore. And that makes the cattle ranchers unhappy.

Stuart Fischer: It's kind of hard to find buffalo meat out here in this sort of wilderness. But now I have to ask you this fascinating question, and I can't wait to get your answer. What do you think of healers in other civilizations, such as Tibetan healers? Have you, in your travels and reading, formed an opinion about these people?

Rolling Thunder: Yes, I have had personal contact with quite a number of them. We are all working for the same thing. I have some wonderful friends who are good doctors, and I know some of the best surgeons in the world. Some people think we should be enemies. But the fact is that a few of them come to me when they want to get well. But don't tell anybody, because I don't have a hospital and if they come here I can't take them. It's that simple. I just can't take them. They can only come here with permission, advanced permission, and I can only take a few because of my condition right now. And even then I don't charge anything. I don't work for money. I work with the Great Spirit only. A lot of people don't know how to approach me. There are certain ways of approaching a medicine man. Good manners help a lot. Anyway, I think I danced all around your question there.

Stuart Fischer: That's the exact thing I was looking for.

Rolling Thunder: I don't look for patients; they look for me—and most of the time they can't find me right now. I'm going to write some books and things like that. I would like to see the public be aware of these silly, stupid laws. The laws have taken some of the best herbal medicines completely off the market.

Stuart Fischer: Tell us more about this.

Rolling Thunder: Live oak, for instance, has been very good for leukemia and other forms of cancer and distemper in animals. But the people who make the laws claim that if you could drink a ton of it as tea at one sitting, it could cause cancer or degeneration of the liver. The same thing could be said about too much water or too much milk.

Stuart Fischer: Or probably half the medications available.

Rolling Thunder: It certainly would apply to Coca-Cola, which has seven spoonfuls of sugar in it, and other cola drinks too. There are seven teaspoons of sugar in each bottle. It is loaded with sugar.

Stuart Fischer: When Stanley Krippner talks about Native American medicine, he often discusses illnesses of the soul. This is something that most medical doctors don't even touch upon. It involves the community; it involves the family and is a recognized malady in many civilizations. I'm sure you've tended to this problem, but we ignore it completely in Western medicine.

Rolling Thunder: Yes, I have treated a lot of these people. There is a certain bad practice that we Native people put on ourselves. We go to funerals or stay around sick people. Medicine men often need to keep the sickness from spreading or else we would all be dead or possessed. But that doesn't happen if there is a medicine person around. Any good medicine person knows what they are doing when they prevent soul illnesses. They know how to protect themselves, and a lot of this will be revealed to the public in my book.

Stuart Fischer: Do you involve the family also in healing?

Rolling Thunder: A few of my little grandchildren have participated in powwows and Indian dances. I'd rather have them dancing and having a good time that way and working off some steam than hanging out on the streets. It makes me feel real good to see these young people get together with some of their white friends too. They are all staying well and are feeling good about themselves too.

Stuart Fischer: Tell me about burning sage and cedar.

Rolling Thunder: Some places we do burn cedar, and other places we burn sage, according to what grows there. It's a form of incense that we use. And we use it just like the incense was used across the "great waters" in Greece many, many years ago. We use it in traditional ways in clamshells sometimes. And we invented a smoke from sage that can fill up the entire house. It seems to be pretty effective for purification. We have hundreds of miles of beautiful sage growing in Nevada. It is the strongest sage in the world, I believe. It works wonders.

Stuart Fischer: Are there different applications for one versus the other?

Rolling Thunder: Yes, whether we use sage or cedar is all according to the region and the area. Another way we used incense was to fill our tepees with smoke after white people would come to visit. You never know, they might be thinking of stealing the children or something like that. A lot of children were stolen and sent to missionary schools.

Stuart Fischer: There is a very strong common bond between what you do and what I have been taught through the books of Carlton Fredericks and in my work with Dr. Robert Atkins. Again, so many of my friends are thrilled that you have done this show. So many people who are listening [to us talk] today are in your debt.

Franklin Fried's Perspective

Franklin Fried provided a very different side of RT during an interview.

Franklin Fried: When RT was in the hospital, Clarence Clemons, the saxophone player from Bruce Springsteen's E Street Band, came to see him. There was a memorial concert for John Cipollina, a musician friend of Mickey's, and I really wanted to go. So Clarence Clemons took my place and stayed with RT that night. I know that when RT and his entourage went to Los Angeles that they met a lot of celebrities down there. And Buffalo Horse told me that one time he met Doris Day, and she was really lots of fun.

It's not good that he was in the hospital, but it's a good story for me to tell you. When they wanted to amputate his leg, RT insisted that he have his medicine bag, his eagle feathers, and any other items that were sacred to him—and they obliged that. Now, I don't know if they put it in a plastic bag or what it was, but he had to have those with him. I think that's quite interesting. Usually hospital staff didn't allow objects that have not been sterilized into the hospital room.

Long ago the Grateful Dead had started a charitable foundation called the Rex Foundation, and one of their first benefit concerts was at the Warfield Theater in San Francisco. The Rex Foundation allotted certain money to different charities. The first charity was Meta Tantay, I believe. I could be wrong, but that was one of the first things to raise money for Meta Tantay. So, basically, the Grateful Dead helped fund the land for Meta Tantay. Mickey and Billy [Grateful Dead band members] went there and recorded parts of the Dead's album called *Shakedown Street.* But sometimes Mickey and Billy did not follow the rules, and once RT told them to get off his land because they were caught smoking marijuana. Have you heard that story?

Sidian Morning Star Jones: I vaguely remember something about that. It wasn't just them though; there were other people that got kicked out for that misbehavior.

Franklin Fried: Oh yeah, other people were caught with things like that. There is a photograph in Jerilyn Brandelius's book, *Grateful Dead Family Album,* of Mickey and Billy at Meta Tantay. Here is something else I can tell you. You know the movie called *Billy Jack,* right? Tom Laughlin produced, directed, and starred in it.

Sidian Morning Star Jones: Yes.

Franklin Fried: Did Buffalo Horse tell you the story about *Billy Jack?*

Sidian Morning Star Jones: What story is this?

Franklin Fried: Well, Meta Tantay was given a *Billy Jack* production truck that the film crew was using to make the movie. While filming the movie some of the local troublemakers walked up to the movie set and started to pick a fight with the production company.

They didn't like the fact that a Hollywood movie was being made about Indians, so they gave the film crew a hard time. But then RT came out and stared them down. He didn't say a word, but they all sulked away.

Sidian Morning Star Jones: Who told you that?

Franklin Fried: Buffalo Horse. Also, in the movie, there is a part where Billy Jack is leading the snake dance as part of this rite of passage. This is a dance that RT borrowed from Iroquois friends; each dancer places his or her hands on the hips of the dancer in front. And during the ceremony he gets bit by a diamondback rattlesnake. Well, they shot the legs of your grandfather when he is actually getting bit by the rattlesnake. You see Tom Laughlin dancing, but the close-up is of RT's legs. He had been trained to assimilate snakebites, and so the poison didn't bother him one bit. In fact, he claimed to have gained the power of the diamondback rattlesnake in this process.

Sidian Morning Star Jones: And he's actually getting bit.

Franklin Fried: He believed he would get some power from the rattle-snake. And another power animal of his was the badger. He liked the badger's sense of smell. I remember Buffalo Horse telling me that when RT was a little baby he always wanted to smell every-thing. Whatever happened, it let him learn to use the sense of smell. That's why for most indigenous people, their senses are more devel-oped than the average human, because when you live in Nature you have to be able to sense things from a distance. You have to learn to feel the vibrations from the Earth. You need to know the scents of the different animals. Plus, you're living among the natural elements. You have to live off the land. You have to hunt so that the wind is going against you. That way your odor won't be going toward the game you are hunting, and so they can't sense you. RT used his sense of smell in his healing sessions. He felt that different sicknesses send out different odors. And he even felt that he could smell the oncoming death of someone.

2 0

The Legacy

On January 23, 1997, Rolling Thunder joined Spotted Fawn in the other world, leaving behind what we consider an impressive legacy. *Shaman's Drum* magazine published a praiseworthy obituary, calling RT "an internationally recognized traditional medicine man, master herbalist, and Native American leader who touched and influenced the lives of many people. His message was simple but profound, urging his audiences to return to the old ways, to abolish war and pollution, and to respect Mother Earth—the life source of all beings." The obituary noted that RT was a lifelong advocate for Native American rights and that even after he was confined to a wheelchair he continued his activism.

Sidian's Comments

Rolling Thunder did not hesitate to talk about death. One of the audiotapes I listened to has several interesting comments on the topic. He said, "There's no death. There's only a crossing over. I know where I'm going. I don't have to come back, even though I've only had three lives. This is common with medicine people.

"On one of my visits to the Happy Hunting Ground my guide took me to a village. Many children were playing and running and laughing, so I know that with so many children they do have sex in the Happy Hunting Ground. What would heaven be without children running, playing, and laughing?"

Another Conversation with Family Members

Several years after RT's death I again interviewed several family members—my aunts, uncles, and cousins. Here are some of the highlights of that interview, and once again I do not identify them here because I encouraged them to speak anonymously.

Sidian Morning Star Jones: Let's take a look at some family photographs. Do you remember this guy who is standing next to you?

First male voice: Sure. I used to chain him up to the ankles. I made him play chain gang.

Sidian Morning Star Jones: What's that?

First male voice: That's where they chain prisoners together and get a sledgehammer, and they make them go and break rocks.

Sidian Morning Star Jones: You would make them go and break rocks? That's pretty funny.

First male voice: Yeah. Well, that was all that I could think of doing with him, because I couldn't kill him. I used to beat him senseless, and he would still keep coming back for more. I'm serious. Mom caught me many times choking him until he turned blue.

Sidian Morning Star Jones: So what did RT think about that?

First male voice: I don't know. I never asked him. He wasn't invited.

Sidian Morning Star Jones: Remember I'm recording this right now.

First male voice: Well, you can't record me without recording that story. It shows how ornery I was as a kid.

Sidian Morning Star Jones: Take a look at this picture. What is that woman wearing?

First male voice: That looks like a badger penis.

Sidian Morning Star Jones: You would know.

First male voice: It's part of a traditional costume. Mom used to wear one.

First female voice: A badger penis?

First male voice: Yes.

Second female voice: I believe she would do that for good luck.

First male voice: It's a bonus. It reminds you that the Great Spirit made all kinds of different penises. Like a pig's penis is a corkscrew.

First female voice: I've heard of it.

First male voice: No, it's true. They have to do cartwheels to get it into a female pig.

Second male voice: You kids used to watch it when we raced those pigs.

First male voice: We had fifty-six of the pigs running. They don't believe me when I say that the pigs had corkscrew penises and they had to do cartwheels to get it in.

Second male voice: They look like corkscrews all right.

First male voice: And they don't believe that some tribes used to wear badger penises that were beaded.

First female voice: Oh, yes they did. That doesn't surprise me about Grandma wearing a badger penis, considering her fascination with sex. It would make a good story. Now, don't you put that in the story.

Sidian Morning Star Jones: No, I want to; it's great. Spotted Fawn had a great sense of humor.

First male voice: Well, you could use the name Meathead when you talk about who I beat up. Yeah, everyone will know whom you are talking about.

Second female voice: Everyone knows who Meathead is.

First male voice: Dead meat from the neck up. I never chained your mom to the telephone pole though.

Sidian Morning Star Jones: What was my mom like back then?

First male voice: She cried every time the police came to arrest us. She'd get us out of it, but she would be crying and went hiding in the bushes 'cause she was little, and the police just kind of felt badly for her.

Sidian Morning Star Jones: Why did the police come?

First male voice: Because we used to fill up bags with shit and put them on the neighbor's door and light them on fire. And the police would come and stomp them out.

Sidian Morning Star Jones: So that's why the police were taking you away?

First male voice: Well, they didn't get me.

First female voice: They didn't catch you because you could run faster and you would leave your little sister behind.

Sidian Morning Star Jones: I'm hearing all sorts of stories tonight.

First male voice: If they pertain to me they are lies.

Sidian Morning Star Jones: How about all these stories about RT that are really mystical and magical?

First male voice: He didn't walk on water. He shit in the toilet just like everyone else.

Sidian Morning Star Jones: I heard that he summoned a bear once to scare off people who bothered him.

First male voice: It must have been a teddy bear.

Sidian Morning Star Jones: So do you have any stories like that?

First male voice: No, he was just normal except he got angry easily.

Second female voice: You heard he brought a bear in to scare off people? Really?

Sidian Morning Star Jones: Yeah.

First female voice: Wow, what do you mean?

Sidian Morning Star Jones: I heard that when he was working on the railroad, he used to get a lot of ridicule for being an Indian because all the rest of them were white, and it escalated into where at some point there was violence or something. And from what I heard, he summoned a bear and scared them all, and they took off and never messed with him again.

Second female voice: That's interesting.

First male voice: Well, if I tell you a story and it goes around the room, it will come back to me a different story. It's just the way humans are.

Second female voice: But I remember being in a sweat lodge ceremony with him, and whoever was running the ceremony wasn't doing it right. And there was a bear on the outside shaking the whole lodge. But it never came in.

First male voice: I've been in peyote ceremonies where strange shit happens outside and you don't want to go outside and look. No sir.

Sidian Morning Star Jones: There was a bear shaking the whole lodge?

Second female voice: Yeah.

First male voice: I was never allowed to go to the sweat lodge ceremony when I was a kid.

Second female voice: Yeah. I remember the bear walking outside the sweat lodge, and the next thing you know the whole lodge was shaking. I don't know if it was because who was running the ceremony wasn't doing it right.

Second male voice: Who was running it?

Second female voice: Some guy from Montana.

Sidian Morning Star Jones: I read on the Internet that a guy shot the world's largest recorded grizzly bear because it was coming to kill him, and when they found his body they said it was big enough to look over a one-story house.

First male voice: That's only ten feet.

First female voice: You say it like it's not tall.

First male voice: The stuffed bear in the Commercial Hotel in Elko is bigger than that.

Sidian Morning Star Jones: This is the world's largest recorded bear. They searched the intestines, and they found that it had eaten two humans previous to attacking this other guy who finally shot it down.

First male voice: Once an animal gets a taste of human flesh, it's like going from peanut butter to ice cream. Human flesh is tasty. That's why there are cannibals. Wild animals are like that too; yeah, they are.

First female voice: I think you make this stuff up.

Second female voice: Dogs are like that.

First male voice: Especially if they start going after cattle and start killing cattle. I put my dogs down. Killed them right there on the spot and left them. That's not a joke.

Sidian Morning Star Jones: I believe you. You have to take care of the cattle.

First male voice: If you don't, the rancher sues you for $300, and back in those days, $300 was a lot of money. That means no Christmas gifts.

Second male voice: Well, we never celebrated Christmas anyway, or any of the other religious holidays. Okay let's think about stories about RT. What did RT ever do? He used to piss me off all the time, making me work.

Sidian Morning Star Jones: Tell me about that.

First male voice: Yeah, we had chores to do. We would have to get up in the morning and run out to the goddamn silver bridge, which was kind of far from the house. You know the house in Carlin? I am talking about the silver bridge down there. And he would set a stupid rock there. In those days they were called sexstones—Indian sexstones. To me they were just another fucking rock.

Sidian Morning Star Jones: What was the whole purpose of putting a rock there?

First male voice: So that when we would run out there and we could prove that we were there to get the stupid rock, bring it back there, do all the chores, and go to school. That's not even a joke. That's the kind of crap he made us do. It's true. Or else he would say, "I want that tree moved over here."

Sidian Morning Star Jones: You would move a tree?

First male voice: Do you remember those big trees in front of the house?

Sidian Morning Star Jones: Yeah.

First male voice: I planted them all, me and my brother. They weren't there originally.

Sidian Morning Star Jones: How big were they when you moved them?

First male voice: Probably about twenty feet tall. I was only three or four feet tall, so they were bigger than I was. They were farther away from the house, and we had to move them out so Mom could have some shade. She lived in the corner bedroom.

Second male voice: It's a good thing you have the tape recorder. None of us remember anything. Those are black days, so we try to block them out. So that's why we can't remember. It's not our fault. We were victims. It's true. He would abuse all of us in one way or another.

Sidian Morning Star Jones: What about working with him when he would go and do the talks?

First male voice: Yeah, that was fun.

Sidian Morning Star Jones: Well, what did you do?

First male voice: Avoided him as much as possible.

Sidian Morning Star Jones: Yeah?

First male voice: Yeah, 'cause he was a jerk.

Sidian Morning Star Jones: Why?

First male voice: Because he always wanted everything his way, and we couldn't talk. We thought he was a prima donna. It was like being with Jesus Christ.

Sidian Morning Star Jones: He'd be like real strict about everything?

First male voice: No, he'd be rude, insulting, irritating, obnoxious, and unruly.

Sidian Morning Star Jones: Yeah, my dad was like that too.

Second male voice: Your dad was just like him. That's why they didn't get along. They were both assholes. I've known your father since he was about sixteen years old.

Sidian Morning Star Jones: Did my dad change throughout the years very much?

First male voice: Yeah, he became more materialistic as he got older.

Sidian Morning Star Jones: Became more materialistic?

First male voice: Yeah, a capitalist, greedy.

Sidian Morning Star Jones: What was he like before that though?

First male voice: He was normal; that was the only reason I hung out with him. I don't believe in capitalism. I don't own anything. You can't own what you can't carry. Do you know about the dresser?

Sidian Morning Star Jones: No, I don't.

First male voice: This was when we went to collect some stuff at Meta Tantay that Carmen was going to give us. But two of the women had a fight about who was going to get the dresser. So we had to draw straws.

Second male voice: We drew names.

First male voice: Whatever. We did a lottery. So we put all the names of both the men and the women in the hat, and then we had someone pull it out. One woman got it, but the other woman still wanted it. There was no way she was going home without it, and it was getting ugly. They were both hitting each other and pulling each other's hair and stuff.

Second female voice: You were the one who was supposed to get it. It was your name that came up.

Second male voice: Yeah, but since there was so much fighting over it, I bowed out. We guys agreed to give it to one of the women even though we put our names in the hat.

First male voice: It was fate when your name came out, but the women did not like that. I saw a side of them I had not seen before. I'm sorry, but it is true. They were materialistic capitalists.

Sidian Morning Star Jones: When was that?

First male voice: Well, let's see. It was right after RT died.

Sidian Morning Star Jones: Okay.

First male voice: See, I didn't find out about RT dying until a friend of mine from Elko called up and told me, "I'm sorry to hear about your father." I said, "What are you talking about?" "Well, he's dead." Well, that dry, little bitch that he married didn't tell us. And then when we came up there to view the body we weren't allowed to go to the funeral. We just got to view the body, and then she cremated it.

Second female voice: This is getting painful.

First male voice: Okay, I won't talk.

Sidian Morning Star Jones: What kind of stuff should I ask you about for the book?

First male voice: We're just talking. You've got to be like your mom's best friend Doug Boyd. He had a photographic memory and remembered all this stuff. Man, he sat and talked just like we're talking now, and he went back to his apartment and wrote down everything word for word without a tape recorder.

Second female voice: I remember when I was born.

Second male voice: Do you really?

Second female voice: I remember where I was and what was around me and what was happening.

First male voice: You were born on the land.

Second female voice: Yes, I know this. I told my mom everything before she even told me. She was born on the land in a wickiup with guys out there drumming.

Second male voice: She says she could remember the drumming.

Sidian Morning Star Jones: That would be a lot more memorable than most people's births.

Second male voice: It's not like we were given a choice for a dad. Do you think we would all choose him?

First male voice: Well, the Great Spirit must have had a reason.

Sidian Morning Star Jones: Do you have any stories about Spotted Fawn?

First male voice: You mean your grandma. You don't call her Spotted Fawn.

Second male voice: Why not?

First male voice: It's his grandmother.

Sidian Morning Star Jones: Stanley said that when she passed away he had a dream that night and she told him that she wasn't going to be seeing him anymore.

First male voice: Well, I believe Stanley.

Sidian Morning Star Jones: So would you say that RT had any special power?

First male voice: We all have power.

Second male voice: I think in the beginning, he actually had something.

First male voice: In the last fifty years of his life he sucked.

Second male voice: I remember seeing him with his eagle feathers and watching the clouds rolling in and stuff, so I do think he had some connection with it.

Sidian Morning Star Jones: That's the story I've heard a number of times. That seems like the most common story so far.

First male voice: Well, that was basically all that he could really do unless he got really pissed.

Sidian Morning Star Jones: He was a rainmaker?

First male voice: Well, you know he could call it down, and he could also stop it. We were coming out of Oklahoma City after visiting an elder out in the mountains, and we were coming back, and all of sudden it started to rain. I couldn't see the reflectors on the side of the road. I was driving this van crammed full of about twelve pesky Natives, and I'm not sure we are going to make it to town. Pretty soon there is water all over the road; it's like a storm, you know, raining and everything. I thought, "Okay, RT, you'd better do something." He made a prayer, and it stopped just long enough for us to get into town, and then it hit again.

Sidian Morning Star Jones: Mom told me that he would have a bowl of peyote and you wouldn't smoke it directly, but he would have you guys turn it into coals and you would just kind of inhale it.

First male voice: We had peyote in our bottles when we were babies.

Sidian Morning Star Jones: Did you really?

First male voice: Yes.

Sidian Morning Star Jones: In your bottles?

First male voice: Yes.

Sidian Morning Star Jones: Wow.

First male voice: But I didn't know what getting high meant until I went to "hippie land" in San Francisco.

Second female voice: Using peyote is sacred, and just like with any other religious sacrament you want to keep your mind focused in a certain way and not let it wander.

First male voice: The hardest thing when you are on peyote is not to think about girls.

Second female voice: We never thought of it like a drug.

First male voice: But I always wandered off to think about girls. That was my problem. No, I'm serious. You're supposed to take peyote and pray.

Second female voice: Mom always beat it in my head, "Keep your mind focused."

First male voice: RT used to tell me that. But I didn't listen to him.

Second female voice: I kept my mind focused.

First male voice: When you take peyote, you drink the tea. Or you take the green buttons, and you eat them. Peal the skin and fur off each button first, and then eat it. If you have the dried buttons, you could eat them. If you have the powdered buttons, you put them in a corn husk and smoke it.

Sidian Morning Star Jones: So did you guys do it a lot or was it every once in a while?

First male voice: When we were younger, we did it on special occasions. But I didn't know what it was all about until I went to hippie land and smoked marijuana. I thought, well, this is the same thing as peyote and that's getting high. I didn't know that I had been "getting high" for years.

Second female voice: There were peyote meetings we used to go to.

First male voice: Right in the house.

Second female voice: We used to have peyote leaders come in, a bunch of Natives . . .

First male voice: Pesky redskins.

Second female voice: . . . and we would have a ceremony.

First male voice: Not getting stoned. You don't use that terminology. That's disrespectful. It's a religious service. We were praying.

Second female voice: It's the Native American Church. That is what it was, and that is what it was called.

First male voice: It still is. It was officially incorporated in about 1918 and is protected by U.S. laws.

Second female voice: It became our mind-set. It's a religion. And it incorporates a lot of Christianity.

First male voice: It is really a way of life.

Second female voice: You don't get high. You simply sit and focus and pray.

Sidian Morning Star Jones: So I'm just trying to understand how you could focus with that many people in the room doing peyote.

First male voice: That's why there were peyote chiefs there to run it.

Second female voice: I've never seen a Native person leave the service once it started.

First male voice: I've seen them walk in there drunk. I've been in meetings where a Native American came in drunk and stuff. The first thing I wanted to do was throw his ass out, but the peyote chief said, "No, let him stay here." He controls the situation, and he makes sure that you stay focused on praying for Mother Earth and relatives and stuff like that. And by praying, the drunken guy pretty soon gets everything out of his system. He's got problems and he's there and he doesn't know why and the Great Spirit is trying to help him. The peyote chief controls that.

Sidian Morning Star Jones: He settles down?

First male voice: Or he gets up, but there is no violence or nothing like that. And if somebody has too much peyote and starts to have problems, that's when the peyote chief controls it. And peyote is where the visions come from and where the power is at. You sing songs and stuff, and there are certain songs that you have to sing, and it takes, you know, all night long.

Second female voice: Usually, there is someone who asks that a meeting be held, because they need help in some way.

Second male voice: And we all help. It's like channeling. We say, "We're going to channel energy for this person."

Second female voice: Or it could be like a celebration, to celebrate the solstice or whatever. It's like giving thanks.

First male voice: And you do that all night, from sunset to sunrise. And then you break after that, and you go and have breakfast. And you walk out of there, and you're fresh, energized. It's like being reborn again. You feel good about yourself. I remember driving home one time from a peyote meeting and I was just not paying attention and a policeman pulls me over and I remember the peyote chief telling us, "Don't worry about nothing when you're driving. We're all going to make it home safe. Just be mellow." And the officer pulled me over, and I just vaguely remember talking to him but not really because I was, as you would say, still "high," but he let me go.

Second female voice: You may have been sleep deprived.

First male voice: The peyote chief always made sure that everyone who went to the meeting always got home safe. And I was speeding along doing about 110 miles per hour. I was in the sixty-five miles-per-hour zone. I remember that the policeman pulled me over for something, I don't remember what, but he never gave me a ticket. He let me go. Normally they write you up for something. But you feel good, and that's what it's all about.

Sidian Morning Star Jones: Did you ever get bad treatment from the police around there because of your background?

Second female voice: Most people in Nevada are prejudiced and narrow-minded.

First male voice: I never felt like I was a welcomed member of the town.

Second male voice: That's a part of life.

First male voice: We were always under suspicion. I was followed home many, many times.

Sidian Morning Star Jones: Because of who you were or because that was just the way it was?

First male voice: Yes, because of RT.

Sidian Morning Star Jones: You got singled out.

First male voice: Yes. And 'cause I had long hair.

Second male voice: If you were different, if you weren't "one of the boys," they were going to get you. That doesn't necessarily mean Indian; you could be a black person, you could be white person with long hair, it didn't matter. You ain't one of them. And that's what's gonna make you stick out.

First male voice: They gotta know you too. Everyone knew everybody back in those days. Hell, Carlin had only 750 people when I grew up there. Elko, Nevada, had only fifteen thousand when we first moved there. We used to live at the end of Idaho Street by Carson Trailer Park. I remember that trailer because RT built it.

Second male voice: When you go and apply for a job, the good ol' boy says, "I don't know why you are filling that out." I said, "Because I'm going to fill it out." I hand it to him and he crushes it up and throws it in the trash right in front of my face. Then you say, "I'll be back next week to fill out another."

Sidian Morning Star Jones: That happened to you?

Second male voice: All the time.

First male voice: And you didn't want to use the last name "Pope." Not a good idea.

Sidian Morning Star Jones: "Pope" had a reputation, huh?

First male voice: Yeah, about as tasteful as the Ku Klux Klan. They didn't like it.

Sidian Morning Star Jones: Where do you think the Pope reputation came from?

Second female voice: It started because RT started going out of the area. Going to San Francisco.

Sidian Morning Star Jones: And his name started getting around.

First male voice: Yeah, when he got in a train wreck in 1964, wasn't it? He was in the caboose along with three other men. They assigned four men to work in the caboose in those days, and you have the engineer and the assistant engineer in the engine car, and there was a head-on collision. About fifty-two train cars went off the tracks.

Sidian Morning Star Jones: That's amazing.

First male voice: Oh, that was a long time ago. And they basically just took a big truck, dug a trench, pushed it all in, and buried them. TVs, French shoes, and all kinds of food products. Thousands of boxes of raisins. After that train wrecked, everybody in Carlin had a garage full of raisin boxes and boxes of evaporated milk too. It was amazing and disgusting. Kids would go to school and open up our lunches and there would be raisins in those little red boxes, and when we would leave the lunchroom all the trash cans were full of raisin boxes. We were all sick of it. It didn't matter what race you were. Well, RT got in that train wreck, and he was in the back end of the caboose, standing in the back by the back door, and he went all the way through the caboose and hit the other door and hurt his back. So they sent him down to San Francisco to get operated on. I think that's when they circumcised him too. Went in for a back operation and they circumcised him.

Sidian Morning Star Jones: This was when he was how old?

First male voice: When he was in his fifties or something. When you go to that hospital they have interns there that do whatever they want. These doctors were getting training on these old railroad bastards, and they figure, "Fuck, nobody likes them." So that was when Dad started to go down to the Golden Gate Park area, right off Haight Street, two blocks away.

Sidian Morning Star Jones: That's where he first met the hippies?

First male voice: Yeah, that's when he would go down there and that's when the hippies started meeting him and he would be talking and that's how people started knowing his name. And the hippies thought, "Whoa, this is cool." And they were all into this flower power stuff and Native American customs. It was by word of mouth, and after that that's how his reputation got built. That's when he met some of the members of the Grateful Dead; actually he met members of the rock band Big Brother and the Holding Company first. And it was Chet Helms, the promoter of hippie events, who really started promoting RT and having him come to the Avalon Ballroom to give the blessing of the stage and have sunrise ceremonies on the top of the Avalon Ballroom, which was the very first rock concert hall. That was a few years before Bill Graham and the Fillmore, Winterland, and the Family Dog.

They were all friends with RT, and they kept him around like a spiritual adviser.

Sidian Morning Star Jones: Wasn't Mickey Hart really fond of RT?

First male voice: Mickey did a lot of good for Dad. That whole Grateful Dead family did. They bought Meta Tantay for him.

Second male voice: I still remember Mickey's Rottweiler dogs.

First male voice: Yeah, but that was after those black dogs, Great Danes. One was just crazy as hell. She would bite everything.

Second male voice: Scared the shit out of me. I was little, you know.

First male voice: I don't know why Mickey had to have all those big dogs over at his ranch.

Second male voice: Yeah, lots of things impressed outsiders. But when you're part of a family you just see people like RT here every day.

First male voice: Or you hear them every day.

Sidian Morning Star Jones: Or you hear about them every day from other people.

Second male voice: Well, that's because he was just a man.

Second female voice: He had a lot of good teachings though.

Second male voice: Not in a lot of people's eyes though.

First male voice: Well, a lot of those people that saw him as a great person were just mental midgets; they were fuckin' crippled. I mean, they looked up to him like he was a shining beacon of light.

Sidian Morning Star Jones: Well, anybody who looks at anybody like that obviously needs to empower themselves instead of giving so much power to somebody else.

Second male voice: It doesn't matter because the problem is that you put them all on top of a pedestal. And I've been with enough of them to know that they are human. They are people. They have gifts. They definitely have gifts, but they have their moments when they have to be men and not medicine men, not anything else.

This family discussion reminded me that RT was a human being with all the strengths and weaknesses, virtues and vices, talents and foibles that all humans share. When conducting the interviews for this book, I discovered many sides of my grandfather that I had never known before. And his legacy inspired me to make the most of my skills and opportunities.

How RT Changed the Lives
of Carolina and Norman Cohen

To balance out the accounts of the family members, I want to include the perspectives of Carolina and Norman Cohen, who spent considerable amounts of time in Carlin with my grandparents and who also ran the Thunder Trading Post in Santa Cruz, California, for many years. This was an enterprise that was inspired by their contact with RT.

Carolina Cohen: Rolling Thunder and Spotted Fawn were, and even in their passing still are, the favorite people for Norman and me. They entered our lives at a moment in time when we were seeking a spiritual direction that would also unfold into our daily lives. The continuing revolutionary spirit of the 1960s and early 1970s was deeply embedded in us. We knew that the world had to change. We came to understand that true change comes from within, in small communities and in a natural setting. Rolling Thunder told us from the very beginning, "Watch your thoughts. Whatever we think, we become, and bring those thoughts into our lives." Every spiritual teacher we admire has expounded on that principle. Rolling Thunder lived that truth and taught us all how to live it too.

The sunrise ceremony was the beginning of the day. Our prayers, our thoughts, our intentions, were infused into the tobacco resting in the palm of our hand, offered to the Four Directions and to Father Sun, Mother Earth, and Grandmother Moon. This is a simple yet extremely powerful ceremony. The smoke from the fire, the drumming, the welcome song, all sent our prayers to the Great Spirit. The circle of community spirals out and up to the Great Beyond, to the land of Spirit. Rolling Thunder taught us that the rising of the sun is one expression of the harmony of the cosmos, a harmony that extends from sky to Earth and can never be fragmented into separate domains.

He was not afraid to tell the long-haired white young folks how to live with the Earth and how to be connected with the Great Spirit. He held no prejudice against us. He told us that when the white man and woman become interested in Indian—Native American—

spirituality and the tribal and clan way of life, then the Earth would begin to change. He hoped to see it, and I guess he did.

Things don't always appear as they seem. Only the Great Spirit knows the right time and place for everything. We can only continue to pray for "what is good and meant to be and to all of our relations," as Rolling Thunder put it in his prayers. RT is our relation in the world of Spirit now. But he is with us every day, because he lives and breathes in the heart of all of his Thunder People.

The first time we went to Carlin was life altering. RT didn't have "the land" yet, but there were wickiups and trailers all over his property in town. There were lots and lots of people sharing a very small kitchen and one bathroom! Coming from Beverly Hills, California, Norm could not have imagined the experience if he had tried. But we loved it!

We loved Spotted Fawn at first sight. She was the matriarch and clan mother to this eclectic crowd of Natives, African Americans, Mexicans, Puerto Ricans, Asians, and whites. She emanated pure unconditional love. But that doesn't mean she was a pushover! She had rules and regulations, and you had to follow them or there would be living hell. And hell existed right here on Mother Earth. But she was so loving, sincere, and wonderful that no one ever wanted to upset her, except maybe her own children. We always have to test our own parents!

Rolling Thunder taught us about love as well. I am not referring to his flirting, because there was lots of that and much was in the spirit of good-natured fun. RT told us that love is not made in a contract. Love does not involve ownership. A man who loves a woman does not own that woman, and neither does a woman own a man she loves—whether they are married or not. Marriage, of course, involves a contract, but the love can exist with or without marriage and is a voluntary coming together of two people without setting up rules and conditions.

I got involved helping cook the food, clean the house, and wash the dishes, all that kind of stuff. I had been involved in the women's consciousness-raising movement at that time, but somehow it seemed so natural to be a part of what was going on in Carlin. The men ate first. I figured it was because there was not much room for everyone to sit, and I enjoyed eating with the women afterward. It was a good bonding time for us.

That very first night we were there, there were a dozen people sitting in the front room listening to RT as he smoked his corncob pipe. He told us, "When I smoke or light a pipe the smoke carries a message. It can show me the right way if I am lost in the woods. It can tell me how much evil there is in the room. I've been in some rooms where there was so much evil you couldn't strike a match and keep it lit. These are some of the ways that the pipe talks to me."

He started to speak about the condition of the Indian people in America. He told us the story of the Trail of Tears, when the Cherokee Nation was sent out of Georgia and walked to Oklahoma under military surveillance. It became a trail of tears for me too. I couldn't stop weeping. He looked over at me, his dark eyes shooting lightning bolts, and he knew that he had found a compatriot and friend.

I never said a word to RT personally during our whole visit, but we were definitely spiritually connected. But Norm was with him the whole time. Norm's experience with RT was one of learning simple, pragmatic life lessons. We all learned how to "walk our talk." We learned how to be quiet, respect one another, respect yourself, and never touch anyone else's belongings without asking. At meetings, if no conclusion could be reached, the women called for a food break, and when the meeting was resumed a consensus was achieved because everyone had time to think, listen to the opinions of their women, and gain from the women's wisdom without losing face.

When an Indian went to war with another tribe, if a killing occurred he was not allowed back into the camp until he purified himself through fasting and prayer and solitude and making amends with the dead. We discussed this in relation to the mass murders happening in Vietnam, when many Indian soldiers returned with what we now call post-traumatic stress disorder. RT knew how to treat them with prayer, with sweat lodge purifications, and with journeying back to Vietnam to ask their victims to release their souls. RT taught us that in all wars, glorified killing should not be the standard.

He also taught us that the positions in the tribe are all equal, because the tribe is a circle. Most medicine people are born gifted, and the tribal elders will look for special markings on babies that indicate their path on the Red Road. But even if they are born to be medicine people, they have to pass the Great Spirit's tests and remain humble enough to be healers. On the other hand, chiefs were appointed by the tribal council for their strength, courage, intelligence, compassion, and leadership. They were committed to the tribal council, always made an offering to the Mother Earth and the Great Spirit when taking something from the Earth—whether it was plants, feathers, or rocks. Both medicine people and chiefs needed to show love and respect for Mother Earth, above all else. It is our home.

When Tom Laughlin finished making the Billy Jack films, he gave RT a huge truck. We took that truck to California and brought it back heavily loaded down with everything we could fit into it, from boxes of nails, to carpets, to tools, to foodstuffs, to furniture, to a huge variety of clothing and donations from our friends and associates in the Topanga Canyon and Los Angeles area. While unloading the truck with RT's sons Buffalo Horse and Mala Spotted Eagle, Norm was thrown a fifty-pound box of nails, which he almost dropped, staggering under the weight.

Norman Cohen: I held on for dear life! And of course all the guys smirked and hid behind their politeness. And then the rolls of carpet just about brought me to my knees. I was an L.A., Beverly Hills guy. I saw RT chewing hard on his pipe to keep from laughing too. I asked myself, "What are these guys doing to me?" But I kept my own sense of humor and told a joke or something, and then everybody could laugh and feel relief, including me. Later RT told me that if the men didn't respect or like me they wouldn't bother to tease me. It was a way of expressing affection. I could relate to that. We all became close friends and brothers over the years. I remember other funny stories as well. I went out to the land one time with Buffalo Horse and Carolina before it was occupied. There was only Greg, the Puerto

Rican guy out there, serving as the caretaker. We were all going to smoke a pipe or two and enjoy the night sky. Well, we got to the gate ,and since I was riding in the front seat I jumped out to unlock and open the gate. Everything went fine on the way in, but on the way out, I jumped out and opened the gate, Buffalo Horse drove through, and I closed and locked the gate with me on the wrong side. I had locked myself in! Well, we all laughed very hard about that!

Another time Buffalo Horse and I were sent to get a load of gravel. RT was having a gathering at the house, and he wanted to gravel all the pathways so folks wouldn't have to walk in the mud. We drove around, and I thought we were going to the gravel yard. We got there and started loading an old Dodge station wagon. Well, I never saw someone shovel so fast in my life. Buffalo Horse shoveled three or four shovelfuls to my one. He was amazing! He got tired of my bragging about him, the greatest shoveler ever. I told that story a hundred times! So one day, much later, he told me, "The truth is, Norman, that gravel wasn't ours! I hurried up and shoveled it into the van before anyone could discover what we were doing." I found out that the gravel belonged to someone else! Go figure!"

One time we were all together with RT, having a fabulous Italian dinner made by a friend of mine at his home. There were about twelve men sitting around the table. It was a great feast and celebration. At the end of the meal a pipe was brought out, and RT loaded it with his famous Five Brothers tobacco. Well, I was excited to be smoking with everyone, so when it came to be my turn I took a puff of this twenty-five-cent-a-package tobacco, inhaling it deeply into my lungs. And I turned red, then green. I didn't want to have a coughing fit, but man, I was dying. RT tells the story that I disappeared, under the table. Maybe I did. I sure felt like disappearing.

Carolina Cohen: When we returned to Santa Cruz, Norman and I opened the Thunder Trading Post. RT came and spent lots of time with us there. He especially enjoyed our homemade bagels. We so much appreciated his visits. He would always do some drumming out in the garden, and he helped us create a great business.

Norman Cohen: One day RT, Grandfather Semu, and I were sitting at a table eating when they started talking about giving me an Indian name. I got very excited but tried hard not to show it. So RT told me about the eagle, its significance, symbology, and its nature. Then Grandfather Semu spoke about the hawk, expounding on its significance and its intelligence. Then they were quiet for a while. When RT spoke again, he said, "We have decided that your name will be Bagel Feather." I wasn't sure whether I should laugh or not. RT said that we should each be proud and honor where we come from. Since I was a Jewish Indian, part of the lost tribe, then I should always be proud of that. I tell everyone that story now, and people always laugh, but for me it has great meaning and sincerity.

Carolina Cohen: Rolling Thunder conducted many healing ceremonies in our presence. It is difficult to recount those events because they were all "otherworldly." The intensity of the drumming and singing, the burning of the cedar and the sage, and the actions of RT were times a powerful witnessing to the work of the Great Spirit coming through the open vessel of RT. They were transcendental and transpersonal experiences. We never talked about it much. It was sacred. RT did heal many people. I saw it and witnessed the transformations that occurred during these events. Many of these healings happened in my home. My home was blessed as a result.

An Interview with Rudy Spangenberg

One of my most informative interviews was with Rudy Spangenberg, a California building contractor who spent a considerable amount of time with RT in his younger days.

Sidian Morning Star Jones: Rudy, how did you first meet Rolling Thunder?

Rudy Spangenberg: Well, I first became aware of him when I was in my freshman year at the University of California, Santa Cruz, in 1976. And there was a symposium in downtown Santa Cruz, and it was called the "Bicentennial Medicine Show." And it was put together by an osteopath, Irving Oyle. Rolling Thunder talked, and there was another Native American elder, Grandfather Semu Huaute.

Sidian Morning Star Jones: Yes, I am familiar with him.

Rudy Spangenberg: Rolling Thunder also did a sunrise ceremony on the campus. They had a big outdoor amphitheater that was kind of a rock quarry. He gave a sunrise ceremony there, and that was my first exposure to him. And I got a copy of Doug Boyd's book at that conference and decided I would like to meet him.

Sidian Morning Star Jones: So how long did it take?

Rudy Spangenberg: The first time I actually met him would have been about fifteen months later, because some good friends and I were going skiing in Park City, Utah, over Christmas vacation. And so I thought, "Wow!" I looked at a map of Nevada and saw the primary route we would take would be Highway 80, and we could stop in Carlin. And I had this really strong impression that we were really going to get a chance to look him up personally. Now, I hadn't told my mother or my brother about this, but I was, like the whole time, knowing I was going to get to meet him.

Sidian Morning Star Jones: It must have been a hard secret to keep, huh?

Rudy Spangenberg: And then when we were driving, my mother asked, "What cities do we go through in Nevada?" And I was saying, "Lovelock, Winnemucca, Battleground, Carlin," and she goes, "Carlin! Someone we know lives in Carlin." And then my brother goes, "Oh! Isn't that where Rolling Thunder lives? We should look him up!" And I said, "We're going to look him up! It's all planned. He's gonna be there. Don't worry. Everything's taken care of."

Sidian Morning Star Jones: So you had all the arrangements before you left.

Rudy Spangenberg: Right. And so we went out to Meta Tantay. But my brother and I have different styles. You know, he's more like the bull in the china shop, and I'm a lot more like the let things flow type. And so he said, "Oh, we want to talk to John Pope." And all the people replied, "Why do you want to talk to John Pope?" And finally I said, "You know, we want to talk to Rolling Thunder. We heard him speak. We read his book." And so it was funny, because we went down to the little kitchen area there—they called it the cook shop—and he came out to greet us, and he just had this look, like he knew we were coming the whole time. He tried to act surprised, but it was like someone who has a surprise party for their birthday, but they knew about it in advance. That's the only way I can describe it.

Sidian Morning Star Jones: Many people got permission to visit Meta Tantay, but there was no guarantee that they would meet RT.

Rudy Spangenberg: I know. We were lucky. So we chatted about various things, and he gave us a little tour of the encampment there. He showed us where the garden would be and the geese and the chickens. And then my mother asked, "Well, do you have any predictions for 1978?" I thought that was a little brash. And he goes, "Oh, yeah. Famine." But there wasn't any particular famine in 1978. But soon after that, there was famine in many parts of the world.

Sidian Morning Star Jones: Eventually, you returned and spent several months at Meta Tantay.

Rudy Spangenberg: Yes, I did, starting in 1982. And I remember when a young guy flew out in his private plane. He had red welts all over his back, and he had come to RT for healing. He offered RT $10,000 for a treatment. RT told him that one never offers money up front to a medicine man. That, he said, is "the white man's way of doing things." RT looked at the bumps and said it was a tropical disease, but that it would take awhile to treat. The rich guy wanted a quick cure and didn't want to spend the time at Meta Tantay that RT required. So RT turned him down, and the guy went off in a huff. But soon after that episode an elderly man without much money showed up. He had a severe case of arthritis. He didn't have much money, but he spent a lot of time talking with RT and following his directions. RT's healing sessions were successful, and the man knew that RT would not take any money. But he gave him a bolo tie that he had made, one with a clasp of a lightning cloud in the middle. RT accepted it and wore it, off and on, for the rest of his life.

Sidian Morning Star Jones: I have seen photographs of RT wearing that tie.

Rudy Spangenberg: There were a lot of jackrabbits and coyotes in the brush at Meta Tantay. Several times I saw a coyote chase a rabbit, and the rabbit headed for Meta Tantay. As soon as the rabbit reached the encampment, the coyote stopped. It was if the coyote had hit a glass wall. Later I found out that RT had set the boundaries of the camp to protect both wild animals and livestock who would have been easy prey. There were never any chickens, geese, or goats lost to coyotes.

Sidian Morning Star Jones: And I've heard that RT negotiated with the coyotes too.

Rudy Spangenberg: He probably did. But RT could also protect himself. He was in Canada for a television interview, and the host began to ask some really silly questions challenging RT to demonstrate his powers. At this point the technician reported that everything had broken down, and they were not getting a recording signal. The host apologized and said that he was sorry for the challenge. RT accepted his apology, and then all the equipment started to work again.

Sidian Morning Star Jones: It would be interesting to get his impressions of everything going on today.

Rudy Spangenberg: Oh, yeah, I'm sure! For example, I happened to be out visiting him when the Loma Prieta earthquake hit in 1989 near Santa Cruz.

Sidian Morning Star Jones: Is that the one that he predicted?

Rudy Spangenberg: So they say. And at that time he was absolutely glued to the TV for, like, two or three days. He wanted to see what had happened, like the collapsed overpasses and some of the buildings. And he just ranted and raved and said, "Oh, that purification is kicking in! You white people! You can try to live apart from Nature, but you can't get away from Mother Earth." So I'm sure his general reaction now would be the same kind of thing.

Sidian Morning Star Jones: He made lots of predictions, didn't he?

Rudy Spangenberg: He made one prediction about two stars changing their positions in the sky. This would be a sign that the outside world would become more receptive to Indian wisdom. And RT told me that he actually saw those stars change positions, something—of course—that would have happened eons ago.

Sidian Morning Star Jones: True. I wonder why those particular stars?

Rudy Spangenberg: And he also predicted a polar shift, that the North Pole and the South Pole would change positions. This would precede four decades of purification both by fire and by water, in other words by forest fires and by floods. People would need to know how to survive those times, and he saw Meta Tantay as a training camp for pulling through those disasters. That's funny, actually, the parallels between that kind of viewpoint and a Christian viewpoint. I don't adhere to any particular religion, myself, but I really see those two playing on the same ideas there, the prediction of an apocalypse. I was raised in a Methodist family. We went to church, but we didn't have any rigorous Bible study or anything like that. But I got interested in the work of Edgar Cayce, and I guess he tried to read the Bible once a year during his whole life.

By the way, RT made this prediction during his visit to Germany, and there were secret police in the audience from Communist East Germany. They came to him afterward and told him that he should not come back to Europe and should not make those predictions. RT told them, "I'll come back as often as I can, and I'll say whatever I want to say."

Sidian Morning Star Jones: Rolling Thunder does not hold back his voice.

Rudy Spangenberg: RT also discussed his training to be a medicine man. The final seven tests were especially severe. If the initiate made a mistake, he might die. One of these tests was to be bitten by a rattlesnake. Another was to know the plants in the area, especially those that would be poisonous if they were used the wrong way. For example, there were two plants that looked very much alike, and both had berries. If you chose the wrong berries to eat, you would get very sick and might die. On a practical basis, the medicine man had the choice of "doctoring" someone, but if that person died, there would be a penalty to pay. And in the old days the penalty was death from the patient's family. So medicine people didn't need malpractice insurance in those days! It wouldn't have helped.

In Conclusion

When I was reading about quantum physics I had no idea that it reflected so many ideas dear to the heart of my grandfather.

As we discussed earlier in this book, quantum physics reveals a basic oneness of the universe. It indicates that the world cannot be split up into independently existing, smaller units. As science penetrates more deeply into the cosmos, it does not show us that Nature is composed of building blocks that can be rearranged to construct larger entities. Nature instead appears to be a complicated web of relationships between the various parts of the whole.

And when I started to read the books by Alan Watts and listened to his audiotapes I heard much the same thing. Everything in the universe is interconnected. Human beings are a part of Nature, not independent units who can get away with manipulating and exploiting the natural environment. The Eastern philosophies that Alan Watts introduced to his readers and listeners placed great emphasis on balance, harmony, and the circular passage of time. And now I understand that this was RT's message as well and realize why the two of them got along when they conducted a seminar together in New Mexico many decades ago.

I talk about my grandfather and his ideas when I give presentations at festivals and conferences, and sometimes I get into heated arguments with "virtual friends" on the World Wide Web. Neither RT nor I could be considered full-blooded Native Americans, but this is the ethnic group with which both of us have identified. We are proud of Indian accomplishments in agriculture, in medicine, and in ecology. The Europeans ignored, destroyed, or stole the Native Americans' endowments. But time has a way of forcing out the truth, and I share my grandfather's passion for the truth. So when you get concerned about global warming, when you want to make the wisest choice of food for yourself and your loved ones, and when you want to be true to your own nature and your own integrity, just listen to the Rolling Thunder. This is what I have learned to do, and the lessons have served me well.

EPILOGUE

Rolling Thunder——Our Greatest Contemporary Shaman?

HARRIS FRIEDMAN, PH.D.

This collection of stories about Rolling Thunder provides a glimpse of this controversial man who some thought to have authentic shamanic powers and others thought to be a charlatan. It also portrays an exciting era filled with charismatic figures and proliferating, innovative ideas, during which many people hungered for the wisdom of non-Western traditions that RT seemed to offer. Some seekers found spiritual riches, and others were sorely disappointed in being deceived by what turned out to be false and corrupt gurus.

The worldview of RT, which comes through loudly in these stories, contrasts with the modern Western worldview, and the question remains open: Who was RT, and what did he really accomplish and represent? Sidian Morning Star Jones and Stanley Krippner attempt to account for the many reported extraordinary occurrences that happened around RT and perhaps were even caused by him in a way incongruent with conventional notions of causation based on interactions in ordinary time and space.

Sidian, with some direct experiences as well as access to many previously unshared secondhand stories as a family insider, shares his understandings about RT, who was his grandfather, while Stanley draws on both his extensive experiences with RT over many years and his scientific insights as a psychologist with a long career studying anomalous phenomena within different cultures. Together they triangulate through their shared insights in attempting to make sense of RT, while largely leaving it to the reader to interpret what might be true, partially true, or perhaps blatantly false.

Sidian and Stanley's writings on RT bring me back to my own coming of age in the mid-1960s, when I first became fascinated with Native American cultures. As a child, I read widely about the so-called mythologies of past traditions and on worldviews across various cultures. Raised as a Jew, I felt that I was an outsider in a predominantly Gentile world, which sensitized me toward diversity issues. As an undergraduate I explored many traditions from the perspectives of comparative literature, religion, and philosophy, as well as from the perspective of social sciences. Like many members of my generation, I discovered Carlos Castaneda's books (starting in 1968 with *The Teachings of Don Juan*, which was based on his master's thesis in anthropology) and avidly read them one at a time, as they were sequentially released, finally coming to the disillusioned conclusion that they were more fictional than based on acceptable anthropological science. I also experimented with many methods of consciousness alteration, from astrology to Zen.

In graduate school I heard of RT but am unsure whether I ever actually crossed paths with him. I attended an Association for Humanistic Psychology regional conference at Rock Eagle, Georgia, in the early 1970s while a beginning doctoral psychology student at Georgia State University. This conference was cosponsored by the humanistic psychology program at West Georgia College, and I recall a charismatic Native American medicine man being present. I have since found out that this is around the time that RT was lecturing in Georgia at a number of venues sponsored by West Georgia College, but I cannot say for sure whether this presenter might have been RT or whether I actually met this presenter in person or just observed him at a distance. Around that time and later I did encounter many who were in his close circle, including Stanley Krippner, who I met in the early 1970s. The litany of interesting, and sometimes very controversial interactions with RT are cited by Stanley and Sidian in this book. The writings of many people they cite were influential in my own life.

One of my major motivations for attending graduate school in psychology (after receiving a master's degree in a department of sociology and anthropology) and for later becoming a transpersonal psychologist was to understand questions brought up in this book, such as how divergent, seemingly incompatible worldviews can simultaneously exist. How they can exist occasionally within one person who can switch back and forth between, and perhaps even integrate, multiple perspectives is even more puzzling. RT was a man who lived in a bicultural world, that of modernity and traditional Native American beliefs.

Since becoming a psychologist I have had the opportunity to become personally acquainted with diverse worldviews through studying and working in many international settings, such as Fiji. I have also had the opportunity to become acquainted with several Native American cultures within the United States, such as serving as the psychological consultant to the Seminole tribe of Florida for several years. In these encounters with people who hold views different from prevailing Western notions, I have learned much about the arbitrariness of any one cultural vantage, especially as power that one culture might hold over another can be used to define what is real and right.

Recently Stanley and I coedited a book, *Debating Psychic Experiences,* in which we juxtaposed the views of opposed scientific experts on parapsychological topics. With considerable rancor, those who were advocates and those who were counteradvocates lined up on different sides of a divide representing their worldview on whether psychic experiences are valid or invalid, respectively. Being able to see comparatively the differences between the two groups, both composed of bright and educated people who were presumably sincere about their differences, gives context to how RT is perceived by some as perhaps the greatest contemporary shaman and by others as a despicable mountebank as the same facts can be interpreted in radically different light depending on perspective.

As a psychological scientist who has had personal experiences with many persons claiming (or having claims made about them) extraordinary powers, including observing firsthand many of what on the surface appeared to be extraordinary events, I remain agnostic about the veridicality of such events. In my own life I have had many seemingly convincing personal experiences that have challenged my own notions of reality, yet I still experience doubt as to their veracity as I realize all too well how easily I can delude myself in myriad ways for a variety of motives.

In another recent book that Stanley and I coedited, *Mysterious Minds,* we presented a number of scientific studies suggesting overall that when people claimed to have extraordinary experiences there were unusual neurological and biological phenomena concomitant with these experiences, as measured by the EEG and other instruments. But this type of research offers little to substantiate or refute events as valid. It should be noted that we did not attempt to verify any objective extraordinary events in this book, but only to demonstrate how subjective experiences related to measurable neurobiological phenomena. And in my other scholarship I have attempted to design scientific ways to discern levels of transpersonal development, as well as to explore implications for applications, such as in clinically differentiating between spiritual enlightenment and psychotic delusion.

I view this book as similar, although less formal, exposition of RT's life, as a type of biographical ethnography of someone who might have been a shaman, presenting data based on historical recollections that provide another type of evidence that the prevailing Western worldview is just one among many possible worldviews. It can be argued, similar to the proverb that fish do not recognize they are immersed in water, that Westerners tend to think that only others have strange worldviews, while concluding that Westerners are in touch with reality through science and other ways of rational knowing.

This is, of course, a very parochial view that privileges one cultural vantage and leads to the type of imperialism that has contributed to the historical decimation of Native Americans as well as atrocities committed to many other non-Western cultures. And, of course, many of the prevailing Western religious beliefs rest on claims of what can be seen as every bit as "magical" as what is related about RT (for example, the Catholic transubstantiation ritual in which wine is turned into sacred blood or the Pentecostal Protestants' claim for "speaking in tongues" while they are possessed by the Holy Spirit).

This type of arrogance, a stance of dismissing the beliefs of some cultures while not even noticing the equally exotic beliefs inherent within Western cultures, represents a collective blindness, leading to discounting alternate worldviews such as those purportedly lived and practiced by RT.

Although Western psychology can help provide tools to understand such differences, it also is too often limited by parochial perspectives. In a recent paper, Joseph Henrich, Steven Heine, and Ara Norenzayan concluded that "behavioral scientists routinely publish broad claims about human psychology and behavior in the world's top journals based on samples drawn entirely from Western, Educated, Industrialized, Rich, and Democratic societies." Even studies in cross-cultural psychology suffer from overreliance on Western assumptions and data collected from research participants who are overwhelmingly Western. And often studies using non-Western samples misinterpret badly what is observed. For example, in some widely cited studies, adult Kpelle tribespeople from Africa were observed to sort objects the way Western children do, leading to the conclusion that adults from this group are childlike (that is, "primitive"); however, one clever researcher thought to ask them to sort the items the way a Westerner would. In his essay titled "Cognitive Development in Cross-Cultural Perspective," Joseph Glick described the process as follows:

> In the sorting task, twenty items representing five types of food, five types of clothing, five types of tools, and five types of cooking utensils were heaped on a table in front of a Kpelle subject. When the

subject had finished sorting, what was present were ten categories composed of two items each—related to each other in a functional, not categorical, manner. Thus, a knife might have been placed with an orange, a potato with a hoe, and so on. When asked, the subject would rationalize the choice with such comments as, "The knife goes with the orange because it cuts it." When questioned further, the subject would often volunteer that a wise man would do things in this way. When an exasperated experimenter asked finally, "how would a fool do it," he was given back sorts of the type that were initially expected—four neat piles with foods in one, tools in another, and so on.

One area of psychology, transpersonal psychology, attempts to appreciate non-Western perspectives on their own merits. In contrast to cynical approaches to psychology that dismiss extraordinary claims, such as have been made about RT, transpersonal psychology tends to take these as valuable data but not as absolute truth. However, transpersonal psychologists sometimes tend to accept such claims too readily, leaving the discipline susceptible to charges of romanticism. However, it provides a counterbalanced perspective to mainstream psychology, which is all too quick to cynically dismiss anything that does not fit within Western preconceived notions of reality. A scientific stance that would allow recognition of Western cultural blind spots without necessarily uncritically accepting all claims from other cultures would be best.

Reading about RT provides an opportunity to ponder such issues about one's worldview. Could RT really shape-shift into an eagle in order to gather a needed medicinal plant from a great distance, or was this simply an anecdote prearranged to dupe a benefactor into lending more financial support to his endeavors? Were perceptions of sudden violent thunderstorms arising and rapidly abating that were attributed by some to RT only a function of selective memory of coincidences, again with the possibility of secondary gains inuring to RT? Or was RT a Native American medicine man with authentic shamanic powers, someone who inhabited two cultures—not just figuratively but in some actuality? Stanley and Sidian have recounted what they experienced and what others have told them, and they both have attempted to make sense of the data as they were presented to them. It is up to the reader to decide the answer to these and the many more questions that this book provocatively raises.

HARRIS FRIEDMAN, PH.D., is a research professor of psychology at University of Florida and a practicing clinical and organizational psychologist. He co-edits the *International Journal of Transpersonal Studies,* associate edits *The Humanistic Psychologist,* and has published extensively within psychology and related fields. He is currently president of the International Transpersonal Association. His most recent book (co-edited with Stanley Krippner) is *Mysterious Minds: The Neurobiology of Psychics, Mediums, and Other Extraordinary People.*

Bibliography

Achterberg, Jeanne. *Imagery in Healing: Shamanism and Modern Medicine.* New York: Shambhala, 1985.

Bernstein, Jerome S. *Living in the Borderland: The Evolution of Consciousness and the Challenge of Healing Trauma.* London: Routledge, 2005.

Boyd, Doug. *Rolling Thunder.* New York: Robert Briggs Associates, 1974.

Brandelius, Jerilyn Lee, ed. *The Grateful Dead Family Album.* New York: Warner Books, 1989.

Brown, Joseph Epes. *The Spiritual Legacy of the American Indian.* Bloomington, Ind.: World Wisdom, 2007.

Castaneda, Carlos. *The Teachings of Don Juan: A Yaqui Way of Knowledge.* Berkeley: University of California Press, 1998.

Cohen, Kenneth. *Honoring the Medicine: The Essential Guide to Native American Healing.* New York: One World/Ballantine Books, 2003.

Corbin, Henry. "Mundus Imaginalis, or the Imaginary and the Imaginal." *Spring* (1972): 1–19.

Cromwell, Mare. *If I Gave You God's Phone Number: Searching for Spirituality in America.* Baltimore, Md.: Parmoon Press, 2002.

Crow Dog, Leonard, and Richard Erdoes. *Crow Dog: Four Generations of Sioux Medicine Men.* New York: HarperCollins, 1995.

Dawkins, Richard. *River Out of Eden: A Darwinian View of Life.* New York: Basic Books, 1995.

DeLoria, Vine, Jr. *The World We Used to Live In.* Golden, Colo.: Fulcrum Publishers, 2006.

DuBois, Thomas A. *An Introduction to Shamanism.* Cambridge, England: Cambridge University Press, 2009.

Eliade, Mircea. *Shamanism: Archaic Techniques of Ecstasy.* Princeton, N.J.: Princeton University Press, 1964.

Feinstein, David, and Stanley Krippner. *Personal Mythology: Using Ritual, Dreams, and Imagination to Discover Your Inner Story.* Santa Rosa, Calif.: Energy Psychology Press/Elite Books, 2008.

Firehart, Nunzio. "Review of *Rolling Thunder Speaks: A Message for Turtle Island,* by Carmen Sun Rising Pope." *Shaman's Drum,* no. 54 (2000): 71–74.

Frank, Jerome, and Julia Frank. *Persuasion and Healing: A Comparative Study of Psychotherapy.* 3rd ed. Baltimore, Md.: Johns Hopkins University Press, 1991.

Friedman, Harris. "Problems of Romanticism in Transpersonal Psychology: A Case Study of Aikido." *The Humanistic Psychologist* 33 (2005): 3–24.

———. "The Self-Expansiveness Level Form: A Conceptualization and Measurement of a Transpersonal Construct." *The Journal of Transpersonal Psychology* 15 (1983): 37–50.

Friedman, Harris, Jerry Glover, and Papalii Failautusi Avegalio. "The Burdens of Other People's Models: A Cultural Perspective on the Current Fiji Crisis." *Harvard Asia Pacific Review* 6 (2002): 86–90.

Giesler, Patric V. "Differential Micro-PK Effects among Afro-Brazilian Umbanda Cultists Using Trance-Significant Symbols as Targets." In *Research in Parapsychology 1983,* edited by William G. Roll, John Beloff, and Rhea A. White. Metuchen, N.J.: Scarecrow Press, 1984.

Glick, Joseph. "Cognitive Development in Cross-Cultural Perspective." In *Review of Child Development Research,* vol. 4, edited by Francis D. Horowitz, 595–654. Chicago, Ill.: University of Chicago, 1975.

Gray, Leslie. "The Looks-Within Place." In *Moonrise: The Power of Women Leading from the Heart,* edited by Nina Simons and Anneke Campbell. Rochester, Vt.: Park Street Press, 2007.

Heinze, Ruth-Inge. "Alternate States of Consciousness: Access to Other Realities." In *Silver Threads: 25 Years of Parapsychology Research,* edited by Beverly Kane, Jean Millay, and Dean Brown. Westport, N.Y.: Praeger, 1993.

Henrich, Joseph, Steven Heine, and Ara Norenzayan. "The Weirdest People in the World?" *Behavioral and Brain Sciences* 33 (2010): 61–135.

Johnson, Chad, and Harris Friedman. "Enlightened or Delusional?

Differentiating Religious, Spiritual, and Transpersonal Experience from Psychopathology." *Journal of Humanistic Psychology* 48, no. 4 (2008): 505–27.

Kohls, Nikola, Sebastian Sauer, Martin Offenbacher, and James Giordano. "Spirituality: An Overlooked Predictor of Placebo Effects?" *Philosophical Transactions of the Royal Society* 366 (2011): 1138–48.

Krippner, Stanley. "The Influence of 'Psychedelic' Experience on Contemporary Art and Music." In *Hallucinogenic Drug Research: Impact on Science and Society,* edited by James R. Gamage and Edmund L. Zerkin. Beloit, Wis.: Stash Press, 1970.

———. *Song of the Siren: A Parapsychological Odyssey.* New York: Harper and Row, 1975.

Krippner, Stanley, Fariba Bogzaran, and Andre Percia de Carvalho. *Extraordinary Dreams and How to Work with Them.* Albany, N.Y.: State University of New York Press, 2002.

Krippner, Stanley, and Harris Friedman, eds. *Debating Psychic Experiences: Human Potential or Human Illusion?* Santa Barbara, Calif.: Praeger, 2010.

———. *Mysterious Minds: The Neurobiology of Psychics, Mediums, and Other Extraordinary People.* Santa Barbara, Calif.: Praeger, 2010.

Krippner, Stanley, Charles Honorton, and Montague Ullman. "An Experiment in Dream Telepathy with the Grateful Dead." *Journal of the American Society of Psychosomatic Dentistry and Medicine* 20 (1973): 3–17.

Krippner, Stanley, and Alberto Villoldo. *The Realms of Healing.* Millbrae, Calif.: Celestial Arts, 1976.

Littlefield, Daniel F., Jr., and James W. Parins, eds. *Encyclopedia of American Indian Removal.* 2 vols. Santa Barbara, Calif.: ABC-CLIO/Greenwood, 2011.

Lyon, William S. *Encyclopedia of Native American Healing.* New York: W. W. Norton, 1996.

McGavigin, L.A. "Interview with Running Wolf." *The Light Connection* (June 2004). Available online at: www.lightconnection.us/Archive/jun04/jun04_article2.htm. Accessed June 15, 2012.

McGovern, William M. *Jungle Paths and Inca Ruins.* New York: Grosse and Dunlap, 1927.

Moerman, Daniel E. *Native American Medicinal Plants: An Ethnobotanical Dictionary.* Portland, Ore.: Timber Press, 2009.

Narby, Jeremy. *The Cosmic Serpent: DNA and the Origins of Knowledge.* New York: Jeremy P. Tarcher/Putnam, 1998.

Narby, Jeremy, and Francis Huxley. *Shamans through Time: 500 Years on the Path to Knowledge.* New York: Jeremy P. Tarcher/Putnam, 2001.

Pope, Carmen Sun Rising, ed. *Rolling Thunder Speaks: A Message for Turtle Island.* Santa Fe, N.M.: Clear Light Publishers, 1999.

Pratt, Christina. *An Encyclopedia of Shamanism.* New York: Rosen Publishing Group, 2007.

Rock, Adam J., and Stanley Krippner. *Demystifying Shamans and Their World: An Interdisciplinary Study.* London: Imprint Academic, 2011.

Rolling Thunder. Foreword to *Song of the Siren: A Parapsychological Odyssey,* by Stanley Krippner, xi–xiii. New York: Harper and Row, 1975.

Rose, Ronald. "A Second Report on Psi Experiments with Australian Aborigines." *Journal of Parapsychology* 19 (1955): 92–98.

Rosenbaum, Robert, and Arthur C. Bohart. "The Art of Experience." In *Healing Stories: The Use of Narrative in Counseling and Psychotherapy,* edited by Stanley Krippner, Michael J. Bova, and Leslie Gray, 295–324. Charlottesville, Va.: Puente Publications, 2007.

Storm, Hyemeyohsts. *Lightningbolt.* New York: One World/Ballantine, 1994.

Storm, Lance, and Adam J. Rock. *Shamanism and Psi: Imagery Cultivation as an Alternative to the Ganzfeld Protocol.* Gladesville, Australia: Australian Institute for Parapsychological Research, 2011.

Torrey, E. Fuller. *The Mind Game: Witchdoctors and Psychiatrists.* New York: Bantam, 1973.

Van de Castle, Robert L. "An Investigation of Psi Abilities among the Cuna Indians in Panama." In *Parapsychology and Anthropology,* edited by Allan Angoff and David Barth, 80–97. New York: Parapsychological Association, 1977.

Vandervelder, Paul. "What Do We Owe the Indians?" *American History* (June 2009): 30–36, 39.

Vogel, Virgil J. *American Indian Medicine.* Norman, Okla.: University of Oklahoma Press, 1970.

Walsh, Roger. *The World of Shamanism: New Views of an Ancient Tradition.* Woodbury, Minn.: Llewellyn Publications, 2007.

Walter, Mariko Namba, and Eva Jane Neumann, eds. *Shamanism: An Encyclopedia of World Beliefs, Practices, and Culture.* Santa Barbara, Calif.: ABC-CLIO, 2004.

Watts, Alan. *In My Own Way: An Autobiography.* New York: New World Library, 2007.

Weiss, Herbert P. "Internationally Renowned Medicine Man John 'Rolling Thunder' Pope Crosses Over." *Shaman's Drum,* no. 45 (1997): 16–17.

White, Rhea A. "Dissociation, Narrative, and Exceptional Human Experiences." In *Broken Images, Broken Selves: Dissociative Narratives in Clinical Practice,* edited by Stanley Krippner and Susan Marie Powers. Washington, D.C.: Brunner/Mazel, 1997.

Williams, Raymond. *The Country and the City.* London: Chatto and Windus, 2011. Original work published in 1978. Williams, Walter L. *The Spirit and the Flesh: Sexual Diversity in American Indian Culture.* Boston: Beacon Press, 1992.

Winkelman, Michael. *Shamanism: A Biosocial Paradigm of Consciousness and Healing.* 2nd ed. Santa Barbara, Calif.: Praeger/ABC-CLIO, 2010.

Index

Books of Related Interest

Original Instructions
Indigenous Teachings for a Sustainable Future
Edited by Melissa K. Nelson

Walking on the Wind
Cherokee Teachings for Harmony and Balance
by Michael Tlanusta Garrett

Medicine of the Cherokee
The Way of Right Relationship
by J. T. Garrett and Michael Tlanusta Garrett

The Cherokee Full Circle
A Practical Guide to Ceremonies and Traditions
by J. T. Garrett and Michael Tlanusta Garrett

Iroquois Supernatural
Talking Animals and Medicine People
by Michael Bastine and Mason Winfield

Sacred Plant Medicine
The Wisdom in Native American Herbalism
by Stephen Harrod Buhner

Coyote Wisdom
The Power of Story in Healing
by Lewis Mehl-Madrona, M.D., Ph.D.

Weather Shamanism
Harmonizing Our Connection with the Elements
by Nan Moss with David Corbin

INNER TRADITIONS • BEAR & COMPANY
P.O. Box 388
Rochester, VT 05767
1-800-246-8648
www.InnerTraditions.com

Or contact your local bookseller